Creative Brainstorms

Creative Brainstorms

The Relationship Between Madness and Genius

Russell R. Monroe

IRVINGTON PUBLISHERS, INC.
New York

Irvington Publishers, Inc.,
Executive offices: 740 Broadway, New York, New York 10003
Customer service and warehouse in care of: Integrated Distribution
Services, 195 McGregor St, Manchester, NH 03102, (603) 669-5933

Library of Congress Cataloging-in-Publication Data

Monroe, Russell R., 1920-
    Creative brainstorms : the relationship between madness and
genius / Russell R. Monroe.
        p.   cm.
    Includes bibliographical references (p.   ) and indexes.
    ISBN 0-8290-1769-0 : $16.95
    1. Artists—Mental health. 2. Authors—Mental health. 3.
Creative ability.   I. Title.
    [DNLM: 1. Creativeness. 2. Mental Disorders. WM 100
M753c]
    RC451.4.A7M66   1992
    153.3'5—dc19
    DNLM/DLC
    for Library of Congress   87-22630
                                                               CIP

First Printing 1992
1 3 5 7 9 10 8 6 4 2

Printed in the United States of America

Acknowledgments

I am indebted to a number of individuals whose expertise I exploited by having them review selected chapters in this book. Particular appreciation is extended to Professor Aaron Sheon in the Department of Fine Arts, University of Pittsburgh, who not only made valuable contributions to my study of van Gogh but also advised me in my review of the 19th Century Marseilles artist Adolph Monticelli. I would also like to thank Reinhold Heller, Professor and Chairman of the Department of Art, the University of Chicago, who reviewed the chapter on Edvard Munch, and Professor Pavel Frankl, Osteras, Norway, for his review of the chapter on August Strindberg, as well as Joanne Trautmann, Ph.D., from the Department of Humanities, the Milton S. Hershey Medical Center, for her suggestions regarding the chapter on Virginia Woolf. Of course, the ultimate responsibility for the printed word must rest on my shoulders. Several psychiatrists whose professional and artistic interests overlapped mine were valuable sounding boards for my ideas, including Paul Miller of Los Angeles, Albert Lubin of San Francisco, Christian Astrup of the Gaustad Sykehus in Oslo, as well as Lutz Von Muehlen of Havre de Grace, Maryland, who translated material from the German literature for me. Other faculty of the Department of Psychiatry, University of Maryland School of Medicine, patiently listened to and commented on my ideas regarding the relationship of madness and genius. Particular gratitude is extended to Robert G. Heath, Department of Psychiatry, Tulane University School of Medicine. During the decade 1950–60, as a member of a research team under his direction, I initiated my studies in mind-brain relationship. Appreciation is also extended to all of my other colleagues who participated in these studies. Furthermore, in 1976 Dr. Heath allowed me to return to investigate the effects of the drug Thujone, the toxic element of absinthe, on some of his animals with chronically implanted subcortical electrodes.

Thanks are extended to the librarians of the Central Reference Library, St. Martins Street, and the Victoria Library, Buckingham Palace Road in London, who helped my review of Virginia Woolf and Mary Lamb. Similar appreciation is expressed to Mr. Hans Van Crimpen, Curator of the Van Gogh Museum, Amsterdam, and Dr. Alf Böe, Director of the Munch Museum in Oslo, as well as their library staffs. The doctoral thesis of Elmyra van Dooren, Amsterdam, provided me with a comprehensive list of the physicians who had written about the illness of Vincent van Gogh. I received considerable help from the staff of the Beaux Arts Museum in Lyon in reviewing the Charbonner collection of Monticelli's paintings and from Monsieur Jean Cailleux at his gallery on Fbg. St. Honoré in Paris, who allowed me to view some of his personal collection of Monticelli's paintings. Finally, I must not neglect the help extended by the local museums including the Walters Gallery and the Baltimore Museum of Art as well as the Corcoran Gallery in Washington, D.C.

Contents

Illustrations

Prologue
Madness *or* Genius

The relationship between madness and genius fascinates the layman and expert alike. Most geniuses are not mad; in fact, except for their extreme dedication and heightened creativity they may be quite normal. In turn, madness in no way guarantees this creativity. Confusion regarding the difference between madness and genius, however, is not surprising when one considers that a mad person has lost contact with reality while a genius presents a new or unusual view of reality. Before the genius's "new reality" has been accepted by society, the difference between madness and genius may be obscure, so a study of geniuses who have become mad should help in clarifying the distinction. The core subjects reported in the first section of this book clearly perceived their madness and distinguished between their madness and their genius. The madness had a precipitous onset, a short but intense duration, and an almost equally abrupt remission. It is these characteristics which led to an insightful self-awareness regarding their madness. The individuals afflicted, having only a hazy recollection of their psychotic symptoms, clearly remembered the events which led up to and followed such experiences. Most have described these in some detail and have elaborated on how such experiences contribute to their creativity. The definitions of genius and madness, however, are complex and will be left for the epilogue of this volume. Vincent van Gogh is presented as the prototype of the creative genius who suffered from episodic madness,[1] but others with a similar affliction are described. These include Virginia Woolf, Edvard Munch, August Strindberg, and Mary Lamb. There is a consistency of both symptoms and creativity among all five.

This episodic disorder which temporarily interrupts the life style and the life flow of the afflicted individual is short-lived and does not seriously limit the quantity of creative output, but it definitely does influence the quality. Two of these subjects, Munch and Strindberg, were "cured" in the sense that these episodes virtually disappeared later in their lives, but long before their deaths. An analysis of their creativity before and after the cure gives clues as to how the episodic disorder influences creativity.

The episodic disorders have been recognized since the middle of the 19th Century. A possible underlying epileptic mechanism has been suspected even though such individuals rarely manifest typical epilepsy. Such disorders were considered "epilepsy without seizures" and referred to in the medical literature as "psychic equivalents" (of epilepsy) or "complex psychic seizures." However, only in the last four decades have we obtained direct empirical evidence, utilizing wire probes in seriously ill patients, that these episodic disorders are correlated with focal epilepsy deep in the brain. The epileptic characteristic of the symptoms before, during, and after the "attacks" provides overwhelming circumstantial evidence for such an explanation in many artists and writers, but, I must add, some episodic disorders reflect hysterical or manipulative behavior rather than epilepsy.[2]

The reader will soon become aware of the double meaning I attribute to the word "brainstorm." In one sense this refers to the storms of electrical activity recorded by the neurophysiologist deep in the brain, while in the other sense, the artists and writers represented by our core subjects report that during these episodic disturbances there often occurs an inspirational or visionary fitting together of percepts or concepts that reveal a new perspective of the world—what is commonly referred to as a "brainstorm."[3] Such a correlation of objectively recorded storms of electrical activity in the brain and this subjectively reported revelation reinforces my opinion that neurophysiology and psychology are complementary rather than contradictory ways of looking at the data reported in this book.

All parts of the brain are susceptible to excessive electrical discharge of neurons, and one area deep in the brain referred to as the limbic system is particularly sensitive. This limbic system stands as a gateway or connection between the new brain serving all higher rational and intellectual functions and the ancient brain of primitive reflexes. Because in lower animals this area of the brain subserves the function of smell, it has been called "the smell brain" and again because it is important for "gut" feelings, in fact, all strong desires and urges such as pleasure, fear, rage, it has also been called the "visceral brain." The limbic system seems to provide a selective-integrative function by which raw emotions are modulated by the cortex and in turn motivate action toward goals as determined by higher cortical functions. The limbic system also influences which experiences are stored as memories and probably which stored memories are recalled because they have some relevance to the emotions elicited by the current situation. At times the core subjects seemed to have an overworking or hyperexcitable and at other times an overworked or exhausted limbic system. The "storms of electrical activity" in the limbic system usually do not spread to the surface of the brain so would not be recorded with an electroencephalographic (brain wave) examination.[4] It is important to realize that only after such seizural activity spreads to the surface of the brain would typical motor seizures result, but seizural activity in the limbic system is frequently limited to the deeper areas of the brain; hence, the patients do not manifest typical epilepsy. Furthermore, studies indicate that the limbic system has the lowest threshold for seisures and is exquisitely susceptible to drugs and toxins which stimulate the nervous system. Neurophysiologists have also discovered that the threshold for seizural activity can be lowered by repeated intermittent electrical stimulation of the

brain—a reaction that has been referred to as "kindling."[5] This
kindling probably can be facilitated by a wide variety of stimuli
and any one of us may wittingly or unwittingly induce such a
kindling phenomenon which ultimately results in focal storms of
electrical nerve activity in the limbic system. When this results
in short bursts of excessive electrical activity, we experience the
inspirational thought or act or an ecstatic or, unfortunately more
often, a very unpleasant transitory emotional state. These intense
emotional outbursts are often acompanied by impulsive acts of
primitive fright-flight or rage-attack behavior. If such bursts persist there may be sustained periods of not only intense and uncomfortable emotions with their associated impulsive acts, but
also hallucinations, delusions, and confusion which can last for
hours, days, weeks, and even several months.[6] Psychic stress
alone can precipitate these bursts of excessive electrical activity
in the limbic system as can physiologic imbalances within the
body. Excessive electrical activity can also be induced by mind
altering drugs such as LSD and Mescaline as well as alcohol and
the toxic element of absinthe, an aperitif that was particularly
favored by several of our subjects.

The perceptual and conceptual distortions induced by these
storms in the brain give unique characteristics to the painting and
writing of our core subjects. The intense dysphoric quality of
their illness led them to look inward for an explanation of their
symptoms leading often to initiation of a self-analysis—some
years before Freud wrote of his own self-analysis. Looking inward
for the meaning of their painful symptoms they also found meaning for the world, which put them in the vanguard of the existential
movement; the epileptoid loss of boundaries between the "self"
and the outside world was conveyed in their works so that, for
example, Virginia Woolf has been called the phenomenologist's
novelist.[7] It is not surprising that these subjects were at the
forefront of the "Expressionism" that seized the imagination of
the intellectual world at the turn of the century.

The strategy for analysis of the core subjects involves foremost a pathography—that is, a detailed description of each
individual's disorder, in the individual's own words as recorded

in their writings, mainly letters and diaries. This then is a self-report that emphasizes the subjective aspect of the the disorder, usually with an elaboration of how such disorders also influenced their creativity. The availability of these data depended on the subjects' willingness to reveal their ''souls'' to the public. Our debt to these individuals in this enterprise of self-revelation can be appreciated by the psychoanalytic patient who accomplished such a self-revelation with great difficulty and only with help and in the privacy of the psychoanalyst's office. The courageousness of our subjects in making their self-revelations public must be part of their genius.

Such an ''autopathography'' cannot stand alone but must be supplemented by a description of the psychopathology as seen through the eyes of those closest at hand—parents, children, spouses, friends, and doctors—but to take such descriptions out of historical and social context would lead to misinterpretations of the data. Furthermore, I cautiously attempt a motivational analysis of the core subjects, a psychodynamic perspective as to what the behavior meant to each individual in the context of his own personal history, even though such psychodynamic reconstructions are fraught with error because they cannot be corrected by a dialogue with the individual. This study then is a psycho-pathography and a psycho-social-history of our subjects.

In Section II of this book, I evaluate creative individuals who probably suffered from a psychosis that was quite unlike the episodic madness of our core subjects.[8] It is not surprising that the interaction between their creativity and their mental disorder was in many ways different than that of the core subjects. This contrast reveals that there is no simple explanation of the relationship between genius and madness. I first discuss Robert Lowell and Ernest Hemingway as examples of manic-depressive disorders, an illness which, like the episodic disorder, intermittently recurs. Nevertheless, there are significant differences between the two. I also discuss Ezra Pound and a Marseilles painter Adolph Monticelli, who was much admired by both van Gogh and Cezanne. These two probably suffered from a paranoid psychosis which, except for fixed delusions, did not seriously impair their intellects. Such an illness usually starts late in life so may have minimal influence on the individuals' early creativity, although it may be quite disruptive to their lives. I also discuss the possibility that their illness was feigned rather than real. Third, I discuss Emily Dickinson, an inhibited recluse with massive neurotic symptoms, whose poetry suggests that she had premonitory or incipient psychotic symptoms and at least one overt psychotic episode. This coincidence offers the opportunity to explore the difference between the psychotic disorganization in thinking and the metaphorical writings of the poet. The next chapter focuses on institutionalized individuals, most suffering from chronic deteriorating schizophrenia, who nevertheless at some time in their lives showed the capacity for talented artistic expression. The last chapter includes vignettes of other creative individuals that elucidate the complexities of the relationship between mental disorders in general and creativity. These include two individuals whose first psychosis inexorably quenched their creative work. These were the German poet Hölderlin and the dancer-choreographer Nijinsky. Brief references are also made to Charles Darwin and Florence Nightingale, both of whom began their productive life with a burst of energy, yet later became chronic neurotic invalids although they remained creative throughout. Proust is included as an example of the severe neurotic who was also physically ill. His creativity may well have been therapeutic. Finally, I briefly consider two of the greatest geniuses of this century, Freud and Einstein, who despite eccentricities and minor neurotic symptoms, certainly would not be considered psychotic.

In Section III I examine the relation between medicine and creativity. The first chapter in this section provides vignettes of patients whose behavior was closely observed, while monitoring electrical activity deep in the brain. Similarities between the behavior of these patients and our subjects with episodic disorders is highlighted as support for my thesis that much of the behavior of the core subjects reflects focal epilepsy deep in the brain. Next I explore the use and misuse of psychiatric and medical labels. Sometimes labels are used to denigrate the genius, but if used properly prolong life and probably enhance creativity. In the next chapter I face the concern often expressed by the subjects and empathically supported by biographers that medical or psychiatric treatment, while it might allay distress, will stifle creativity. This is a close scrutiny of the doctor-patient relationship of each subject, with particular emphasis on the obvious failures—those who committed suicide.

The Epilogue presents the essence of creativity and why this creativity can be mistaken as madness. It describes exciting new medical techniques which in the not-too-distant future may move my hypothesis regarding the contribution of mini-fits to creativity above proof by circumstantial evidence to proof by objective measures of brain activity.

My credentials for undertaking such a study are based on my experience as a psychiatrist and psychoanalyst who has treated many patients with episodic disorders (as well as other illnesses), some of whom were artists and writers. Furthermore, my research involved correlations between brain and behavior, including neurophysiologically recorded brain activity as well as the influence of such drugs as alcohol and the psychedelics on both brain activity and behavior. My most valuable insights, however, have been provided by the reported introspection of my patients.

How can psychiatrists assure the validity of retrospective clinical evaluation of historical figures? They cannot talk to these individuals and, in fact, may have difficulty in projecting themselves into the proper historical perspective. The psychiatrist usually does not have access to medical records, even if they are extant. However, the psychiatrist's most important source of information is the self report of patients, and this is available in the sense that the core subjects in this book wrote copiously: letters, diaries, poetry, novels, autobiography—and some painted. It is surprising how many did all of these and also surprising how many interacted either directly or indirectly with each other. Needless to say, writers' and artists' creative work in some sense is autobiographical and occasionally is overtly presented as such. This data must be interpreted cautiously, as the creative individual has poetic license to exaggerate for dramatic effect and, like Munch, may openly admit this.

If at times I seem to emphasize the neurophysiologic or medical model, I must add the caveat that any neurophysiologic explanation of madness or genius, no matter how elegant, is still simplistic in trying to understand both creativity and madness—that is the "soul" of our subjects. Whether we can ever completely understand this soul is unlikely, but our best effort utilizes the biopsychosocial perspective presented here.

Section I

Episodic
Madness

Chapter I

Vincent van Gogh
—Storms in the Brain

"Aberrations suddenly seized me," said Vincent in a letter to Theo[620]* and so they did at least seven times in the 18 months between December 24th, 1888, when Vincent mutilated his ear and his tragic suicide at age 37, July 29th, 1890. During this period Vincent was phenomenally productive, completing over 450 works. What was his aberration, and how did it interfere—or could it have contributed—to his creativity? Almost every conceivable psychiatric diagnosis has been applied to Vincent's illness, so the Dutch psychiatrist, Professor C. Kraus, says that since Vincent was unique in every other way, perhaps he was unique in his illness. However, it is hard to believe that even Vincent could invent a unique mental illness just for himself. To comprehend Vincent's genius one must try to understand not only his personality but also his illness. Like so many geniuses, his life was seen as an aberration by ordinary persons, but to him only these episodes were. He felt them as something alien and a threat to his productivity.[2]

The experienced physician in trying to understand his patient first listens to his patient. Vincent wrote over 700 letters to his

* 3 digit # refers to a letter # in reference 1.

brother Theo, which revealed him as a genius with words as well as paint.[(1)] Early in this correspondence Vincent wrote to Theo, "Do you want me to continue writing about everything the way I have lately, tellling you the thoughts that come into my mind, without being afraid of letting myself go, without keeping back my thoughts or censoring them?"[(169)] These letters then are an act of self-revelation comparable to that of the psychoanalytic patient, a technique of psychological investigation that had yet to be discovered when they were written. What then did Vincent say about his illness? Between attacks he wrote not only to his friends but almost daily to his brother Theo. Although he did not describe in detail the content of his hallucinations and delusions, he did describe his subjective life. He often called these episodes "fits" or "spells" elaborating further as "fits of excitement" or else "sluggishness"[(591)] or "inner seizures of despair,"[(583)] "painful hallucinations and perverted religious superstitions."[(605 & 606)] In one of his more detailed descriptions he says, "I gather from others that during their attacks they have also heard strange sounds and voices as I did and that in their eyes too, things seemed to be changing. And that lessens the horror that I retained at first of the attack I have had, and which when it comes on you unawares, cannot but frighten you beyond measure. Once you know that it is part of the disease, you take it like anything else. If I had not seen other lunatics close-up, I should not have been able to free myself from dwelling on it constantly. For the anguish and suffering are no joke once you are caught by an attack. . . . I really think that once you know what it is, once you are conscious of your condition of being subject to attacks then you can do something yourself to prevent your being taken unawares by the suffering or terror. Now that it has gone on decreasing for five months, I have good hope of getting over it, or at least not having such violent attacks."[(592)] Thus, to Vincent madness was not a myth as others have proposed. Unfortunately, despite his optimism he suffered further attacks no less severe in the near future.

Vincent did not want to dwell on the painful recollections of his attacks; in fact, he had difficulty in recalling events that occurred. In one letter he stated "I have completely lost the recollection of those days," [597] Perhaps like ordinary mortals he too found it necessary to repress painful experiences. However, this forgetfulness may have been more than repression because Vincent wrote to his friend, Aurier, that he "loses consciousness for a fortnight"[626A] or he states, "I am dazed in the head."[628] This sounds like a true confusion or the altered level of consciousness one experiences in a toxic psychosis or seizure.

Awed by the suddenness of these attacks, Vincent wrote to Theo "My work was going well, the canvas of branches in bloom . . . you will see that it is perhaps the best, the most patiently worked thing that I've done, painted with calm and with a greater firmness of touch. And the next day, down like a brute."[628] He was equally impressed with the sometimes precipitous remission of the symptoms, saying "the whole horrible attack has disappeared like a thunderstorm."[633]

Vincent was optimistically surprised with his rapid recovery, "It astonishes me already when I compare my condition today with what it was a month ago. Before that I knew well enough that one could fracture one's leg and arm and recover afterward, but I did not know that you could fracture the brain in your head and recover from that too."[574] This optimism was tempered by his insight, "I know they will come back and I know that they will go."[605] He seemed to have premonitions of getting sick, saying, "I must beware of my nerves,"[556] as well as an equal awareness of the persistence of his episodic disorder, "I shall always need a doctor."[572] Not only did Vincent predict recurring attacks but he correctly anticipated an attack at Christmas, 1889, significantly the anniversary of his first episode.

Most of Vincent's attacks were of short duration, as he said he generally "loses consciousness for a fortnight."[626A] In fact some episodes were actually shorter and even the longer ones apparently waxed and waned including lucid intervals. As an example, a letter dated December 23, 1888, the day before Vincent mutilated his ear, implies difficulty with Gauguin, but does not reveal evidence of an impending psychosis. Again, a letter to Theo on January 1st seems to be quite rational, so that the period of his episodic psychosis was less than one week's duration. His second attack February 4th must have lasted less than two weeks as he was discharged from the hospital on the 18th, although he slept and ate there for some days thereafter. There is also a report of a brief episode following his forced commitment on February 24th, but until his discharge from the hospital in April he was clearly rational, although his insecurity is revealed in his statement, "paralyzed when it comes to acting and shifting for myself."[590] This led to his voluntary commitment to the asylum at St. Remy in May, 1889. However, to understand Vincent's illness and his creativity we must put them in the context of his personal history.[3]

EARLY YEARS

Vincent van Gogh was born March 30, 1853, at the vicarage of Zundert in Brabant, Holland, located on the Belgian frontier.* His father, Theodorus, a minister in the Dutch Reform church, was a man of "fine spiritual qualities," but not a successful preacher as his calling was limited to small village parishes. Vincent's mother, Anna, is described as a strong-willed, devout woman who was the only member of the family other than Vincent to possess artistic talent.

Information on Vincent is particularly sparse concerning his early formative years, and I see nothing in his youth that would suggest either his genius or his illness. Retrospectively, the most important clues to Vincent's future development were his devotion to and astute observations of nature, and a competence in

For this chapter, I have relied heavily on the "Memoirs of Vincent van Gogh," by his sister-in-law, in Volume I of the complete letters of Vincent van Gogh,1 and the scholarly treatise on Vincent van Gogh, by Mark Tralbaut,2 who devoted a lifetime to the study of van Gogh. These should be reliable sources, although they are at variance with some of the psycho-histories written by Lubin,4 Nagera,5 Westerman-Holstijn,6 Perry,7 Welsch-Ovcharov,8 and Evensen.9 The interested reader will find these writings valuable supplements to what is reported here.

sketching. His early years suggest numerous traumas, such as the austerity of life in a Calvinistic parsonage, the birth of siblings with attendant rivalries, and the difficulties of being sent off at a young age to boarding school. Although all of these experiences must have left their mark, none seems particularly unique except for one event that occurred before Vincent was born. Ironically, Vincent's birth occurred one year to the day after a previous male sibling, also named Vincent, died at birth. The first Vincent was buried in the cemetery adjacent to the vicarage. A tombstone bearing one's own name, viewed daily from early childhood, must have had a significant effect on Vincent's development and adult personality.

Subsequent to Vincent's birth, three sisters and two brothers were born into the family. As the eldest brother, all of the children looked up to Vincent, and the younger children, not surprisingly, were the butt of considerable teasing by Vincent. Little else is known about these early years except that Vincent was described as a "willful child of difficult temper."[1] He had a great love of nature and made numerous collections of birds' nests, flowers, etc. At the age of eight, he modeled a clay elephant, but destroyed it when his family praised his work. This also occurred another time when he sketched a cat.[2] These are early examples of Vincent's intolerance of praise (as well as criticism) which recurred throughout his life. As he approached adolescence he was described by contemporaries as intense, stubborn, a loner, always serious and never smiling, a description that does not suggest a charming person. He was of medium build, broad shoulders, head covered with disheveled red hair carried down and forward. His eyes were narrow, wide-set, and flashing blue. In 1864, at age eleven, Vincent was sent away to school, continuing his education in this boarding school atmosphere until it was terminated, although no one seems to know why, at the rather young age of 15.

In January, 1869, at the age of sixteen, Vincent began an apprenticeship in the firm of Goupil et Cie, Paris art dealers, with branches in leading European cities, one of which was under the direction of an uncle. Vincent continued in their employment for the next five years. His boss, Tersteeg, gave good reports of Vincent's behavior, describing his diligent, studious attitude which everybody liked. One gets the impression then, that until Vincent's twenty-first year, his development was unexceptional. Significant for Vincent's artistic career, his younger brother, Theo, joined the firm in 1873. From that time onward the brothers shared a common interest and initiated a correspondence which was to continue for the rest of their lives.

Vincent was transferred from the Hauge office to London in 1873 and there experienced the first of several ill fated love affairs, this one with Ursula, his landlady's daughter.* Vincent's love affairs, like most other aspects of his later life, seemed to have a unique quality. For instance, the affair with Ursula was most illusory in that Vincent, for many months, kept his love a secret, meanwhile indulging in an elaborate fantasy about his future life as Ursula's spouse. When he finally declared his love in June 1874, Ursula informed him that she was already engaged, a fact that most men would have discovered much sooner. Vincent urged her to break this engagement and when she refused, he plunged from idyllic happiness to deepest gloom and turned more into himself and into religion. Prior to this he had been highly regarded in the world of commerce by both employer and customers. the epitome of conservatism, he was always neatly attired in the standard London businessman's suit and top hat. Now he became disheveled in dress, irritated with his customers, socially isolated, and disinterested in material success. For the first time he was considered eccentric, and he would continue to be until his death sixteen years later. As might be expected, his work at Goupil's deteriorated so that in 1875 the firm found it expedient to dismiss him.

Some historians see this as the onset of Vincent's neurosis or even a schizophrenic or manic-depressive psychosis. Certainly, he must have lost confidence in his ability to attract women, or to become a successful businessman. Perry's evaluation was that

---

* Recent research by Kenneth Wilkie[10] reveals that Ursula was the landlady and the daughter's name was Eugenie. However, as Ursula is referred to as the object of Vincent's love in most biographies, I will do likewise.

Vincent's repeated failures were not only painful but that he lacked insight; "He saw how he felt, not how he did.''[7] Vincent, who had to play the adult at age sixteen, now at twenty-one entered a delayed adolescence, struggling with his identity crisis, a process which continued for the next five years until the fall of 1880 when he decided to become an artist. During the years in London and subsequently in Paris, Vincent had been sketching and expressing mild interest in art when writing to Theo but his psychological conflicts interfered with an orderly resolution of this identity crisis.

After his dismissal from Goupil's, Vincent sought new means of support. For a short period he was content to teach in a boys school outside London, and then combined his teaching with a new religious zeal, working as a part time curate for a Methodist minister near London. He even preached his first sermon, reporting the event to Theo with considerable pride.[1] Now, Vincent's letters suddenly reflected his need to serve mankind and his contact with the slums of London initiated an evangelistic zeal for ministering to the downtrodden.

Apparently, the joy and satisfaction with preaching was also short-lived, as during a visit home, in 1876, he experienced one of several "Christmas crises,''[7] deciding not to return to London. With his family rallying around him, giving moral and financial support, he worked for a short period as a bookseller, but the world of commerce as a bookseller was no more satisfying than that of an art dealer. His mother commented, "I wish he could find some work in connection with art or nature.''[1] Much to the satisfaction of his father, he undertook preparations for admission examinations to the University, being tutored in Latin and Greek under the watchful eye of Amsterdam relatives. At this time Vincent idolized his father and sought to please him by following in his footsteps. For one as brilliant as Vincent this task should not have been difficult, but studying Latin and Greek seemed a circuitous route to his goal of ministering to the poor. Nevertheless, he persisted in his academic endeavors for one year, fearing failure and desperately hoping not to disappoint his family again. It was during this period that his physical masochism first became overt, manifest by beating himself with sticks, sleeping on a plank, eating dry bread, and expressing concern that he was unclean. To Westerman-Holstijn,[6] the meaning of this uncleanliness is clear—he could not control his masturbation, which he must have perceived as unclean and sinful, hence his lust for suffering. At this time there occurred a strange act wherein Vincent threw his gold watch into the collection bag at church and then stuffed in his gloves as well; evidence that his sacrifice was not just monetary but symbolic, and perhaps, as Westerman-Holstijn suggests, symbolic of autocastration, the watch and gloves representing Vincent's genitals. His religious fervor in attending three to four church services on a Sunday and reading the Bible far into the night, plus his social isolation, brooding sadness, and intense concern for the underdog set him apart from his fellow man—a distance that grew greater during the few remaining years of his life.

In the Spring of 1878, Vincent could no longer tolerate the classical preparation for a theological career, returning briefly to his parent's home. Then with family encouragement, he entered a missionary school near Brussels, this being a more direct path to his goal of ministering to the poor. A significant event occurred at this school. While Vincent was drawing on a blackboard a fellow student teased him by pulling his coattails and Vincent whirled on his tormentor in a blazing rage, striking him a "brutal blow." As Tralbaut discerns, this was "the first murmur of the fury and indeed madness that was to come later,"[2] an event quite similar to one which occurred shortly before Vincent committed suicide when colleagues placed salt instead of sugar in his coffee and again he flew into an uncontrollable rage. Basically a gentle soul, such rage turned outward and was rare for Vincent, whose anger would more often be reflected on himself and expressed through mortification, self-mutilation, and ultimately suicide.

Vincent was dismissed from the missionary school at the end of his three-month probationary period. Failure plagued him until his death and failure during this period was no exception. However, this was particularly devastating because, unlike so many previous failures, Vincent desperately wanted to reach his goal. We often explain the failures of children as due to the inadequacy of their parents. However, at this time, as well as in the past and the future, Vincent's parents consistently rallied to help him in times of stress, giving him as much financial and moral support as possible, while not understanding the deepest secrets of his soul. Vincent's failures were usually more emotional than intellecutal as his intense eccentric behavior was not easily tolerated by the mundane world, particularly as he had not yet demonstrated any creative talent which might excuse such behavior. One of his sisters, writing to Theo, says, "You think that he is something more than an ordinary human being, but I think it would be much better if he thought himself just an ordinary being," while his father wrote, "He will spoil everything by his eccentricity, his queer ideas and views of life;" and his mother said, "It grieves us to see that he literally knows no joy of life, but always walks with bent head, whilst we did all in our power to bring him to an honorable position! It seems as if he deliberately chooses the most difficult path."[1]

Through the intervention of his family, Vincent realized his evangelistic aspirations by securing a temporary appointment ministering to miners in the Borinage region of Belgium. Vincent's dramatic mortification was never more apparent than during this period. He gave up his comfortable lodging to live in a hut, slept on straw, rejected soap as sinful, and literally wore sackcloth and ashes as garments. He nursed the sick and gave his clothes to the poor, leaving inadequate food, clothing, and shelter for himself. In this situation his masochism may have proved useful, for instead of preaching faith he performed good works—perhaps the best way to impress his flock of wretched coal miners and their families. As Tralbaut says, Vincent was seen as a "madman or a simpleton, but they loved him all the same."[2] To the poor, the exploited and the miserable, he became a friend despite his eccentricity, but no matter how loved by the workers, authorities saw his behavior as undignified and setting a bad example, so once again Vincent failed his probationary period, allegedly because of his difficulty with public speaking.

Vincent did have difficulty in public speaking, but, as Tralbaut points out, his failure was more likely because he was dirty.[2] During this time he had little contact with either Theo or his family. When he finally began writing again, after Theo had chided him for his idleness, his comments were touching and revealed his innermost self. He wrote, ''I am good for something, my life has purpose after all. I know that I could be quite a different man, how can I be useful, of what service can I be? There is something inside of me, what can it be? This is quite a different kind of idle man; if you like, you may take me for such a one! The caged bird in Spring, knows quite well that he might serve some end; he is well aware that there is something for him to do, but he cannot do it, what is it? He does not quite remember. Then some vague ideas occur to him, and he says to himself, the others build their nests and lay their eggs and bring up their little ones, and he knocks his head against the bars of the cage, but the cage remains, and the bird is maddened by anguish. Look at the lazy animal, says another bird in passing, he seems to be living at ease . . . A certain idle man resembles this idle bird.''[133] Earlier, in the same letter he says, ''Therefore above all I think the best and most reasonable thing for me to do is to go away, and keep at a convenient distance, so that I may cease to exist for all of you. As molting time—when they change their feathers—is for birds, so adversity or misfortune is a difficult time for us human beings. One cannot stay in it—in that time of molting—one can also emerge renewed; but any how it must not be done in public and it is not at all amusing, therefore the only thing to do is to hide oneself, well so be it.'' One wonders what saved Vincent from utter despair; ''One feels an emptiness where there might be friendship, and strong and serious affections, and one feels a terrible discouragement gnawing at ones very moral energy, and fate seems to put a barrier to the instincts of affection, and a flood of disgust rises to choke one, and one exclaims, 'How long, My God' . . . There may be a great fire in our soul, but no one ever comes to warm himself at it.''[133]

COMMITMENT TO ART

In the fall of 1880 Vincent changed course for the final time, leaving the church for good and devoting all energies to his artistic studies. During the remaining years of his life the road was direct and clear. He was no longer trying to follow in his father's footsteps; but was perhaps more under his mother's influence, for she was the one with artistic talent who had encouraged him in this even as a child. At the age of twenty-seven the delayed adolescent identity crisis was over and Vincent was convinced that he had found his calling. This did not mean that his anguish was relieved; someone as intense and as uncompromising as Vincent could not help but suffer one life crisis after another. His stubborn persistence, undoubtedly part of his genius, did not make life easy for himself nor for those who loved him although it did inspire an undying devotion in those who recognized his genius. The Reverend Mr. Petersen, one of Vincent's teachers in Brussels, wrote to his parents, "Vincent impresses me as somebody who stands in his own light."[1] Although Vincent's sudden vocational change appeared impulsive, his letters reveal that he had spent many months considering this, as they increasingly included sketches and references to artists.

Leaving the Borinage after this last failure, he began his career as an artist. Vincent moved to Brussels where he studied anatomy, sketched models, took lessons in perspective, and for the first time developed close associations with other artists, particularly a young aristocratic Dutch painter, van Rappard, who remained a steadfast friend and supporter even though at times critical of the "crudeness" of Vincent's art. In the summer of 1881, to minimize expenses, Vincent returned to his family home, now in Etten. He was still limiting himself to sketching, not using oils until 1883. His career as a painter then spanned less than seven years; however, during these seven years he completed over 800 paintings, 450 in the final eighteen months of his life.

In view of his past history it is not surprising that Vincent had little tolerance for academic art. When he did study in such a formal setting, he absorbed what he could quickly and then moved on, refusing to bow to the demands for conformity, yet he was not a primitive. With self-discipline he put himself through an intensive period of training, proceeding step-by-step from simple sketching to oils until he reached the apex of his career with his post-impressionistic style in which as much is conveyed by color as by form, particularly the complementary colors of yellow and blue-violet, red and green.

During the summer of 1881, the second of Vincent's ill fated love affairs occurred. A cousin, Kee, who had been recently widowed, visited the van Goghs accompanied by her young son. Once again Vincent silently fell in love, expressing this love only through his tenderness towards the young child. When he did openly profess his love, Kee rejected him, not surprisingly, as she was still mourning her late husband. Vincent, who was consistently insensitive to others, became so intensely persistent that she fled home to Amsterdam. Undaunted, he pursued her, but she refused to see him or answer his letters. In front of Kee's parents, Vincent plunged his hand into the flame of a candle until one could smell burning flesh, asking to see her for only as long as he could hold his hand in the flame. Perhaps this was a prodrome of his more famous mutilation in slicing off a part of his ear. His own family, as well as hers, protested his unseemly persistence; Vincent blamed them for his failure in wooing Kee, and became increasingly irritable with his parents. On Christmas Day of 1881 he had a violent argument with his father and left immediately for further studies at the Hague. This was another one of Vincent's Christmas crises.[7]

In the Hague Vincent found the only women with whom he was to live. She was a pregnant prostitute named Sien whom Vincent nursed through her confinement and whose child he joyously welcomed as his own. For one-and-a-half years he lived with and prided himself in this family despite the fact that Sien was uncouth and of inferior intellect. Vincent's rescue efforts were inevitably doomed as Sien ultimately resumed her old ways. In the fall of 1883, dejected and destitute, Vincent moved to Drenthe. It may be significant that it was only after the birth of Sien's child that Vincent finally began using oils. Vincent's father wrote at this time, "Whenever he (Vincent) looks back into the past and recalls how he has broken with all former relations, it must be very painful to him. If he only had the courage to think of the possibility that the cause of much of which has resulted from his eccentricity, lies in himself. I don't think he ever feels any self reproach, only spite against others, especially against the gentlemen in the Hague."[1]

In December of 1883, poverty again necessitated a return to his family home. His father at this time held the parsonage in Neunan. Vincent's eccentric, irritable behavior became a constant source of strain to his parents and the community. His parents tried to be sympathetic, but this was complicated by Vincent's relationship with Margo, a somewhat older spinster living in the neighborhood. This relationship was terminated when she attempted suicide and was committed to a hospital. Vincent became estranged from both his family and community—the former felt helpless in the face of his impulsive verbal abuse and both blamed him for Margo's illness, assuming that it was the result of an affair which he had initiated. Again, a relationship between Vincent and a woman ended in disaster, leaving him bitter and depressed. From the comments he made regarding Margo's mental illness, it seems reasonable to assume that Vincent was born with or soon developed more than the usual assertiveness, for he was referred to in these early years as "willful" and "unruly." The probability that this willfulness was crushed is reflected in his empathy with Margo wherein he wrote to Theo, "That it is a confounded pity for her that in her youth she let herself be crushed by disappointments, crushed in the sense that the Orthodox religious family felt that they had to supress the active, gay, brilliant quality in her and have made her utterly passive."[378] Several sentences later he reflects, "I used to be very passive and very soft hearted and quiet; I'm not anymore, but it is true I'm no longer a child now that I sometimes feel my ego." He expressed his new rebelliousness in a letter to Theo, "I tackle things seriously and will not let myself be forced to give the world work that does not show my own character."[180] We also perceive his extreme loneliness, an alienation from society which he realized was self-inflicted as he wrote, "I try to act indifferently, speak sharply, and often even pour oil on the fire."[212]

It would seem that much of Vincent's life was devoted to abortive rebellion against his father, as was also true of many of the other subjects described later. Several years before his father's actual death he had symbolically killed off the idealized image of his father as a messenger of God, giving up the conventional theological training which would have established him, like his father, as clergyman in a typical Dutch parsonage. Instead, he sought the life of missionary-evangelist, expressing his religious fervor through good works and ministering to the poor, as preferable to living in a snug parsonage and preaching homilies to a middle class congregation. Only when his missionary efforts also failed did he embark on an artistic career. His early years as an artist were characterized by constant violent arguments with his family, particularly his father, leading to separation from the family home, soon followed by a return allegedly due to a financial crisis. During these "returns," Vincent tormented his family and recognizing this, he wrote to Theo that he was viewed as a "foul beast" and a "big rough dog who would run into the room with wet paws."[346] He realized that he was considered uncouth by his parents. This vacillating guilty rage and guilty fear in relationship to parents delayed the development of Vincent's creative genius.

During the years prior to Neunan, Vincent painted gloomy pictures of peasants and weavers entitled "Melancholy," "Sorrow," "Worn Out," "Regrets," while at Neunan the titles were less dolorous, but still heavy with social protest such as "Weavers," "Digging Potatoes," and "Potato Eaters." Theo wrote to his family at the time that Vincent left Neunan, "Vincent is one of those who has gone through all the experiences of life, and has retired from the world; now we must wait and see if he has genius. I think he has . . . if he succeeds in his work he will be a great man . . . appreciated by some but not understood by the public at large. Those, however, who care whether there is really something in an artist more than mere superficial brilliance will respect him; and in my opinion that will be sufficient revenge for the animosity of so many others."[1] Vincent now renounced all thoughts of marriage, so that unfettered by a wife and family, he could give up all thought of worldly goods or conventional success and pursue his career with increasing fervor. Even though Vincent, when he gave up his religion aspirations for art, had long since abandoned the idealized father, it was not until March 25, 1885, that his father actually died. Vincent was now completely free of his father's influence so it is perhaps significant that his first masterpiece, "The Potato Eaters"[(F82)]* was finished in April 1885, one month after his father's death. (Illustration # 1)

In November 1885, Vincent left his home forever, proceeding to Antwerp. Shortly after his arrival there he wrote to Theo of his desire to move to Paris in February, 1886. By the following summer Vincent's health was much improved and his spirits gayer. The following winter, however, he became irritable and argumentative with increasingly frequent "outbursts of temper."

While in Paris, Vincent studied briefly in Cormon's studio, but again he rebelled against the controlled atmosphere of formal teaching. He did, however, become acquainted with the works of impressionists and the artists of the Salon des Independents. At this time we see the lightening of the palette with experimentation in using the bright colors that characterized his future work as well as brief experimentation in the brush techniques of the impressionists as he rapidly progressed to his own unique style. These were heady years for Vincent as he had personal contact with artists who already were or soon became famous: including Degas, Pissarro, Bernard, Gauguin, Toulouse-Lautrec, Seurat, and Signac. Theo wrote to his family, "If we can continue to live together like this, I think the most difficult period is past and he will find his ways."[1] As already mentioned, during the next winter in Paris, Vincent's health deteriorated. He felt that this was due to alcohol or perhaps absinthe. Theo's optimism had dissipated for he wrote, "My own life is almost unbearable. . . . It seems to me as if he were two persons, one marvelously gifted, tender, and refined, the other, egotistic and hard hearted. They present themselves in turn, so that one hears him talk first in one

*Numbers preceded by the letter F refer to reference 11.

THE POTATO EATERS—Lithograph similar to van Gogh's painting with the same title. The latter is considered his firstmasterpiece.

#1

way, then in the other, and always with arguments on both sides. It is a pity that he is his own enemy, for he makes life hard, not only for others, but also for himself."[1] Vincent left for Arles, in Southern France, in February of 1889. Theo wrote that perhaps this was a stop on the way to Marseilles because it was in Marseilles that the artist Adolph Monticelli, whom Vincent much admired, had lived (see Chapter 7). Theo wrote prophetically to his sister, "He is certainly an artist and if what he makes now is not always beautiful, it will certainly be of use to him later; then his work will perhaps be sublime, and it would be a shame to have kept him from his regular study, however unpractical he may be, if he succeeds in his work there will certainly come a day when he will begin to sell his pictures . . ."[2]

Arles was Vincent's most creative period. Here in the sunny Provence his spirits revived. This was a happy time accompanied by immense productivity, painting landscapes including spring blossoms, orchards in bloom, wheat fields under the burning sun, autumn colors, and starry nights. Vincent said, "Life is almost enchanted after all." He rented a little house of his own (the yellow house), decorating it with his own pictures. Vincent was engaged in a period of feverish productivity accompanied by grandiose plans to establish as a joint venture with Gauguin an art studio where young sympathetic artists could gather and work. In part, Vincent's productivity during this period was to impress Gauguin and although Gauguin was dubious concerning the proposed studio, he finally consented to come to Arles because of severe financial straits and desperate need of help from Vincent's brother Theo in selling his paintings. On the surface it seems odd that Vincent chose Gauguin as his partner in this enterprise because they had little in common regarding artistic style except that both were innovative and poorly understood artists who were trying to supercede the impressionistic movement. In Paris Vincent had only minimal contact with Gauguin and they had disagreed vehemently as to the capabilities or contributions of other artists. The fervor with which Vincent pursued this alliance suggests that it met some dimly perceived (if perceived at all) archaic

*In 1985 one of his paintings sold for 9.9 million dollars

need. Gauguin was to be the leader or father of the studio and Vincent second in command, or the mother—an only thinly disguised family with prospective young artists representing the children. As Nagera suggests,[4] the arrangement was probably sublimated homosexuality with Gauguin the dominant masculine figure and Vincent the submissive female. Symbolically, this is represented in Vincent's art; for example, the painting of Gauguin's grand armchair with book and erect candle on the seat,[F499]* contrasting to Vincent's smaller chair with supine pipe and tobacco pouch.[F498] The relationship between the two artists was strained from the start because, as Tralbaut points out, Vincent could not help but be hurt by Gauguin's "instinctive provocations and malicious smiling scarcasm."[5] It is unlikely that Gauguin recognized Vincent's genius and for this reason did not accept Vincent as an equal. It was also out of character for Vincent to be obsequious, so during this period he was often obstinate and disagreeable.

Prior to the ear mutilation several acts of Vincent's are important as they represent abortive impulsive acts. Details are vague and the reliability of Gauguin's reporting is sometimes questioned, but it has such clinical validity that it must be taken seriously even though more details would be desired. Gauguin reported that on several occasions during the night Vincent would approach his (Gauguin's) bed as if walking in his sleep and when called by name would immediately "awaken" and return to his own bed.[2] Could this have been an unconscious expression of a homosexual overture?

On another occasion there was the unexplained episode where Vincent threw a glass of absinthe at Gauguin's head and finally, on the night of the tragedy, Vincent approached Gauguin with an open razor. Gauguin reported, "I must have looked at him with a very commanding eye for he stopped, lowered his head, and then turned around and ran back toward the house."[5] It was then that Vincent cut his earlobe off, walked a few hundred yards to a brothel where he presented it to a prostitute he and Gauguin shared saying, "Guard this well." Later he was found

* Numbers preceded by the letter F refer to reference 11.

by the gendarmes bleeding and unconscious on his bed. This is a classic example of aggression when thwarted being turned on oneself.

Tralbaut's theory regarding the symbolic meaning of the ear mutilation is the most parsimonious, namely that Vincent suffered from auditory hallucinations (as he later admitted) and was responding to the command "Kill him, kill him." When thwarted he then responded with a biblical injunction, "If thine ear offend thee, cast it forth," behavior that is surprisingly common among psychotic individuals. This explanation, however, ignores the significance of the ear presentation to the prostitute. It makes more psycho-dynamic sense to consider this act as symbolic of the bull-ring, as proposed by J. Oliver.[2] In this sense, the bull-fighter after demonstrating his prowess (manliness) is presented the ear of the vanquished bull as a token of esteem for his performance and in turn presents the ear to the lady of his choice. Undoubtedly, Vincent's self-esteem had been severely deflated by Gauguin's malice. Did not the act of ear mutilation reflect Vincent's vacillating identification with first the vanquished and then the vanquisher (in this case the bull and the matador respectively)?

HOSPITALIZATION

On December 24, 1888, he was hospitalized after mutilating his ear. By January 1st he had physically recovered and seemed rational; however, he was not discharged from the hospital until January 19, 1889. He had another relapse February 4th and was hospitalized until February 18th. After leaving the hospital the townspeople of Arles signed a petition for his commitment but he was discharged from the hospital on March 19th.* Vincent

* This sequence is somewhat different than reported by Hemphill[12] who does not reference his source—mine was Tralbaut.[2]

no longer felt capable of handling the mundane affairs of living as well as keeping up a studio, so in May he volunteered to go into the asylum at St. Remy where he stayed for one year.

During the year at St. Remy there were at least four more attacks, one occurring July 8th and lasting perhaps for forty-five days, but other attacks were of shorter duration, except the last, which persisted from mid-February until mid-April, 1890. Vincent's illness then was a recurrent episodic disturbance with a precipitous onset and an equally abrupt remission of varying but usually brief duration. This is what I have described elsewhere as episodic psychoses.[13] Such reactions, if accompanied by confusion, are generally the result of storms of electrical aactivity occurring deep in the brain and thus in the neurophysiologic sense are true electrical brainstorms. This excessive electrical activity deep in the brain seldom results in a typical epileptic seizure as it does not involve the areas of the brain that control muscle action, so when Vincent said, "I am a madman or an epileptic"[589] he was, in fact, neither most of the time, but during the episodes in some sense he had a little of both. This should be considered neither schizophrenia nor epilepsy in the usual sense, but something quite distinct because the peculiar combination of madness related to an epileptoid mechanism deep in the brain results in behavior both qualitatively and quantitatively quite different from typical epilepsy or classical schizophrenia.

Dr. Hans Evensen,[9] a Norwegian psychiatrist demonstrating persistence and guile, managed to review the stored handwritten notes of Dr. Peyron at the asylum of St. Remy shortly after World War I. Dr. Peyron suggested that Vincent's diagnosis was epilepsy but Dr. Evensen comments on the fact that there is no documentation of any grand mal (or for that matter any other typical forms of seizure) in Vincent's life. Apparently, unaware of the current French concept of "epilepsy without seizures" Evensen considers the lack of documentation regarding seizures merely an oversight, particularly because van Gogh told Peyron that other memebers of his family had epilepsy. I can find no documentation of a family history of seizures and we must remember that van Gogh thought he had epilepsy so that in reporting this family history he probably meant that other members in his family had an illness more or less similar to his own. His sister Wilhelmena was hospitalized two years after his death, and remained there until her own death at age seventy-nine, which means that she spent over fifty years in an institution. Her illness does not sound like an episodic psychosis such as Vincent experienced, unless she remained in the institution even when her illness remitted. Vincent's youngest brother died in the Boer War and it is not clear whether this was in battle or a suicide, but this was ten years after Vincent's death, so Vincent could not have been referring to this episode unless the younger brother had earlier episodic disorders.

On the other hand, Peyron described in some detail Vincent's symptoms and these symptoms are characteristic of the episodic psychoses related to epilepsy. Peyron mentions that at the time of Vincent's arrival at the sanitarium he was perfectly normal but had suffered "acute mania and delirium" in the recent past. He continues that these episodes came "out of the blue," that he had only vague memories of these episodes, and was only partially conscious during the attacks. Peyron noted that the attacks lasted fifteen days to one month, although he mentioned that the last one persisted for two months, but that Vincent was well when he left the asylum.

CAUSE OF ILLNESS

Vincent believed he had epilepsy, for in writing to Theo he stated that he had heard there were 40,000 epileptics in France, but only 5,000 in the hospital, which suggested to him that if he did have epilepsy the prognosis for his own recovery and early departure from the hospital at St. Remy was excellent.[589] Two of his doctors, Rey, the resident physician (intern) in Arles, and Peyron, his Physician at St. Remy, felt that Vincent's symptoms represented an epileptoid phenomenon,[591] describing his illness either as an epileptic crisis or an attack of epilepsy. Surprisingly, most modern neurologists would reject this diagnosis because of the lack of typical seizures; however, today we have data (often ignored) which would support the diagnosis of his own physicians that there was probably a significant epileptoid mechanism behind Vincent's "fits" or "spells."

One can only conjecture why Vincent's doctors during that era diagnosed epilepsy in the absence of overt seizures, but perhaps it was the precipitous onset and abrupt remissions of his symptoms with a clouding of senses and partial memory loss that accompanied these episodes, all suggestive of epilepsy, that led to their diagnosis. The French physician Esquirol, in the early 1800's, popularized the concept of "epileptic furor" and it was believed that this could occur not only before and after typical seizures, but even without such seizures.[14] Hemphill[12] says that Vincent undoubtedly had fits, although I can find no evidence for this. Vincent did have episodic confusional states and I believe that most people who diagnose Vincent as an epileptic are referring to these. It may have been the seeming lack of precipitating factors for the episodes that suggested the diagnosis of epilepsy to Vincent's doctors, although with our modern knowledge of psychodynamics we can identify a number of precipitating psychological events, such as the engagement of Theo, the birth and subsequent illness of his nephew, and finally the illness of Theo, all temporarily related to an episodic psychosis or a dyscontrol act.

We should take seriously what Vincent felt was the "unaccountable involuntary"[492] nature of his attacks for there seemed to be a compelling force beyond his control; a feeling which is typically expressed by epileptics when they describe their seizures. Vincent also had a number of minor symptoms which are significant because they occur so frequently in patients with seizures. These are dizziness, sensitivity to bright lights, and the sensation of nearby sounds coming from a great distance as well as objects changing shape before his eyes. Perhaps his doctors were ahead of their time and were willing to recognize what so many modern physicians still refuse to—that there is an epileptoid basis for episodic behavioral disorders. Lubin[5] says that the episodic symptoms might have resulted from seizural activity in the temporal lobes, while I believe it is more precise to say that such behavioral changes are due to seizural activity in the limbic system, only a part of which is located in the temporal lobes.

This hypothesis seems to be supported by Vincent's experience, for when treated with bromide his "hallucinations were converted to nightmares."[574] Bromide, which in excessive amounts can itself precipitate a toxic psychosis, was in years past utilized as a sedative and an anti-epileptic drug.[14] It would have elevated the seizural threshold within the limbic system and in this way could have aborted episodic psychotic behavior.

It has been demonstrated that even purely psychological but stressful events eliciting emotions will precipitate such seizures; therefore, it is obvious that the psycho-dynamic and neurophysiologic theories are complementary and not contradictory. In Vincent's case, perhaps, it was the anxiety of losing Theo's support in anticipation of his impending marriage, combined with the sexual dominance-submission conflict with Gauguin, that proved the final straw, eliciting limbic seizures followed by the dyscontrol act of severing his ear. It may also be that the limbic system was particularly susceptible in Vincent because of his notorious neglect of his physical well-being. We know that such susceptibility can occur as a result of improper diet, or hypoglycemia (low blood sugar), and perhaps vitamin deficiencies, leaving the limbic system particularly vulnerable to excessive neuronal discharges. Furthermore, alcohol can precipitate limbic seizures as well as precipitate dyscontrol acts. Could it be possible then that Vincent intuitively recognized this when he writes about the "Night Café,"[F463] "I've tried to express the idea that the Café is a place where one can ruin oneself, go mad or commit a crime." (See Illustration #2) On other occasions Vincent reported the deleterious effects of alcohol on himself, recalling that when he left Paris he was "almost an invalid and almost a drunkard."[544] It was upon his arrival in Paris that Vincent began drinking excessively and it was especially in Paris where he

#2

THE NIGHT CAFE—van Gogh said, "I have tried to express the idea that the cafe is a place where one can ruin oneself, go mad, or commit crime. . . ."

became so obstreperous that his brother Theo reported living with him most difficult, writing to his younger sister, "My home life is almost unbearable, no one wants to come and see me anymore because it always ends in quarrels and besides he is so untidy that the room looks far from attractive." He continues, "It seems as if he were two persons: one marvelously gifted, tender and refined; the other egoistic and hard-headed. They present themselves in turns so that one hears him talk first in one way and then in the other and always with arguments on both sides."[2]

There are other factors which could have induced a hypersensitive limbic system, leading to focal seizural activity in that area. Vincent makes a startling revelation in a letter dated January 9, 1889 when he writes, "I fight this insomnia by a very strong dose of camphor in my pillow and if ever you can't sleep I recommend it to you."[570] This was written shortly after his first attack, which resulted in the ear mutilation. Camphor is a convulsant so there is a possibility that this could have aggravated his condition. Camphor poisoning produces headaches, warm feelings, confusion, excitement, restlessness, delirium, and hallucinations, all quite typical of Vincent's attacks. It is unclear how long he persisted in this treatment or how much camphor could have been inhaled in this manner. Far more likely is that thujone, a known convulsant that is similar to camphor and the toxic constituent of absinthe, might have stimulated the limbic system to the point of seizural activity. We have confirmed in our own laboratory that this is a potent convulsant in animals, and in low doses induces spindling activity within the limbic system without concomitant generalized motor seizures.[3] We know that Vincent began drinking absinthe heavily in Paris at the very time when he was becoming increasingly irritable and continued in Arles where he imbibed even more than in Paris. It was here that he suffered his first psychotic episode. Signac, who visited Vincent in Arles after the first attack, noted that he was drinking absinthe and cognac every afternoon. In the 1957 Dutch edition of Vincent's letters it was proposed that "bad" absinthe was the cause of Vincent's attack and Lubin and others mention this possibility as a precipitating cause for his episodic madness.[1,3,5,12,15] It is therefore worthwhile investigating the effect of absinthe in more detail.

This drink called the "green muse" by the poet Verlaine (an absinthe addict) or "Water of the Star Wormwood," was supposed to produce lunatics. As the author of "Notes for a Cellar-Book"[16] says, only a madman would drink it "neat" so it was consumed in a ratio of one part absinthe to three to five parts water. As absinthe, particularly the thujone, is relatively insoluble in water, it induces a pearly precipitant when in contact with water. Before 1905 absinthe was allegedly the best selling "before dinner drink" in the world. Its popularity in France was initiated by the Algerian War of 1847 when French soldiers were given absinthe in their wine as a protection against malaria and many of the soldiers developd a fondness for the anise flavored liqueur at that time. Absinthe is a concoction of fifteen herbs including the leaves of wormwood (Artemisia Absinthium) in neutral grape spirits, the best product being 136 proof.[17] It was originally used as a medicine supposedly effective for chills, fever, poor appetite, bronchial inflammation, and about any other discomfort which befell man. It is considered an aphrodisiac, and as Hemingway pointed out, "It works by changing ideas and not be irritating the sexual glands."[18] Intellectuals liked it because it stimulated the mind and assisted in the flow of ideas. In the fashionable Café de la Paix and also in Montmartre, intellectuals and artists spent hours sipping their absinthe, many in a constant state of intoxication, and most of Vincent's artist friends imbibed. Supposedly Vincent's own private mixture was one part absinthe, five parts water, and one part black ink which he claimed augmented the flavor.[17] The French poet, Verlaine, described the exultation, freedom from inhibition, wildness of ideas and sensations, sexual excitement, and the raging fires of hostility that were induced by this drink. Apparently, it brought out Verlaine's cruelty, particularly toward his wife, and ultimately he served a prison sentence for shooting his homosexual lover, the poet Rimbaud.[17] The painter Adolph Monticelli, much admired by Vincent because of his use of colors, was also an absinthe addict, as was Strindberg (See Chapters 7 and 4 respectively).

In 1909 a Swiss peasant shot himself and his wife as well as his young daughters and then made an unsuccessful suicidal attempt. When confronted with the bodies of his victims he said, "It is not me who did this, tell me oh God, please tell me, I have not done this. I love my wife and children so much."[17] This sounds like a rather typical, although extreme, dyscontrol act. It is a moot point of how much can be blamed on the two absinthe drinks he had during the day of the crime and how much should be blamed on six quarts of other spirits consumed during the same day, but we know that either alone can induce limbic seizures. The Swiss made absinthe the scapegoat for this crime and shortly thereafter banned the manufacture of this liqueur. It was not until 1915, six years later, that the French followed suit and then only after claims that reverses early in World War I were due to the debilitation of French culture by the excessive use of absinthe.[17]

At least indirectly relevant to Vincent's illness is a consideration of other drugs which induce limbic seizural activity as well as behavioral disorders, particularly dyscontrol acts or episodic psychotic reactions. These are the so called psychedelic drugs or hallucinogens such as lysergic acid diethylamide (LSD), psilocybin (from mushrooms), and mescaline (from peyote cactus). It is interesting to note, too, how the experiences of toxicity under these drugs is much desired by artists and writers as a creative experience. This lends support to the theory that Vincent, during the intervening lucid periods, might have utilized symptoms occurring with limbic seizures in his artistic work. My colleagues and I have shown in the laboratory that not only in animals but also in humans, toxicity under these psychedelic drugs is accompanied by spindling activity in the limbic system.[3,13] It is also well documented that acts of impulsive nature sometimes destructive to self or to others take place when an individual is toxic from psychedelic drugs.

However, such infrequent but tragic consequences of these drugs have obscured the well known fact that there also occur remarkable perceptual, conceptual, and emotional changes during these transitory toxic states of an exceptionally pleasant nature, leading artists to seek out such experiences to enhance their creativity (see Chapter 11). It suffices at this point to mention only that Vincent's life left ample opportunity for the developemnt of limbic system dysfunction. It may well have been that this area was particularly susceptible in Vincent to seizural activity from birth onward as we know that he showed impulsive behavior (dsycontrol acts) early in his life, long before his episodic psychotic reactions first occurred at Christmas 1888.

EFFECT ON CREATIVITY

During Vincent's episodic psychotic states he was not artistically productive. He did make numerous sketches all reflecting his exquisite artistic talent, but these sketches were simple and fragmented [F1600 Verto]. At times they represented what was for Vincent a unique confusion, that is, combining aspects of the scenery of Holland with those of Provence [F1593]. One of the few works known to be painted during a psychotic episode were his three versions of "Reminiscence of the North" painted in April, 1890; therefore, completed toward the end of an episode [F673-5]. To me these appear to represent Vincent's lesser accomplishments. By this I mean that there seems to be little suggestion of what is the foreground and the background, the important from the unimportant. For example, it is difficult to separate the green foliage from the green village houses from the green sky or the orange flowers from the orange clouds. Such confusion is not apparent in the paintings he completed immediately before and immediately after this psychotic episode. Apparently, these episodic psychotic reactions were devastating and accompanied by too much confusion for productive work. Lubin says, ''Vincent's case does not aid those who wish to prove that a psychotic man can create great pictures,''[5] yet Lubin speculates that perhaps Vincent used the symptoms of his illness in the creative process rather than passively accepting them. This is certainly possible inasmuch as there were long lucid periods between psychic episodes during which he was unusually productive.

The psychedelic drugs such as LSD and Mescaline induce changes in neuronal activity within the limbic system suggesting "fitting" activity. Those who have experienced the toxic effect of these drugs describe the lucid feelings and thoughts as though one is truly awakened to a new perception of the world. The perception of color as reported by persons under the influence of such drugs is, "It was as if we were surrounded by a golden glow"; "I emerged alone in the radiant white light"; "Sparkling lights flashed across the darkness"; "It began to glow a dull purple which turned to a deep cherry and the heat of it was overwhelming"; "Colors seemed to flow"; "Colors seemed to hold great and uncanny significance"; "Fields had a kind of luminescence"; "Whirling colors into color, angle into angle"; "There was no glow in them but only activity and revolution."[18] Vincent describes the colors even more vividly regarding his painting "Night Café,"[F463] "In all of this, an atmosphere like a devil's furnace of pure sulfur."[534] Or describing the first starry night,[F474] "On the blue-green expanse of sky the great bear sparkles green and pink, its discrete pallor contrast with the harsh gold of the gas."[533B] Of himself and the other impressionists, Vincent wrote to his sister Wilhelmina, "We are all of us more or less neurotic. This renders us very sensitive to colors and their particular language, the effects of complementary colors and of their contrasts and harmony."[W23]* Vincent repeatedly said he wanted to portray feelings by color alone as did Edvard Munch (see Chapter 3).

If we assume correctly that Vincent's storms in the limbic system, although present early in his life, increased in frequency, perhaps, under the influence of toxins in absinthe, then his art should have changed during the periods he was in Paris, Arles, St. Remy, and Auvers. Not an art critic, I hesitate to evaluate Vincent's paintings in this historical perspective but can only describe my personal experience in visiting a van Gogh exhibit on three different occasions when his paintings hung in chron-

* Reference 1

ological order. As I moved from room to room starting with his earliest paintingss to the final ones at Auvers, I experienced a mounting tension and excitement. For me his creativity heightened throughout his life as a painter. His art was particularly meaningful because of the bold strokes, vivid colors, sparkling exaggerations, all of which create a reality beyond photographic reproductions of the scenes themselves. Perhaps, Vincent would have been considered a great artist had he never painted after the "Potato Eaters,"[F82] but to me his exciting creativity progressed exponetially in the subsequent years, precisely at the time he was becoming sicker, suffering from increasingly frequent episodic psychotic reactions. We must keep in perspective, however, the years of preparation for this beautiful, spontanéous, and creative effort. It was the preceding, plodding methodical work done in an atmosphere of unbelievable privation and anguish which was necessary so that Vincent in his feverish activity could transfer from palette to canvas the kind of unique experience all of us can enjoy. As Barker says, "Having great ideas seems to question whether one is creative or crazy, blessed or damned."[19]

The use of absinthe alone, of course, cannot explain Vincent's artistic genius because he painted masterpieces before he used absinthe. Nevertheless, during the period of his absinthe drinking, his artistic endeavors suddenly took on new and unique characteristics, such as the swirling kinetic quality, the vivid complementary colors, and the sparkling halo effects which were only vaguely suggested in earlier works. Yet absinthe was extensively used by the French population in general and also by many of the post-impressionistic artists, but they did not paint like Vincent. However Monticelli, an artist much admired by Vincent for his use of color, was also an absinthe addict, and there is considerable in Monticelli's painting that reminds me of Vincent's art (see Chapter 7).

VINCENT'S ART

Let us briefly examine a number of Vincent's paintings to see what these painting can tell us about the artist's feelings and how they are related to this psychedelic experience.*

* Unless otherwise referenced these are reproduced in Tralbaut's book.[2]

The lithograph, "The Potato Eaters"[(F1661)] completed at Ein-
dhoven, April 1885, long before Vincent was addicted to absinthe, was similar to the painting with the same title and generally
considered to be Vincent's first masterpiece. It is also thought
by some to be the first expressionistic art work. Although the
social message is present, Vincent was particularly concerned
with the play of light as was reflected in his later paintings. Note
the halo effect about the girl's head as the steam rises out of the
potatoes. This halo effect is a common experience under the
psychedelic drugs. Also, note the human caricature, an almost
simian quality to the faces, which one also experiences under
psychedelic drugs. Vincent said of this painting, "It is a subject
that I tried to paint, being inspired by the peculiar light effect in
that grimy cottage." This lithograph of the painting was sent to
Theo and Vincent's colleague, van Rappard. van Rappard in
viewing the lithograph wrote, [(1)] "The people's movements had
not been properly studied and their positions were
awkward . . . there was no proper connection between the kettle,
the table, and the hand on the handle; and what was the kettle
doing floating in the air? Why had the man on the right no knee,
belly or lung? Why was his arm a yard too short? And he only
had half a nose. Why did the woman on the left have a nose like
a cube on the end of a tobacco pipe?"[(2)] Vincent, not surprisingly,
was hurt by van Rappard's critique and replied, "I've just received your letter . . . you are herewith getting it back." This
led to an alienation which persisted until Vincent's death.

"Roulin the Postman,"[(F432)] painted in Arles, August 1888,
was commented upon by Vincent, "I am now engaged on a
portrait of a postman in his dark blue uniform with yellow, a
head somewhat like Socrates, hardly any nose at all, a high
forehead, bald crown, little grey eyes, bright red chubby cheeks,
a pepper and salt beard, and large ears. This man is an ardent
republican and socialist, reasons quite well and knows a lot of
things."[(1)] Note the power of this portrait despite the fact that
some consider the draftsmanship inadequate, as evidenced in the
distortion in the right leg, right arm, and the right hand as well.

"The Night Café," [(F463)] painted in Arles, September 1888, about which Vincent said; "I have tried to express the idea that the Café is a place where one can ruin one's self, go mad or commit a crime, so I have tried to express, as it were, the powers of darkness in a low public house, by soft Louis XV green and malachite, contrasting with yellow-green and harsh blue-green and this is an atmosphere like a devil's furnace of pale sulphur."[534] I have suggested earlier that this description of "The Night Café" may reflect Vincent's own awareness that alcohol and absinthe could send him into madness. Perhaps, more than any other picture, this condenses all of the perceptual distortions of the psychedelic experience. To some, the most striking aspect of this painting is the distorted perspective and increased depth of the picture, particularly dramatic if one views the picture under the influence of one of the psychedelic drugs. We also see ominous and depressive effects despite the sensuous beauty—all characteristic of the psychedelic distortion.

"The Starry Night," [F612] painted at Saint-Remy, June 1889, remains an enigma to most of Vincent's biographers. He says about it, ". . . I am sending you . . . a study of night . . . the olives with a white cloud and the night effect are exaggerations from the point of view of arrangement, their lines are warped as in old wood." [607] In reply Theo says, "I understand quite well what it is that preoccupies you in your new canvas, like the villages in the moonlight."[2] Apparently, Theo understood something Vincent's biographers find hard to comprehend. Canaday describes "The Starry Night" (Illustration #3) as follows: "If the starry night seems to burst, to explode, to race, it does not run away; it is built on a great rushing movement from left to right; this movement courses upward through the landscape, into the hills and on into the sky, and floods into the picture like a swollen river in the galaxy beginning at the border of the upper left, but this movement curls back on itself in the center of the picture then it rushes forward again at reduced pace; and finally curls back once more to join other rhythms instead of running out of the picture . . . The cypress rise abruptly and lean slightly in the opposite direction as a brake; their own motion spiraling upward is another check to the horizontal lunge of the earth and

#3

STARRY NIGHT—John Canaday comments on the dynamic intensity of this painting, suggesting that something like an inspiration which was present at the time of the painting accounts for the extraordinary immediacy of the picture.

sky; a church steeple less conspicuously across the sweep of a hill on the horizon, to the same effect.'' This, then, reflects the extreme kinetic quality to Vincent's pictures, attention which can be either exciting or painful, perhaps, more dependent upon the mood of the viewer than that of the artist. As Canaday points out, the dynamic intensity of ''The Starry Night'' suggests something like ''inspiration'' which was present at the time of the painting and accounts for the extraordinary immediacy of the picture.[20] Canaday adds, ''This inspiration flowed from the reservoir of study and experience, even if it was released by the passionate absorption of the moment.''

''Reminiscence of the North,'' [F675] painted at Saint Remy, April 1890, is the best of three paintings with the same title which were probably the only ones completed during the height of a psychotic episode. Vincent said after his recovery from his illness, ''I nevertheless did some little canvasses from memory.'' To me, personally, the interest and quality of this painting is minimal compared with those painted before or after psychotic episodes Sketches done by Vincent during the same period are F1600, F1601, F1599.[11] All show the lack of concentration and persistence necessary for creative artisitc effort. Also, ''Hut with Cypress in Winter: Three Peasants Working''—Saint-Remy, January-April 1890, indicates, perhaps, Vincent's disorganization in thought. In view of Vincent's realism, it is significant that the thatched roofs of the north, but unknown in the Provence, were surrounded by cypresses common in the Provence but unknown in the north. The artistic products during his psychosis hardly support the idea proposed by some that Vincent's psychosis directly contributed to his creativity; rather it seems that the psychosis interfered with this creativity.

Of ''Almond Tree Branch in Blossom,'' [F671] painted at Saint-Remy, February, 1890, Vincent says, ''I started right away to make a picture for him (his newly born nephew, also named Vincent) to hang in your bedroom. Big branches of white almond blossoms against the blue sky.'' He goes on to say, ''In the canvas of branches in blossom you will see that it was perhaps the best and most patiently worked thing that I have done, painted with calm and with a greater firmness of touch.'' In the next sentence Vincent says, 'And the next day down like a brute.''[628] By that Vincent meant that he suddenly became psychotic and entered one of his most prolonged psychotic periods, lasting from February to April 1890. Particularly striking to me is the meticulous, almost oriental flavor,* quite different from what Vincent was painting just prior to this. Does this represent a special effort for this young nephew and namesake or could this perhaps be a defensive, obsessive, meticulous attempt to control his usually impetuous painting at a time when he was ominously expecting a psychotic break? The latter seems possible because after recovery from his psychotic episode in April, Vincent mentioned to his brother that he felt ill while doing this painting.

"Crows on the Cornfield,"[F775] painted at Auvers, July 1890: Although often presented as such, is not Vincent's last painting. Some critics suggest that it represents a disorganization in perspective, reflecting a psychotic break shortly before his successful suicide; however, his letters at that time reveal no psychotic ideation and a photograph from the same perspective in Tralbaut's book suggests that the scene still retained what I have referred to as Vincent's realism. What can be discerned is the ominous sky rolling forward to engulf one, probably a fair reflection of Vincent's deep depression shortly before his suicide. It is interesting to ask one's self which way the crows are flying.

At Vincent's insistence he was released from St. Remy in May 1890. He traveled alone to Paris, where he met with his brother briefly, and then proceeded to Auvers, where Theo had arranged for him to be under the medical care of a Doctor Paul Ferdinand Gachet. The physician had been recommended by Pissaro because of the doctor's own interest in painting. Unfortunately this ended two months later with Vincent's suicide.

---

* My impression of the oriental meticulous quality was derived from the reproduction of this painting in Tralbaut,[2] and was not so apparent when I viewed the original in the Van Gogh Museum in Amsterdam.

SUICIDE

On the afternoon of July 27, 1890, Vincent shot himself in the stomach. Walking home wounded he stumbled up to his room where he was found groaning in pain. His doctors agreed that it would be impossible to extract the bullet. Theo was summoned and early on the morning of July 29th Vincent died in his brother's arms. In a letter to his mother Theo wrote, "One cannot write how grieved one is, nor find comfort, it is a grief that will last in which I certainly shall never forget as long as I live. The only thing one might say is that he himself has the rest he was longing for . . . life was such a burden to him; but now as often happens, everybody is full of praise for his talents . . . Oh Mother! he was so my own, own brother." [1] Theo's own health, which had been poor prior to this, failed rapidly. Six months later, on January 25, 1891 Theo also died. Perhaps, the symbiotic relationship of their lives continued unto death.

A profound aspect of Vincent's personality, basically a reflection of this destructive ambivalence towards his parents, was his extreme child-like dependent neediness, e.g., his persistent, extractive behavior with Theo. Although this had some practical value, because he could continue his artistic life unhampered by mundane activities necessary for his subsistence, it was even more meaningful to Vincent as it reflected an early childhood neurotic conflict—the continuing struggle to be the favorite child. Such arrested development may have contributed to his genius, for it is said that most of us lose our childhood spontaneity, but that it is the true mark of a genius to carry this spontaneity into adulthood. This arrest in development was a part of Vincent's creativeness which did not become maladaptive as long as Theo acquiesced to Vincent's demands. We have Theo to thank for having contributed almost as much to Vincent's productivity as Vincent himself. Despite Vincent's humble protest during periods of depression, he, like most geniuses, had a conviction of the worthiness of his art and felt that by sharing this with Theo both would be rewarded. He saw himself as the mother of the painting and Theo the father. One must realize that the demands Vincent placed on Theo were not for personal luxury, for the extra money Vincent extracted went for paints, canvases, or models. He made equally arduous demands upon himself and I think it is reasonable to assume that these demands killed them both. It is characteristic of geniuses to believe in their importance and this is matched by perseverance, energy, and self-sacrifice, devoted to reaching their creative goal even under the most adverse circumstances.

The events leading to Vincent's suicide contribute to our understanding of this dependency. It does not seem likely that Vincent was suffering another "attack" or was even fearful of an imminent one. Vincent had premonitions regarding these attacks, but described calm intervals of three to four months following attacks. A letter found on his person after his death did not indicate the disorganization in thinking that preceded past psychotic episodes. Vincent had made suicidal attempts during previous psychotic reactions, but they were bizarre, poorly planned, impetuously and ineffectually carried out through means closest at hand—such as eating paints or drinking turpentine, although he would have realized that these were ineffective in his rational moments. These attempts are in contrast to his successful suicide. No matter how impetuous the act of pulling the trigger might have been, the last attempt required considerable forethought and planning and that is why it was successful. Vincent borrowed the gun several days prior to his suicide, obviously not for the purpose he espoused—to shoot crows. The Town Hall in Auvers, painted shortly before his suicide, does not suggest that Vincent was psychotic. (Illustration #4)

Retrospectively, there were many premonitions of the impending suicide. Vincent wrote to Theo, "If I were without your friendship, they would remorselessly drive me to suicide, and however cowardly I am, I should end by doing it."(588) This was written when Vincent was in the hospital at St. Remy, at a time when Vincent's dependency needs were seriously threatened. His studio in Arles had failed, his furniture was gone, Theo was soon to be married, and Vincent could perhaps anticipate future children who would compete with his own childish needs. The marriage did occur with the subsequent birth of his nephew and

THE TOWN HALL IN AUVERS—this is one of van Gogh's last paintings which belies the implication that van Gogh's artistic accomplishments had deteriorated shortly before his suicide.

#4

namesake, and simultaneously there were ominous stories of Theo's ill health. A letter Vincent wrote pleading to be released from the sanitorium at St. Remy two months before the suicide reflects his desperation, "I can't stand anymore, I must make a change, even a desperate one."[(631)] This is certainly no man to give a gun to.

Another possible reason for Vincent's suicide was his increasing reknown as an artist and his fear of this success. Vincent's neurosis of being "wrecked by success" is suggested in the following letter to his mother and sister, written shortly after a favorable review of his art, "As soon as I heard that my work was having some success and read the article in question, I feared at once that I should be punished for it; this is how things nearly always go in a painter's life: success is about the worst thing that can happen."[(629a)] This reaction to praise was similar to what he had shown in his childhood when he destroyed any artistic efforts after his parents had spoken well of them.

I propose then that Vincent's pervasive childish dependency was his outstanding character trait, which may have contributed to his artistic creativity in maintaining a spontaneity that most of us lose as we mature. This was also the basis of Vincent's persisting melancholia and his need for an all consuming mystical union with another person (mother substitute) which in its childishness was destined for failure. These neurotic conflicts, not the electrical "storms in the brain," resulted in his premature death through suicide.[(3)]

Chapter 2

Virginia Woolf—Another Suicide

Virginia Woolf who had her first mental breakdown in the summer of 1895 (age 13) and drowned herself on the 28th day of March, 1941 (age 59), was considered to have suffered from a manic-depressive psychosis.[1] During the forty-six years between her first and last attack, by my count, she had at least twenty other episodes. In terms of standards delineated in the current Psychiatric Diagnostic and Statistical Manual (DSM III), Virginia would be diagnosed as suffering from a bipolar affective (manic-depressive) disorder with mood incongruent hallucinations and delusions. Utilizing the strictest definition of manic-depressive psychosis, her illness was not typical. Many of her episodes had an abrupt onset and short duration while others showed a mixture of rapidly cyclic mania and depression with hallucinations and delusions so bizarre that it would suggest a diagnosis of schizophrenia. The combination of the two would lead to the diagnosis of a schizo-affective disorder implying that it would be difficult to assign Virginia to either a schizophrenic or manic-depressive diagnosis. By the diagnostic standards current in the United States in the 1940's, she would have been considered a schizophrenic rather than a manic-depressive because of the bizareness of her hallucinations and delusions.

Poole[2] believes that mental illness is a myth, denying that she was ill at all, claiming that she was just misunderstood, but Virginia herself during her rational interludes admitted to her madness. The data to support the concept that Virginia Woolf suffered from an atypical or episodic psychosis distinct from either schizophrenia or manic-depressive psychosis, probably associated with an underlying focal seizure deep in the brain (limbic area), will be reviewed.

The deaths of loved ones close to Virginia, including her father and mother, have been identified as precipitating causes at least for her first two psychotic episodes, although these seem more likely to have been prodromal or predisposing causes as her illness occurred several months after the death of her parents. On the other hand, more direct precipitating causes in later years were Virginia's anxiety about the publication of her novels; i.e., the breakdown occurring after the novels had been submitted for publication but while she was awaiting critical reviews.

The data available for making my analysis of Virginia's illnesses depend to a large extent on her own published comments, although Virginia did not write a systematic autobiography. These statements are scattered throughout six volumes of collected letters[3] and four volumes of diaries.[4] Other information is obtained from the autobiography of her husband Leonard Woolf, particularly the volume entitled *The Journey Not the Arrival Matters*[5] and brief autobiographical sketches by Virginia regarding her adolescent life contained in the volume *Moment of Being*.[6] Autobiographical material was included in many of Virginia's writings, particularly her second novel, *Mrs. Dalloway*,[7] and the last, *Between the Acts*.[8] Finally, details of her life are reviewed in the two volume biography of Virginia by her nephew, Quentin Bell.[1] Her family background and childhood were extensively covered in the biography by Love.[9] Some of Virginia's episodes may have been precipitated by medications prescribed by her physician, but unlike Vincent van Gogh, Edvard Munch, and August Strindberg, alcohol did not seem to play a significant precipitating role. At least Vita Sackville-West stated that Virginia only drank light wines and seldom did she even do this.[5]

EARLY YEARS

Virginia was born on the 25th of January, 1882, to Leslie Stephens and Julia Duckworth. This was both her mother's and father's second marriage, so that Virginia had four half siblings, George, Stella, and Gerald Duckworth on her mother's side and Laura on her father's. There were also three full siblings. Vanessa three years older, Julian Thoby, two years older, and Adrian, one year younger.

Laura, who was the daughter of Leslie Stephens by his first wife, was Thackeray's granddaughter. Bell described the child as mentally defective, but one gets a somewhat different point of view from Love. She is described as a vacant-eyed girl who could hardly read and was tongue-tied. She was part of the household until sometime between 1887 and 1891 at which time she was institutionalized and apparently relatively ignored after that. Other descriptions of the child were that she was mulish, obstinate, perverse, but that she was verbal. She was known to howl, shriek, exhibit a fiendish temper, and is considered by some as a childhood schizophrenic. [9]

Virginia showed traits of an episodic disorder as a young girl. It was said that she had sudden extremes of emotion which would range from rage, to gloom, to ecstacy. It was also noted that Virginia herself realized that she had a problem with her sense of "self" as she reports having memories without a "self." Thus, she apparently had periods which would be technically referred to as depersonalizations as well as a sense that the inner world and the outer world could quite literally flow into each other. According to Love, [9] Virginia had a disproportionate balance in thinking away from the rational empirical to the nonrational and mythic. Poole agrees but feels this was an asset whereas Love sees it as a liability. This lack of subject-object boundaries must be one of the reasons Poole refers to Virginia as "the phenomenologist novelist" in the sense that Husserl, the founder of Phenomenology, attempted to transcend the Cartesian dichotomy between the subject and object. [2] Apparently Virginia experienced such transcendence and at times used this in her novels.

There are some rather startling descriptions of Virginia's childhood based on her own recollections. How distorted these are is not clear, but if accurate, Virginia was always a very strange and complex creature, but even early her uniqueness was recognized as possible genius. She remembers having the feeling that the mind is a receptacle into which "moments of time" and "segments of space" actually entered. She had complex fantasies of worlds, within worlds, within worlds—she herself being one of these worlds. If the episodic disorders are correlated with electrical storms deep in the brain Virginia describes this well when she refers to both unpleasant and pleasant fantasies as "shocks." Virginia developed language skills late but by the age of five she would entertain both siblings and adults with long speeches and story telling. The strength of her character and nonverbal communication was such that she could cast gloom or joy over the house just by her facial expression and action.

On the 5th of May, 1895, when Virginia was thirteen, her mother died. In the summer of that year Virginia had her first psychotic episode. Virginia in later years described her first illness as "gigantic chaos streaked with lightning." She remembers her symptoms as anger, irritability, mental confusion, physical pain, racing pulse, delusion, illusions, and difficulty in keeping track of time. There is also some question as to whether or not even in this earliest episode she made an attempt at suicide. Virginia felt that her early psychosis was a mixed blessing; at least it gave her the motivation to write. Even in early childhood she had an existential preoccupation with death, nothingness and non-being.[9]

Virginia indulged in much "scene making," enjoying a vivid imagination or eidetic imagery that sometimes would tip over to madness but at other times, when she coordinated these scenes with language, turned toward genius. Again, Poole[2] feels that people around her would call this madness because they didn't understand her, but Love rightly approves of this imagery only as long as it was "coordinated and controlled." Virginia also seemed to recognize when such "scene making" got out of control, as she said when writing the end of *The Waves* her own voice seemed to "fly ahead of her, . . ."

The time following her mother's death was a trying period for the girls within the Stephens family. Their father remained chronically depressed and self-pitying, demanding constant attention from the females, first from Virginia's older half-sister Stella, who married two years after her step-mother's death, leaving Virginia and her sister Vanessa to meet their father's incessant demands for care and attention. In the meantime, her brothers were off to public schools and then Cambridge. Virginia was envious of her male siblings who were offered such educational opportunities while she was limited to tutoring or occasional classes within the confines of London. In 1897, Virginia had some sort of illness because it is reported that her doctor prescribed "milk and medicine." We don't know whether this was a psychologic or physical illness except that she was reported as "feverish and ill." Because of this illness, it was necessary for Virginia to give up her private tutoring.

In 1904 (age 22), Virginia experienced her second loss when on the 22nd of February her father died. On the 10th of May, Virginia had her second serious breakdown described as going into a "nightmare." She became maniacal, thought that her nurses were fiends, heard voices urging her to starve herself, and made a suicidal attempt by throwing herself from a window which was not high enough above the ground to cause serious harm. Illusions were reported in that as she lay in bed listening to the birds singing outside her window they seemed to be singing in Greek and she imagined that King Edward VII was lurking behind the azaleas calling out to her in the "foulest . . . language."[1] She remained mad until August, then "thin and shaken," she was well enough to reside under the care of her sister Vanessa. Although this illness is thought to have been precipitated by her father's death, one should note that there was at least a three-month interval between his death and the onset. During those three months, she was traveling in Europe with family and friends, returning to London the day before she became ill.

During her adolescence and early childhood, Virginia and her sister Vanessa were subjected to the sexual advances of their half-brothers Gerald and George Duckworth, ten or more years their senior. Virginia herself wrote about these seductions in her autobiographical writings, *Moments of Being*.[6] She was vague about the details but obviously considered it a true seduction whether or not it actually involved coital activity. What influence this had on Virginia's later sexual life remains problematical, but it was doubtful whether Virginia was ever orgasmic and certainly in later life was more likely to have erotic feelings toward women than men. Her sister Vanessa, who was also subjected to the same advances from her half-brothers, certainly was not as inhibited as Virginia by these experiences. What is pertinent at ths point is that during the travels between her father's death and her breakdown, George Duckworth was among the relatives accompanying the Stephens girls on their travels in Europe. It was mentioned that when Vanessa and Virginia returned to London they were escorted by George and it was the next day that her second serious breakdown occurred. This may be important in view of the sexual encounters forced on Virginia by her stepbrothers. This year was another landmark in Virginia's life because in December she published her first writing, an unsigned review in the Guardian.

After their father's death, the Stephens children moved to 46 Gordon Square in Bloomsbury and began having regular Thursday evening meetings which included a number of her brother's Cambridge friends. This could be considered the birth of the Bloomsbury group. In November 1906, her older brother Thoby died. This was a significant loss to Virginia but one that did not precipitate a psychotic break, although she pretended for some time that a death did not happen, just as she did when her mother died. In February of 1907, Vanessa married Clive Bell, so the two sisters separated in their living arrangement. This too did not precipitate a psychosis but it was another landmark year because Virginia began work on her first novel, ultimately published under the title *The Voyage Out*. Throughout this period of her life, and in fact throughout most of her life thereafter, the modern reader can only wonder about the hectic life of the independently wealthy British intelligentsia. Their lives were filled with frequent trips, both within England and on the continent, as well as incessant socializing. Nevertheless, Virginia and her friends, all authors and painters, were creatively productive despite this hectic social life. On the 29th of May 1912, Virginia agreed to marry Leonard Woolf and the wedding took place on the 10th of August. It was reported that Virginia had periods of being "unwell" immediately before and after her marriage.

As one reflection of Leonard's dominance over Virginia, Love comments on Leonard's behavior in going behind her back to seek medical and psychiatric consultation regarding Virginia's condition. It is astounding that Leonard had his first consultation with Virginia's doctor even before they were engaged. This process of seeking medical consultation regarding a third party without the collaboration and knowledge of the third party is something that would be considered at least untherapeutic, even unethical today. But in the early part of the century insane patients were treated like children who could not care for themselves. This, Love believes, was responsible for Virginia's frequent denial that she was ill and the violent struggle she put up when she was hauled off to a nursing home. One feels that her paranoid ideas that everybody, including her doctors, was against her was to some degree justified.[9] Poole believes that nobody asked Virginia the reasons behind her behavior and in this sense our definition of madness as behavior not understood by those in the patient's environment must include the caveat that one must make an effort to understand the allegedly mad individual before one comes to such a conclusion.[2]

There were obvious sexual problems from the onset of Virginia's marriage and at one point Virginia discussed with her older sister Vanessa as to when one could expect one's first orgasm. Vanessa, recognizing Virginia's inhibition, was reluctant to confide that she (Vanessa) had experienced her first orgasm at age four. It was decided shortly after the marriage that because of Virginia's predisposition to psychotic episodes there would be no children.

ILLNESS AND CREATIVITY

In the winter of 1913 (age 31), Virginia became agitated while awaiting acceptance by the publisher of her first novel. As she said, "How when one longs for sleep does one learn to be sensible? Does one command the brain to lie still and lose consciousness? After such nights there were days of headaches, drilling the occiput as though it were a rotten tooth and then come worse nights of anxiety and depression."[1] In the last week of July, Virginia became ill again and spent several weeks in a nursing home; however, she wrote daily to Leonard, but by the 22nd of August had delusions and resisted food. Her last letter was dated August 5th and Leonard said that she was "slipping into madness." On the 7th of September, Virginia attempted suicide for the second time by taking an overdose of the sedative Veronal. In Leonard's diary,[5] he describes day-by-day changes as follows:

> September 10th–Unconscious all day.
> September 11th–Spoke to me.
> September 12th–Fully conscious, fairly happy.
> September 13th–Cheerful, very cheerful even.
> September 14th–Calm and cheerful, but began worrying later in the day.
> September 16th–Cheerful, but not a good night.
> September 17th–After tea much worry and a bad night.
> September 18th–Depressed and much worried. Slept badly.
> September 19th–Much worried, bad night.
> September 20th–Bad night.
> September 21th–Very excited and worried, trouble with food.
> September 22nd–Very depressed, continued trouble with food, bad night.
> September 23rd–Depressed, great trouble with all meals, re-
> ' quired paraldehyde.
> September 24th–Fair day, lunch great, difficult dinner, again paraldehyde.

September 25th–Excited all day, Two hours over each meal, did not sleep at all.

September 26th–Queer on walk, hardly walked for a moment and then jumpy, lay down. Much calmer in the afternoon.

September 27th–Excited, violent with nurse, 5 ½ hours natural sleep.

These brief comments certainly indicate the rapid cycles between depression, calmness, agitation, and violence which characterized most of Virginia's psychotic episodes. In describing this illness to Violet Dickinson following her recovery she said, "I think the blood has really been getting into my brain at last. It is the oddest feeling as though a dead part of me were coming to life. I can't tell you how delightful it is—and I don't mind how much I eat. All the voices I used to hear telling me to do all kinds of wild things have gone—and Nessa says they were always only my imagination. They used to drive me nearly mad at Welwin and I thought they came from overeating but they can't, as I still stuff and they are gone."[3]

Many years later (1930), in a letter to Ethel Smyth, Virginia describes her madness, "After intermittent rages, then I married and then my brains went up into a shower of fireworks. As an experience madness is terrific . . . and in its lava I still find most of the things I wrote about. It shoots out of one everything shaped, final, not in mere driblets sanity does and six months I lay; it taught me a good deal about what is called ones self."[3] This is pertinent because in his autobiography Leonard discusses whether psychoanalysis might have helped Virginia control her psychotic episodes. Virginia and Leonard did not particularly believe in psychoanalysis although Hogarth Press, owned by the Woolfs, published the Stracheys' translation of Freud's work. In fact, Virginia described psychiatry as a "rape of the mind."

It was obvious that Virginia felt her illness contributed to her creativity, and this was supported by both Leonard and even later the psychoanalyst Alex Strachey (Mrs. James Strachey), who thought that an analysis would be too much for Virginia. Both believed that madness contributed to Virginia's creativity and that it would be better for Virginia to be periodically psychotic than being "analyzed and ordinary." I would also question the value of any intensive insight psychotherapy during Virginia's acute episodes, but believe some expert psychological guidance during the intervals between episodes might have prolonged the periods of remission and lengthened Virginia's life without severely interfering with her creative productivity. Poole[2] says that what Virginia needed was a therapist with an existential or even a religious point of view (see discussion p259).

During the next two years (1914–1915), Virginia had intermittent relapses. In April 1914, she consulted with Dr. Craig and it was reported that she had bursts of excitement and despair. She recovered by December of that year. In 1915, Virginia resumed keeping a diary. On the 18th of February, she complained of headaches. On the 25th, she was at one moment depressed, languid, and at another violent, suicidal, and garrulous, and then finally sank into a coma. The coma seemed more like catatonia, as she refused to talk with Leonard, and sometimes acted as though she did not even recognize him. By March 4th she was excited and violent and taken off to the nursing home on March 25th. Throughout April and May she was almost continuously violent and raving. By June there was a gradual improvement in her condition. In August, Leonard was able to take her out for a drive or take her in a wheelchair. By the 11th of November, all nurses were dismissed. Throughout these years one can follow the periods when Virginia was ill by the sudden interruption in her correspondence, or the fact that Leonard would write letters for her. Looking back on these intermittent psychotic episodes, Virginia wrote some years later (1927), "Suppose one woke and found oneself a fraud? It was part of my madness that horror."

During the years following this 1915 episode, the Woolfs were preoccupied with esablishing the Hogarth Press and Virginia did not have a significant relapse until 1921 (age 39). In 1918, she finished the novel *Night and Day;* in 1920, she began writing *Jacob's Room*. In 1921, there were no entries in her diary between June 7th and August 8th and the first entry after the lapse says, "These, this morning, are the first words I have written to call writing for sixty days; and these days spent in wearisome head-aches, jumping pulse, aching back, frets, fidgets, lying awake, sleeping draughts, sedatives, digitalis, going for a little walk, and plunging into bed again—all of the horrors of the dark cupboard of illness once more displayed for my diversion. Let me make a vow that this will never happen again; and then confess that there is some compensation. To be tired and authorized to lie in bed is pleasant; . . . that I can take stock of things in a leisurely way. Then the dark underworld has its fascination as well as its terror.''

In January, February and March of 1922, she again had the ''flu'' and a murmur of the heart as well as high temperatures. She was in bed much of the time, but felt that by having three teeth extracted her recovery was expedited. Because of her re-current fever TB was suspected. Such physical symptoms, in-cluding fever, can also be symptoms of the epileptoid episodic disorders particularly when the ''storms of electrical activity'' spread to the hypothalamus—one of the deeper areas of the brain controlling the body's physiologic functions.

In January 1923, she was again ''struck by temperature'' and ''sinks her head into the mud.'' On the 19th of August, there was yet another sudden collapse and she remained in bed until December, suffering intermittently from headaches and exhaus-tion. During this period she wrote to friends complaining of frequent nightmares. On July 17, 1926 (age 44) she recorded being exhausted and a ''battlefield of emotions.'' In a diary entry on the 15th of September, entitled ''States of Mind'' she wrote:[4]

''Woke up, perhaps, at three. Oh! it's beginning, its com-ing—the horror—physically like a painful wave swelling about the heart—tossing me up. I'm unhappy! Down—God, I wish I were dead. Pause. But why am I feeling this? Let me watch the wave rise, I watch. Vanessa. Children, failure. Yes; I detect that. Failure, failure (the wave rises). Wave crashes. I wish I were dead! I've only a few years to live, I hope. I can't face this horror anymore. (This is the wave spreading over me.) This goes on; several times, with va-

rieties of horror. Then at the crisis, instead of the pain
remaining intense it becomes rather vague. I doze. I wake
up with a start. The wave again. The irrational pain; the
sense of failure; generally some specific incidents, as for
example my taste in green paint, or buying a new
dress . . . tacked on.''

In this description we see the characteristics of an ictal phenomenon, e.g., waves of dysphoria overwhelming her, periods
of dream-like states or calm and then another wave again. The
stress, however, seems to be psychological—here the sense of
failure for not having children like Vanessa.

In January 1929 (age 47) she had another relapse. This was
attributed to the sedative drug Somnifene which Vanessa gave
her to overcome seasickness on a boat trip back from Germany.
However, the doctor said there was nothing in the dose of Somnifene which was sufficient to have caused such an extreme reaction. The morning after taking the drug she felt ''completely
drugged, my legs staggered, my head reeled—slept on
train—Leonard had to drag me—remained in a state of nervous
exhaustion, e.g., pain, heart jumping, backache.''[4] She also
mentioned at this time that she was taking bromides for her
insomnia and complained again of frequent headaches and ''heart
jumps.'' In July of that year, there were intermittent attacks of
both headaches and melancholia and she said that she didn't know
why.

In August-September 1930 (age 48) she fainted and was ill
for ten days. Her diary includes several comments about her
illness and the process, ''But I have now earned the right to some
months of fiction and my melancholy is brushed away so—soon
as I can get my mind forging and not circling around.''[4] She
also says, ''And so the unconscious part now expands. In walking
I notice the red corn and the blue of the plain an infinite number
of things without naming them; because I'm not thinking of any
special thing. Now and again I feel my mind take shape, like a
cloud with a sun on it, as some idea, plan or image wells up, but
they travel on over the horizon like clouds and I await peacefully

for another to form or nothing—it matters not which." "I believe that these illnesses are in my case—how shall I express it—partly mystical, something happens in my mind. It refuses to go on registering impressions. It shuts itself up. It becomes a chrysalis. I lie quiet, often the acute physical pain—as last year. Only discomfort this then suddenly something springs."[4] In her letters written in 1930 she describes her headaches in three stages as including pain; numb; and visionary. The latter is perplexing but I assume what she means by visionary is that she has hallucinations or maybe transcendental insight. A description of these experiences might be, "after being ill and suffering every form and variety of nightmares an extravagant intensity of perceptions—for I used to make up poems, stories, profoundly and inspired phrases all day long as I lay in bed."[3] This is similar to the subjective sensations of a person under the influence of psychedelic drugs, which have been shown to introduce excessive nerve firing deep in the brain. Thus, like Munch, she seemed acutely aware of the intensity of her perceptions and insights; and also like Munch, she "awakened in the night suddenly terrified." In another letter she says, "my whole body feels . . . twitchy and saggy."[3]

In February 1931, Virginia finished the final chapter of her novel *The Waves*. In the recollection of John Leyman he quotes Virginia as describing the last days of writing this novel as follows: "Reeled across the last ten pages was some moments of such intensity and intoxication that I seemed to stumble after my own voice or almost after some sort of speakers (as when I was mad) I was almost afraid remembering that I used to fly ahead." This sounds similar to the frenzy that engulfed van Gogh while he was painting. The fact is Virginia finished *The Waves* while in bed and reported that she was nearer a "climax of despair" than she had been in the preceding six years.[10]

In 1932 she had a fainting spell and it took several days for her to recover. She also had an episode of "galloping heart" and later in the year reported, "my spine swollen and burning and tender at the third knob from the top."[4] In 1934 she again had two severe episodes of the "flu." In 1936 and 1937, having completed a manuscript, she collapsed into bed in a state of despair needing constant reassurance from Leonard that her work was a masterpiece.

Despite recurrent physical illnesses and nervous exhaustion during the fifteen years from 1926 to 1941, she was particularly productive, publishing almost yearly, including the novels *Mrs. Dalloway* (1926); *To the Lighthouse* (1927); *Orlando* (1928); *A Room of One's Own* (1929); *The Waves* (1931); *Flush* (1933); *The Years* (1937); *Three Guineas* (1938); and her last novel *Between the Acts* (1941). Although there were no protracted psychotic episodes, she refers to many intense emotional experiences that were close to, if not actually, transitory psychotic experiences.

THE "MYTH" OF MADNESS

Roger Poole in his book, *The Unknown Virginia Woolf,* presents a somewhat different view of Virginia's illnesses than the above. Poole approaches Virginia's life from the viewpoint that she was a phenomenologic novelist.[2] There are several prejudices that enter into his appraisal, namely the "myth" of mental illness and the inadequacies of the medical model as well as the limitations of psychiatric treatment for the psychiatric patient during Virginia's life. Although I can agree with many of Poole's conclusions regarding Virginia's relationship to her husband and to her doctors, I find it unnecessary to fall back on these prejudices to come to similar conclusions. His analysis rests heavily on Virginia's novels and identifying in these novels the personas of Virginia and Leonard. Most of his analysis is limited to two serious "breakdowns": the one in 1913 a year after Virginia's marriage and the final episode leading to Virginia's suicide in 1941. Virginia's letters and diaries are largely ignored, but most had not been published at the time he wrote his book.

Poole also believes that Virginia was molested sexually by

both half-brothers, Gerald and George Duckworth, starting when she was five or six years old and continuing until Virginia's father died when she was 22.[2] On the basis of Virginia's recollection in *Moments of Being*,[6] I would agree with him. Furthermore, and I would again agree, he thinks Virginia's serious sexual fears probably stem from these episodes, reaching their apogee at the time that she accepted Leonard's proposal in March, 1912. This is supported by the fact that Virginia had at least two minor breaks directly before and after she finally accepted Leonard's proposal. In further support, Poole discovered that the severe break in 1913 occurred when Virginia and Leonard were visiting the Plough Inn, just one year after they had spent the early days of their honeymoon in the same hotel. The presumed sexual abstinence that existed between Virginia and Leonard may have been easier for Leonard to bear than Virginia and one wonders whether Leonard, through gentle, subtle encouragement could not have overcome Virginia's preconception of the lustful, animal-like behavior of the sexually aroused male. This, plus the astounding lack of communication between spouses as well as the decidedly different world view between the rationalist Leonard and the existentialist Virginia, belies the view of Bell and others that the marriage was idealistically romantic despite the lack of sex. This seems to be supported by Virginia's one letter (already mentioned) when she expresses "failure" for not having children as her sister Vanessa did. Poole feels the decision not to have children was largely Leonard's—based on Dr. Hyslop's (Virginia's doctor) eugenic bias that mental illness should be a bred out of society, particularly English society, so they could continue to fulfill their colonial destiny.

It is astounding that Leonard never bothered to talk with Virginia about her symptoms and never appreciated Virginia's concern about eating and remaining thin. Unlike Poole, I think Virginia should be held responsible as well, for she, as far as we know, never volunteered her thoughts and never confided in him her early sexual experiences with the Duckworth boys. It was ironic and probably tragic that during one of Virginia's convalescences she was sent to George Duckworth's home and slept in his bed, a trauma that could have been avoided had Leonard known or Virginia protested and explained why.

In Poole's analysis of both Virginia and Leonard's writings *(Mrs. Dalloway, To the Lighthouse, The Waves, Orlando, Between the Acts* for Virginia and *The Wise Virgins* for Leonard) the marital conflict of the Woolfs was exposed in only a thinly disguised form.[2] Each, of course, had read the novels of the other and why this wasn't sufficient to communicate their disparate points of view is hard to understand.

Love, in describing Virginia's novels, says that she was determinedly honest when writing them, but because she adopted poetic fiction, her novels employing metaphor and myth and using hyerbole freely, these can hardly be treated as biographical fact. [9] Poole would argue that it was only other people who didn't recognize what to Virginia was fact.

Poole's analysis could explain why Virginia in her excitement became both physically and verbally abusive toward Leonard, although neither Leonard nor Virginia nor Quentin Bell reported this abuse verbatum. Perhaps Poole is right—the best data available is in Virginia's novels, with their recurrent theme of hostility between men and women. This also would explain why Virginia at times would not recognize Leonard nor communicate with him at all.

Virginia did not describe in detail her ''symptoms'' during her episodic madness and this also is true of some of our other subjects, particularly van Gogh. However, they were good reporters on the prodroma or sequelae of the episodic disorder, so data from letters or diaries should be supplemented by the artistic production of the individuals involved. However, we must remember that the artist is a poet and may not be reporting accurately; in fact, may be exaggerating or generalizing. Munch openly admitted this and everybody believes that Strindberg's so-called autobiographical writings were considerably dramatized.

Poole believes that there is no such thing as madness and he considers insanity and madness as just insulting words, insisting that madness is a myth.[2] He is perfectly right that sometimes madness is a myth and we will see how this was probably

true for Monticelli and may have been true for Pound, and even
on some occasions the others; but not all madness is a myth and
one only has to review Virginia's letters to realize that she herself
knew when she was mad. It would be hard to convince me that
she accepted her madness only because Leonard and her doctors
insisted that she was mad. If this were true, she might have saved
herself from such a judgment by being more realistically self-
assertive. I believe that Poole does not help his analysis through
his hyperbole describing Leonard as having a "witch doctor"
point of view. Poole quotes from Virginia's novels to show that
males are repeatedly portrayed as egocentric, gruff, bruising,
insensitve, hammering, dominant, fact-obsessed, cynical, reduc-
tive,ironical, and contemptuous, while women seem not so much
to think but to know, not rationally separate but joined together.
Women do not use logic at the expense of other people but arrive
at conclusions which make the lives of other people easier. So
Poole feels that Virginia's life was hidden from even the person
allegedly closest to her, that is Leonard.

VIRGINIA'S SUICIDE

With the onset of World War II, the Woolfs moved out of
London, visiting only rarely, and Leonard, being Jewish, expressed concern over a possible Axis invasion of England. the
Woolfs actually prepared themselves for suicide should this occur. On February 26, 1941, Virginia finished her novel *Between
the Acts* and by the 24th of March Leonard became seriously
alarmed by Virginia's deteriorating state, although prior to this
she seemed to be quite tranquil and planning her future writing.
In retrospect there is some question as to whether Virginia had
attempted suicide on March 18th, but on the 24th she was talking
about her new book. Nevertheless, Leonard was concerned because he thought she looked seriously depressed. Louie Mayer,
the Woolfs cook, noted Virginia's peculiar behavior reporting,

"She would often come into the kitchen and sit down and then looking perplexed would wonder what it was that she had come to talk about."[10] She also remarked that Virginia bumped into trees or stumbled over rocks as if she did not see them. On the 27th of March, at Leonard's request, Virginia consulted Dr. Wilberforce, who reassured Leonard that she did not need hospitalization.

Quentin Bell reports that on Friday, March 28th, a bright, clear cold day, Virginia went as usual to her studio in the garden where she wrote two letters, she explained that she was again hearing voices and this time had the conviction she would never recover. The letter to Leonard said:

> "Dearest, I feel certain I'm going mad again. I feel we can't go through another of these terrible times and I shan't recover this time. I begin to hear voices and I can't concentrate so I'm doing what seems the best thing to do. You have been in every way all that anyone could be. I don't think two people could have been happier till this terrible disease came. I can't fight any longer. I know that I'm spoiling your life, that without me you could work. And you will I know. You see I can't even write this properly. I can't read. What I want to say is I owe all the happiness of my life to you. You have been entirely patient with me and incredibly good. I want to say that—everybody knows it. If anybody could have saved me it would have been you. Everything is gone for me but the cetainty of your goodness. I can't go on spoiling your life any longer. I don't think two people could have been happier than we have been."[3]

This convinces me that Virginia did not believe mental illness was a myth. She put the letter on the mantle and then picked up her walking stick and made her way across the meadow to the river. Leonard, missing her a short time later, rushed out to the meadow and not seeing her, continued to the bank of the river where he found her walking stick stuck in the mud, but no Virginia. Several days later her body was found on the banks of the river, the pockets of her coat filled with stones. She had once said to Vita Sackville-West that her death would be "one experience I shall never describe." (For a further discussion on Virginia's suicide see pp.256)

How can we explain why Virginia committed suicide when she did? I agree with Poole (and this seems to be supported by Nicholsen's and Trautmann's analysis of Virginia's letters [3], Appendix Vol. 6) that the suicide had been contemplated for some time. The mounting hopelessness can be traced to, at least, three factors. First, Virginia's feeling that the world as she knew it was coming to an end with World War II and in this she was quite right. Second, her most recent novel, *Between the Acts*, was really a scathing analysis of her marital relationship. Then the closing line in her last letter to Leonard, "I don't think two people could have been happier than we have been," must be to some degree a denial of her true feelings. Finally, Virginia's isolation in the country with the lack of social companionship that she needed so badly left little opportunity to sublimate or compensate for the incompatibility in her relationship with Leonard. She could communicate with women, but by moving to the country she lost this companionship.

In summary, what is the evidence that Virginia had an episodic psychosis similar to van Gogh? First, of course, is the recurrent nature of her illness. Rosenthal, in reporting that Virginia had only four manic-depressive episodes, must have considered only the first at age thirteen, the two in which she attempted suicide, as well as the final one when she did commit suicide.[11] However, she had at least four other episodes that were severe enough to require relocation in a nursing home or, at least, constant nursing attention. Furthermore, in eight other years she had one or more attacks that were significantly incapacitating, at least, leading to several months in bed, and these episodes do not include the frequent transitory frightening nightmares, dysphoric feelings, and panic reactions which she reported in both her diaries and letters.

The second symptom that is typical of the episodic disorder is the intense dysphoric experience during the episodes themselves. The panic, terror, rage, and deep depression are all frequently reported by Virginia and those in attendance. Periods of euphoria are either insignificant or short-lived, as they are rarely mentioned. The attacks occurred abrubtly, developing over a period of no more than several days. Although the remissions appear more gradual, this is partly an artifact as her doctors insisted on several months confinement to bed, even though the acute symptoms had subsided and she was obviously clear in the head and no longer delusional. During the intervals between attacks she was not only clear headed but immensely creative and productive, while also leading an active social life.

Typical prodromal symptoms that Virginia reported were her restlessness and sensitivity to external stimuli. This is probably one reason that she willingly accepted the doctor's advice to retire to bed, seeing nobody except her nurses and Leonard. Another common prodromal was Virginia's recurrent headaches; in fact, other physical symptoms including cardiac arrhythmia and chronic insomnia. The nightmares and fainting spells suggest formes frustus of epilepsy, typical of the episodic disorders, and were all symptoms she shared with van Gogh and others.

Not only were her psychotic episodes characterized by intense emotions, violence, and excitation, but at other times there was stupor or negativism in refusing to talk with Leonard or even failing to recognize him. This excessive inhibition of motor behavior alternated with hyperactivity, irritability, and violence that occasionally would last for several months; but most often there would be rapid swings hour-by-hour or day-by-day between the hyperactive and the hypoactive state.

Most of these episodes were accompanied by hallucinations with a bizarreness that is inconsistent with typical manic-depressive psychosis. As, for example, the illness of Robert Lowell (Chap. 6). Finally, following most of these episodes there was a calmness as well as an appreciation of the experience, a realization that durirng some part of the episode a fully formed creative idea occurred to her and there were bursts of inspired thoughts with ideas flowing through her head in "full form."

Again, as we have noted in van Gogh, not only were there

no residual defects during the intervals between attacks, but also both Virginia and van Gogh utilized these experiences through reflection and introspection to find out about one's ''self,'' as we will see did Munch and Strindberg. The serious question arises as to whether Virginia Woolf would have been as creative if she had not had an episodic psychosis. Were these experiences crucial to her constant exploration of new forms and new content in her novels? Would she have been productive if she had not been ill? Such questions, unfortunately, are only speculation with regard to Virginia, but some clues are provided by the experience of Edvard Munch and August Strindberg, who were ''cured'' of their episodic disorder but continued with their artistic creativity for many years thereafter.

Chapter 3

Edvard Munch—A Cure

It is not clear whether Munch had repeated psychotic episodes inasmuch as he had only one psychiatric hospitalization,
but then van Gogh also had only one hospitalization, although
we could identify at least seven discrete psychotic episodes during
the last two years of van Gogh's life. Even Munch's one psychotic
episode may have been a simple toxic psychosis due to alcohol.
He did have paranoid delusions which may have persisted for
some years or may have been bouts of paranoid panic similar to
Strindberg's. Also, Munch admitted himself to spas or a sanitarium on several occasions, although details for his reasons,
except for "exhaustion," is lacking. There is no doubt that
Munch was a severe neurotic, and this neurosis was amply expressed in his paintings, particularly in the years prior to 1908.
There is considerable evidence that these episodic bouts of fear
and rage were sometimes precipitated by, and probably at other
times allayed by, alcohol. It is also not clear whether his alcoholism was a true chronic alcoholism or excessively frequent
spree drinking. One point is clear throughout Munch's life: regardless of his psychopathology, he was persistently productive
in terms of his artistic output and this would have been highly
unlikely if he was a chronic disorganized psychotic, a chronic
inhibited neurotic, or a chronic alcoholic.

Munch himself, as well as his colleagues, mentions the episodic quality of his disorder. Furthermore, Munch's life is of interest because he was "cured" of this disorder with no significant relapses in the last thirty-five years of his life. Whether the cure was due to his own self-discipline in restraining his drinking or the result of his physician's intervention is not clear, but the fact that his artistic output was considerable during these latter years gives us clues as to how the episodic disorders contributed to or interfered with his creativity. A question that is often raised about van Gogh is whether successful treatment by Dr. Gachet would have prevented his premature death due to suicide at thirty-nine and what effect this would have had on his subsequent creativity. Perhaps Munch's life will give us some clues. In this chapter we will examine the data which demonstrate the episodic nature of Munch's illness, utilizing whenever possible Munch's own self-revelations.

It was mentioned in the chapter on Vincent van Gogh that he was an ideal subject for a psychohistorical and a pathographic study inasmuch as he wrote to his brother Theo: "Do you want me to continue writing about everything the way I have lately telling you the thoughts that come into my mind without being afraid of letting myself go, without keeping back my thoughts or censuring them,"[169] I pointed out that this constitutes an act of self-revelation comparable in many ways to that of the modern psychoanalytic patient. The data of Edvard Munch should be even better raw material for a psychohistorical and a pathographic study than that of van Gogh's. First, Munch expressed his feelings very directly in his painting and these paintings resulted from an obsessive process of self-analysis.[1] Furthermore, Munch wrote condensed prose poems about the meaning of his paintings. He probably had plans to publish these prose poems together with the corresponding pictures.[2] Also, Munch, under the influence of his mentor Hans Jaeger, the leader of the Kristiania (Oslo) Bohemians, had been exhorted to personally experience all that was possible and to publicize these experiences. Munch was one of the few of Jaeger's students who dared to lay bare his life. This style of life was a protest against the realistic philosophers

*3 digit # refers to letter in reference 1, chapter 1.

such as Hegel and reflects a conviction that immediate experience reveals more completely the nature of reality than man's cognitive experience. Although Munch's early writings were mostly realistic descriptions of an autobiographical nature, later, perhaps under the influence of a well known writer Knut Hamsum (see pp.148), who in 1890 gave a lecture entitled "From the Life of the Unconscious," Munch as well as other writers and artists, including Strindberg, explored the deeper layers of consciousness or what Munch called "The Life of the Soul."[2] He wrote:

> When I write these notes with drawings—it is not in order to tell about my own life—to me it is a question of studying certain heredity phenomena that determine the life and fate of a human being—just like phenomena indicating insanity in general. It is a study of the soul. I have since I practically can study myself—used myself as an anatomical soul preparation. But, since it in the main is to create a work of art and a study of the soul, I have altered and exaggerated—and have used others for the studies—it is thus wrong to look upon these notes as a confession. I therefore divide—like Soren Kirkagaard—the work in two parts—the painter and his neurotic friend, the poet.[2]

Of course, Munch was both the painter and the neurotic friend. Furthermore, Munch, who considered himself an author as well as an artist, did write an illustrated essay, *Alpha and Omega,* as well as a whimsical playlet entitled, *The City of Free Love,* during his hospitalization.

Until the end of Munch's life he tried to organize his notes, comments, diary, and letters into a coherent statement regarding his life and philosophy, but unfortunately, and inexplicably, because he had the time, he never completed the task. Much of the scattered notes are undated, so that it will take years of scholarly research to fit all of the pieces together, and much remains unpublished and untranslated. Some of the data may be lost in that his letters were willed to his sister Inger and she may have edited or destroyed those she felt detrimental to Munch's reputation.

Nevertheless, what remains gives a detailed picture of Munch. It has been said that Inger arranged with Munch's physician to destroy the hospital records at the clinic in Copenhagen. In his final efforts to collate his notes he planned to write one text entitled *The Tree of Knowledge* and another interwoven with this entitled *The Notes of a Madman*. Unfortunately, this project was never completed. Thus, much valuable data still requires scholarly analysis and the coherency of the introspective material typical of van Gogh's letters is not available to us without such an analysis.

We discovered that van Gogh's episodic disorder, at least on some occasions, was precipitated by absinthe and we know that Munch's alcoholism may have precipitated a number of his episodic disorders. It is not clear, however, whether Munch himself abused absinthe, although we do know that a number of his friends were heavy users, including one of his alleged mistresses, Dagny Juell (Ducha in Munch's portrait of her), as was his mentor Hans Jaeger and also Strindberg. The only comment about Munch's drinking pattern I uncovered was that he preferred whiskey.

EARLY YEARS

Munch realized that his personality was determined to a large extent by childhood events so it is too bad that we do not have more details regarding his childhood. We do know of several traumatic experiences which probably led Munch to say that he does not paint, ". . . what I see, but what I saw."[3] Munch was born December 12, 1863 in Löten, Norway, the son of an army doctor. He was the second of five children. During his childhood he lived in Oslo and the first trauma occurred at the age of four when his mother died of tuberculosis. His mother anticipated her death and discussed this openly with her children. Based upon what Munch painted in later years, he must have at least imagined that he had been present at her death, and this experience was repeated again at age thirteen when his sister Sophie also died of tuberculosis. It is said that several times during Munch's childhood he himself coughed up blood so it is not surprising that he was quite hypochondriacal and particularly worried about his health, often mentioning that he had inherited a predisposition for insanity from his father (one of Munch's sisters and his grandfather were psychotic) and tuberculosis from his mother. On the other hand, Munch's family was one of high intellectual distinction.

Munch felt deprived following his mother's death even though an aunt became a surrogate mother and, in fact, she was the one responsible for encouraging him at age sixteen to leave technical college against his father's wishes to enter the school of design. His father was reported to have a difficult temper with periods of nervousness and religious anxiety which bordered on insanity. Munch said, "When he punished us he could be almost insane in his violence."[3] At the age of eighteen, Munch joined several other artists under the supervision of Christian Krogh who was a highly respected naturalist and impressionist painter. Krogh had surprisingly avant garde attitudes toward his young pupils and their art. In both his lectures and articles, he proposed that fantasy, intensity of feeling, and clarity of communication were the qualities to be recommended to the modern painter. He predicted that the next generation of artist would project its own moods and feelings and he argued that art should not "impress" but "move" people. In writing on modern art he said, "Your duty is to take the stubborn public by the collar and make it stop to look at what you want to show."

From the start Munch demonstrated his talents, showing remarkably mature style even in his adolescence. In fact, Munch sold his first paintings at age nineteen. Thus, Munch, ten years younger than van Gogh, started painting almost the same year that van Gogh did, but unlike van Gogh, Munch's talent was immediately recognized, at least by his teachers, and he was encouraged by family and friends to continue in his artistic efforts.

Much to his father's despair, Munch became involved with

the Kristiana (Oslo) Bohemians under the leadership of Hans
Jaeger. This was an anarchist-atheist-antibourgeois group particularly promoting "free love." As I said, one attribute of the
group was to experience life fully and to lay bare these experiences through autobiography. At the age of nineteen Munch began
an affair with an older woman, Milly Thaulow (identified as Mrs.
Heilberg in Munch's autobiographical notes). In 1889, discov-
ering that she had been unfaithful to him as she had been to her
husband, he was devastated, and this experience colored his attitude toward women for the rest of his life, much of it being
expressed in his paintings as well as in the prose poems that
describe these paintings (quoted below). This was the first of a
series of affairs that all ended with the same disastrous result.
Another alleged mistress, Dagny Juell, was introduced to his
comrades in Berlin, but he was quickly disillusioned again by her
promiscuity and ultimate marriage to his good friend Przybyszewski. He had another affair with a well-to-do Norwegian
woman, Tula Larsen, which ended when she attempted to shoot
herself because of Munch's refusal to marry her. In the struggle
to wrench the gun from her, she shot off the terminal phalanx
of his left ring finger, a bodily mutilation that was a constant
reminder to Munch of the dangerousness of women. Munch remained a bachelor until the end of his life; in fact, Munch had
very little to do with his two spinster sisters. Inger, the sister who
survived Munch, was said to have been invited to his home only
twice in the last six years of Munch's life.

Although Munch's art was not accepted by his countrymen
until he was fifty, in 1885, at age twenty-one, he received the
first of several scholarships which allowed him to travel to Paris.
It was at this time that he began three major works: "The Sick
Child," "The Morning After," and "Puberty." Again, continuing the parallel with van Gogh, this was the year that van Gogh
painted his first masterpeice, "The Potato Eaters." It was in
Paris, in December of 1889 that he learned of his father's death.
The depression that followed this was deepened even more by
the final breakup with his mistress Milly Thaulow. He said of
his father, "I would give anything if I could just once hold his

#5

THE SCREAM—a woodcut similar to Munch's painting on the same subject. He commented that only an insane person could have painted such a picture.

MELONCHOLIA—this lithograph reflects Arne Eggum's observation that Munch focuses on the "transmission of empathetic experience."

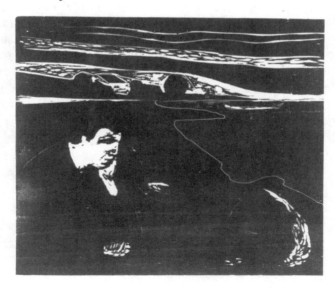

#6

gray head in my arms and tell him how much I care for him. There was always a stupid sense of embarrassment; it is not so much all the worries that I caused him, it is more all of the small things, that I rejected him when he was compassionate towards me.''[4] It was at this time that he painted his famous "Night." Heller feels that this painting represented a dramatic change in style, "The painting no longer is mimetic of an external world subjectively comprehended, but rather of subjective state or idea interpreted in or forced into the remnant of nature's forms."[5] He adds, "The painting becomes an artificial construct focused on the transmission of empathetic experience." (see Illustrations 5, 6) Continuing our parallels between Munch and van Gogh, it is interesting that both artists painted significant masterpieces immediately following their fathers' deaths (van Gogh's, "The Potato Eaters" and Munch's, "The Night"), and that in both instances the fathers were extremely powerful, deeply religious individuals, distant and authoritative with their sons. Munch then was going through a depression just several months prior to van Gogh's suicide.

Despite his depression, Munch stayed in Paris through the spring of 1890, attending an exhibit at the Salon de Independents. The works exhibited included Seurat, van Gogh, and Toulouse-Lautrec. The following December, on his way to Paris again, Munch became ill with what was supposedly rheumatic fever. After some weeks in the hospital he went to Nice to recover. Over the years Munch made a number of retreats to spas and sanitariums allegedly for physical reasons, but often as not there were reports that these retreats were preceded by periods of "nervous exhaustion."

SECESSION

In 1892 Munch moved to Berlin and began a new phase in his life. An exhibit of Munch's paintings was arranged but this caused such a violent protest that it was closed after several days. The critics stated that it was not art, although the German artists who supported him, founding the Berlin secession group, arranged for the exhibit to be shown at Dusseldorf and Cologne. It then returned to Berlin and went on to Copenhagen, Dresden, and Munich. The howls of protests from the critics gave him a notoriety that was the best possible advertisement for his art, so that for a time he prospered both from admissions fees to the exhibit and from paintings that he sold. Seeing his paintings hung together, Munch realized that there was a common theme and began to think in terms of a frieze entitled, "Love and Death." Although Munch eschewed "isms" of any kind saying, "There are no styles there are only tasks,"[8] art historians consider that he went through a series of experimental periods from naturalism to impressionism and symbolism to become one of the fathers of expressionism. In fact, Munch is considered the only Scandinavian artist who had any significant impact on world art.

In Berlin Munch joined a group of Scandinavian and German artists, poets, writers, and professionals who were similar to the Kristiana Boheme. They met regularly in a bar-restaurant that Strindberg called zum Schwarzen Ferkel—"The Black Pig" (see pp. 103). In March Munch introduced his mistress, Dagny Juell. This could only cause trouble among this closely knit group of artistic geniuses, who for a time enjoyed each others camaraderie, but all of whom equated their superior genius to an irresistible appeal to women. As Heller said, "Once again . . . he found himself rejected, cast off by the women, only to be occasionally reeled back as Dagny in her expertly practiced roundelle of free love fished . . . for suitor after suitor."[1] This was even too much for others within the group and so, despite their close kinship, within a few months all (including Strindberg) were "fleeing separately and desperately on trains heading North, South, and East."

By 1894 Munch's prosperity had waned and he was often seen on the street following eviction from his quarters, not having money for either food or lodging. Despite this, or perhaps because of this, he took up a new task and learned other artistic techniques including dry point, wood cuts, and lithography. One of his few patrons during this period (1895), sitting for a portrait, noted, "Munch is still young but already seems worn out, tired and both in a psychic and a physical sense hungry."[1] From 1895 until his hospitalization in 1908, Munch restlessly traveled throughout Europe, drinking heavily and arguing with friends. He was frequently described as in a state of terrible emotional exhaustion. From 1902 to 1905 he engaged in a series of violent barroom brawls. A physician friend was so concerned that he wanted to heal Munch of his neurosis and sleeplessness, but Munch opposed this, feeling it might interfere with his creativity. Despite this neurosis, however, Munch exhibited 106 times during the years between 1892 and 1903 in Scandinavia, Germany, France, Belgium, Australia, Italy, Russia, and Czechoslovakia. His psychosis (described below) led to his hospitalization in Dr. Daniel Jacobson's clinic in Copenhagen in October of 1908, from which he was discharged in the spring of 1909. He returned to Oslo at that time and, except for brief trips abroad, evidenced little of the hectic pace in traveling that preceded his hospitalization. In fact, after 1916 he seldom left Norway. He gave up drinking, became a recluse, and treated his paintings almost as if they were children, often refusing to sell them, although by this time they brought high prices. In 1912 he was an "honorary guest" at an exhibit in Cologne which meant that like Cezanne, van Gogh, and Gauguin his paintings were hung in a room by themselves. He won the commission for painting the murals at the University of Oslo, completing this in 1916. He was represented in the armory show in New York City in 1913 and by 1915 was prosperous enough to support several young German artists. He continued his social isolation throughout both World Wars, living quietly during the German occupation of Norway. On January 23, 1944, a little more than a month after his 80th birthday, Munch died, bequeathing all of his works to the City of Oslo—including over 1,000 paintings. 15,000 prints, 4,000 drawings, watercolors and six sculptures.

PHILOSOPHY

Munch was primarily concerned with life, love, and death. The superficiality of this statement does not reflect the intensity of his commitment nor the complexity of his philosophy. Life triumphs over death through sexuality, so the erotic relationship between a man and woman became a central theme in his art. He saw this relationship going through several stages—a process of attraction, followed by possession, followed by jealousy, and then separation and isolation. This struggle between man and woman was not only reflected in his paintings but also in the prose poems which accompanied these paintings and, not surprisingly, were related closely to Munch's own sexual experience. One of his earliest comments regarding the painting, ''The Voice,'' follows:

> The summer night shed gold over your face and your hair. Only your eyes were dark and sparkled with a mystical glow—a gold pillar stood in the water and rocked back and forth—it melted because of its own brilliance—and gold flowed on the surface—when our eyes met invisible hands tied fine threads—that went through your large eyes in through my eyes and bound our hearts together.[2]

He soon expressed a more ambivalent but still romantic view of the relation between a man and a woman as reflected in his description of his ''Madonna.''

> Your face contains all the tenderness in the world, your eyes dark like the bluish green sea—stuck me to you—your mouth has a painful tender smile—as if you wanted to ask my forgiveness for something—your lips are sensual—like two blood snakes—there is piety in your face under the moonlit lamp—from your pure forehead your hair is brushed back—your profile is that of a Madonna—your lips glide apart as in pain.[2]

The tender pain is a reflection on Munch's ambivalent attitude toward sexuality and apparently was present from his earliest erotic experiences onward.

The year after Munch's breakup with Milly Thaulow he wrote,

> Its been a long time since I thought of her, but still the feeling is there. What a deep mark she has left on my heart. No other picture can ever totally replace her. Was it because she took my first kiss, that she took the sweetness of life from me? Was it because she lied and deceived that one day she suddenly took the scales from my eyes so that I saw Medusa's head, saw life as a great horror, everything that I had seen in a rose colored mist now seemed empty and gray. Here I felt burning love's happiness . . . I felt an executioner (as if as . . . and I was almost insane for several years . . . nature screamed in my blood . . . I was going to burst.)[1]

At another time he wrote, ". . . . then the experienced woman of the world came on the scene and I received my baptism by fire. I was made to feel the entire unhappiness of love . . . and for several years it was as if I were nearly crazy. The horrible face of mental illness then raised its twisted head . . . and after that I gave up the hope of being able to love."[1] The shift to pessimism and futility was now quite evident.

He could still express and idolize woman, as reflected in a memorial he wrote for Dagny Juell upon her death: "She moved among us freely and probably encouraging us constantly, comforting us as only a woman can and her presence alone was sufficient to calm and inspire us. It was as if the simple fact that she was near by gave us new inspiration, new ideas so that the desire to create flamed up fresh and new."

For Munch the process of obtaining eternal life through procreation consisted of a savage battle between the sexes. "Thus now life reaches out its hand to death. The chain is forged that binds the thousands of generations that have died to the thousands of generations yet to come.''[1] Munch carried this even further and one of his themes was the transubstantiation—''dead life provides nourishment for new life and generations follow generations as a result of love between man and woman.''[2] The only ''religious'' theme in Munch's painting was ''The Empty Cross'' which Munch describes:

> The red sun—purple red as though smokey as through a smokey glass and the sun shines upon the world. On the heights in the background the cross stands empty and weeping women pray to the empty cross—lover—whores—drunkards—criminals fill the terrain below—and to the right in the picture a steep slope goes down to the sea. The human beings fall down the steep slope—and terror stricken—they hug the ledge of the precipice—in the center of the chaos stands Munch staring ahead, bewildered and with the frightened eyes of a child at all this—and says why why—it was here—passion and the vices are raging all over the city—the terror of death lurked behind—a blood red sun shines down on everything—and the cross is empty.[2]

It can hardly be said that Munch was an atheist, although undoubtedly he was agnostic, and what religion he had was terrifying. Munch developed an existential philosophy which, to his surprise and delight, he later discovered was quite compatible with Soren Kierkegaard. One of his drawings was named ''The Road Leading to Nothing,'' which seems to reflect Munch's view of mankind's condition. Munch also described his own fear of open spaces in much the same way that Kierkegaard mentions ''the dizziness of freedom.'' Munch, like Kierkegaard, believed that truth is achieved by intensity of feeling. Munch saw man in three parts, tied to the earth through his legs, while the body with heart, stomach, and sex organs linked him with other living beings and the head connected him with higher spheres. Even though man through his body is inevitably bound to the earth, ''each man's brain may be capable of soaring thoughts and yearning

towards something bigger and more pure than itself.''[2] He even
expressed a more basic phenomenologic point of view stating,
''The chair (to have meaning) must be seen by a man.''[6]

Munch was quite outspoken about his philosophy of painting. In his *St. Cloud Manifesto,* written in 1889, Munch asserted
the importance of real life as a source for the arts, ''There ought
no longer to be painted interiors, people who read and women
knitting—they ought to be living human beings who breathe and
feel, suffer and love.'' He said, ''. . . all art, literature as well
as music must be created with ones heart blood.'' At another
time, ''We want something other than mere photography of nature
nor is it in order to paint pretty pictures to be hung on the parlor
wall. We want to try if we can whether we might not succeed
in such a way that we lay the groundwork for art devoted to man,
an art that seizes and takes hold of one, art that is created with
ones heart blood.'' Thus in the sense that an existential thinker
is a passionate thinker, Munch was an existentialist. It is startling
how the central figures in Munch's paintings are staring out at
the audience as if conveying a message directly to the viewer.
(see illustrations 4, 5) Recognizing the importance of ones past
experiences in the individuals perception of reality, he said that
he painted, ''not what I see but what I saw.''[3] The marked
sensualism and primitive child-like quality of his paintings and
the use of background landscapes for depicting human emotions
have all been commented on by art critics. Munch was convinced
that he must paint his inner vision of reality and he openly expressed his emotions in his art.[4] It is not surprising then that he
is considered the first expressionist. He spoke of his desire to
overwhelm others saying, ''I want the viewer of my paintings
to have a profound experience to feel in awe as though they were
in church.''[7] It was when first seeing a group of his paintings
hung together that he recognized the common theme of life, love,
and death that run through his paintings and so he became interested in being a creator of modern allegories.

In Munch's coterie of friends there were a number of writers
and a symbiotic relation developed between these writers and
Munch. They wrote about what he painted and he painted about

what they wrote. One of these was Stanislaw Przybyszewski, a medical student who had taken a special interest in neurology, but he gave up his medical studies to become an author. Przybyszewski had denied the external world and reduced his plots to a sequence of mood and random workings of the mind. In his book *Ascension,* published in 1894, he said, ". . . thoughts described wide elliptical lines, they stretched out, they whirled and glowed and darted around"—this sounds much like an experience with psychedelic drugs. He often cross-referenced Munch's painting when he wanted to suggest certain sensations of pain or pleasure. In fact, he wrote a novel about a painter who wanted to paint a scream he had heard from a woman who threw herself over the railings of a bridge into the water below. Przybyszewski visited Nietzsche in the winter of 1892–93 and remembers this as one of the tragic impressions of his life. Nietzsche was in a wheelchair on his veranda, helpless, apparently bereft of speech and sight. Munch, too, was enamored by Nietzsche although he never met him, but knew his sister and drew a posthumous portrait of the philosopher with the help of photographs.

Munch said of Strindberg, "He and his circle were preoccupied with the deepest problems of mankind." Some of Munch's paintings were a reflection of Strindberg's own texts. He painted several portraits of Strindberg, and in 1896 reported that Strindberg was mad because he (Strindberg) thought that his friends were trying to gas him. Although Henrik Ibsen was thirty-five years older than Munch, and a contemporary of Munch's father, Ibsen encouraged young rebels, including Munch, by telling them that if they caused offense they were sure to have talent. Munch made a number of drawings related to Ibsen's plays. His first portrait of Ibsen was drawn in 1897 for a theatre advertisement for the play "John Gabriel Borkman" and Ibsen's themes in his plays, "Ghosts," "Peer Gynt," and "Pretenders" have much in common with Munch's paintings. Munch's favorite writers were Jaeger, Ibsen, Obstfelder, Strindberg, Nietzsche, Dostoevski and Poe.[4] Munch, like Strindberg, had an instinctive sense of the unconscious and how to use this in learning about one's self. This anticipated Freud and his psychoanalytic teaching by some years.

ILLNESS

Munch believed he was cursed with undesirable, inherited traits that created conflicts in his relations with other people. Reflecting on his fate he said, "a German asked me but you can get rid of many of your afflictions then I answered they belong to me and my art—they have become one with me and it will ruin my art—I want to keep these sufferings."[2] But, after his sojourn in the psychiatric clinic, there was a dramatic change in his personality. Munch who had been a dissolute roustabout with many friends, traveling incessantly and drinking heavily, became a quiet recluse, living only for his art and pictures, no longer drinking, only rarely allowing visits by friends, and then no more than one at a time. There were some differences in his paintings, too. He seemed to shift from the suffering artist to the reflective artist. These later paintings enticed one into the picture rather than screaming out at one. He said that he "no longer wished to paint individual man's sorrows and joys seen in close quarters, but rather the great eternal powers."[8] He painted two pictures entitled "Ashes." The one before his treatment shows a girl with an unbuttoned dress and straggly hair, looking painfully out of the picture with the adjacent man stooped with his hands clutching his head. The second "Ashes," painted after his illness, shows a voluptuous nude standing next to an older man who has an ecstatic expression on his face. He painted twenty epic pictures of workmen and the labor movement, identifying with the struggles of the working class against the bourgeois, which is an interesting reversal of the pattern of van Gogh, who when painting him Brabant was preoccupied with the plight of the miners and peasants and later painted his joyful, brightly colored landscapes from Provence. (See Illustration 7)

There is considerable difference between Munch, who had only one clearly defined psychotic episode, and the other individuals discussed in this section. Van Gogh had at least seven episodes, Virginia Woolf probably twenty, and Mary Lamb over thirty-two. However, the episodic disorders can be episodic neurotic reactions as well as episodic psychosis. Such episodic neu-

#7

WORKERS IN THE SNOW—after Munch's "cure" there were many paintings of a heavy dark mass of workers moving slowly toward the viewer like a force of nature.

rotic reaction is reflected in spells of panic, rage, and depression, and even, on occasion, erotomania.[9] Actually, Munch may have had more psychotic episodes because, as mentioned earlier, he entered sanitariums in Norway and Switzerland and retired to German spas on several occasions. He frequently referred to himself as being close to madness when one of his love affairs was disrupted and said that only an insane person could have painted "The Scream." Although he was hospitalized in Dr. Jacobson's clinic in Copenhagen from October 1, 1908 until May of 1909, letters dated October 22nd revealed that he had already resumed his creative activities. There is considerable evidence for not only episodic agoraphobia and melancholia, but also transitory periods of paranoia and intermittent explosive rages particularly during the years 1902–1905. These emotional disturbances must have been transitory because they did not seriously interfere with his artistic productivity, although between 1897 and 1900 he did little painting or lithography. However, in these years he was exhibiting frequently and traveling extensively throughout Europe. Many feel that Munch used his painting as an attempt to master his intense emotional states.[1] Heller describes Munch's illness as "a recurring schizoid psychosis actualized by alcoholic over-indulgence" and states "that Munch was forced to paint out of fear—to gain through his paintings renewed actualization of his ego which could withstand the pressures of sensual stimuli."[6] He notes that Munch's diary often refers to the idea of suicide but he never made any suicidal attempts, although his behavior at times was certainly self-destructive.

My proposal that these episodic disorders are related to a focal epileptic process deep in the brain (limbic system) no way contradicts the possible interplay between psychological and neurophysiologic mechanisms.[9] These are complementary and not contradictory. Munch and his friends were amazingly sophisticated on this biopsycho-social perspective of medicine, probably influenced by several physicians in Munch's circle of friends who were far ahead of their time in perceiving such complex interactions. One characteristic of the episodic reactions as well as the dyscontrol syndrome is that there are often prodromal symptoms which allow both the afflicted individual and those in his environment to predict when an episode is going to occur. Munch showed a number of these, particularly his restlessness and insomnia, and may have been using sedatives to treat the latter. He was extremely sensitive to external stimuli and often when walking outside seemed to be in a daze or almost asleep as if the scenic beauty around him was too much to bear.[10]

Synesthesia, i.e., the transformation of one sensory modality into another (e.g., sound into visual perceptions and vice versa), which is characteristic of the limbic hypersynchrony as induced by psychedelic drugs (mescaline, lysergic acid, etc.), was frequently reported by Munch as was another common experience, the feeling of an overwhelming sense of calmness following an attack. Munch often referred to the fact that alcohol precipitated his derangement and we have seen how alcohol and particularly absinthe precipitates episodic disorders. At the same time alcohol on occasion may have a calming or dampening affect and is used by such individuals to treat themselves. It is not clear whether Munch's alcoholism was chronic alcoholism or spree drinking. There is evidence to support both ideas and in fact they are not necessarily contradictory. One anecdote suggests the "treatment" possibility. Because of Munch's agoraphobia he sometimes became dizzy when crossing a broad boulevard and had to retreat to the nearest bar for a drink before he could acomplish the crossing. Another anecdote would suggest a more chronic state of alcoholism—that was when one of his patrons arrived early to pose for a portrait, Munch opened the door and stared at him in wide-eyed terror telling him he could not possibly work then but to come back in an hour or two. The patron observed a full bottle of wine on the table. When he returned several hours later, Munch sat down to do the portrait and the patron noticed that the bottle of wine was now empty.

An example of an episodic panic reaction is described by Munch in events which precipitated the painting "The Scream." He said, "I walked along the road with two friends. The sun went down. The sky was blood red—and I felt a breath of sadness—I stood still tired unto death—over the blue-black fjord and city lay blood and tongues of fire. My friends continued on—I remained—trembling from fear—I felt the great scream—nature."[2] (See Illustration # 5)

Between 1902 and 1905 it was reported that Munch had a series of barroom brawls. He describes one of these. "Once after a heavy drinking bout, Karsten and I had a fist fight having thrown him down the stairs—he wasn't much of a fighter you see—I brought out my rifle, aimed at him and fired. What if I hadn't missed?" During the period immediately prior to hospitalization, Munch wrote malicious lampoons of his friends. For instance:[11]

Then Gunnar Heiberg
—sailing along
with his fat little pouch
—winking his pinky eyes
—a cross between
a pig and a toad—
—always crawling with worms
—always sniffing out
marital abstention—

. . .

Gunnar H. had
a pointed and rather fleshy stomach
—with it he cruised
slowly towards his goal
—his nostrils
rose and picked up the scent—
where there was food—there was female flesh.

His fighting, plus this lampooning and bouts of paranoia, alienated his friends. In fact, his old mentor Kristian Krogh was about to sue Munch until he found that he had been hospitalized for psychiatric care. A series of lithographs reflecting Munch's persecutory ideas during the years 1902–1908 entitled "The History of Assault" reveals this paranoia. He made such statements as, "Something extraordinarily remarkable, as you know, happened to me some years ago—when people failed in their attempts to starve me or insult me they hit on the idea of butchering me and selling my flesh and blood.'' Other comments reflecting his paranoia are the following: ''Friends are enemies in disguise—they sneak into your house eating your food, drinking your wine, and stabbing you in the back.''

It is alleged that what precipitated hospitalization in the Fall of 1908 at Jacobson's Clinic in Copenhagen was an acute delirium, probably an alcoholic hallucinosis. Munch blamed many of his problems on alcohol and at one time described this as follows:

> The influence of alcohol carried the split in the mind or the soul to its outermost limits until the two states like two wild birds tied together pulled in different directions and threatened to dissolve to tear apart the chain. With the violent split of these two mental states there was created a powerful inner tension—an intense inner struggle—a horrible fight in the soul's cage—the value to the artist or the philosopher of this condition depends upon the things in a way being seen by two persons—in two mental states—the things were seen from two sides the periphery—the thoughts moved toward the periphery of the soul—and were threatened to be flung outside of the effective range of the centrifugal force—out into space or darkness or insanity. Then at the same time these touched—the finest and most remarkable only dimly perceived life truths and life forces—I imagine the two mental states was a desire for peace and rest and the other a desire for that which drives one to motion and action—normally these two work together in ones life's work like a negative and positive force as in the cylinder of a locomotive and normally as split and divided states they have a destructive effect on the machinery. [2]

Arne Eggum[11] describes the precipitating or immediate events which preceded the hospitalization as follows. Munch reported an experience on the train to Copenhagen of a bird-like pursuer introducing himself as a psychoanalyst from Vienna, with whom he discussed his problems. However, Eggum says: "We have no idea whether Munch like Peer Gynt in the 5th Act is speaking with his alter ego or whether he actually hallucinated a person of this kind."

The night before entering the hospital, Munch went on a formidable spree with a fellow spirit, the author Sigurd Mathiesen, an enthusiastic admirer of Edgar Allan Poe. At this time Munch's hallucinations became violent and protracted. Outbursts of anxiety were accompanied by stabbing pains in the chest and Munch tried to treat these pains with more alcohol. Munch describes his situation himself as follows:

Sitting drinking one brandy-and-soda after another—alcohol excites me still more—especially in the evening—excites me—I feel it eating its way into my delicate nerves—and then tobacco—lots of strong cigars—nicotine—the funeral pyre of the tobacco plant eating its way into the channels of the arteries—converting in the labyrinth of the brain—the subtlest workshop of thought—and in the passage of the heart—the most delicate nerves are affected—I feel it—and the most delicate of all has been attacked. I feel that this is my vital nerve—it is burning—Yes—let it burn—let us get it over—and there will be an end to all pain—an end of to all fear—brandy-and-soda burning up pain, fear—everything—and that's the end."[11]

In the morning his legs refused to support him and his hand was numb. Munch said: "I staggered about on the floor with my rightside paralyzed—I hobbled on my right leg—My left arm hung limp—my hand was numb—I couldn't take hold of anything—a stroke—."[11] Munch's description would make the symptoms hysterical and not organic. His friend Emanual Goldstein, the poet, took him to the clinic where he was given a strong sedative and slept for eight days. In December Munch wrote to his friend Jappe Nilssen: "My innards are like a glass of muddy water—I'm allowing it to stand now and clear up—whatever it will be like when the sediment sinks to the bottom."[11]

ALPHA'S PROGENY—the format but not content of his publication Alpha and Omega is similar to an illustrated children's book.

#8

In the hospital he began work on Alpha and Omega,[11] with eighteen lithographs and two pages of text describing the last (or the first)—at least the only—humans on earth who have an idyllic love relation until the woman is seduced by animals—in sequence a snake, a bear, a lion, a donkey, a pig, and then she escapes from an island on the back of a deer. Subsequently, Omega, the man, is confronted by Alpha's progeny, half animal/half human. (See Illustration 8) He runs to the beach in great fear and when one day the deer brings Alpha back he drowns her, and while still looking at her, he is attacked from behind and killed by her progeny. The format and writing style—but hardly the content—is like a child's fairy tale. Perhaps this description of the vile female was helpful as a catharsis in Munch's recovery. His treatment was described as not only rest but also electric by which I assume it means faradic stimulations and massage. I suspect that there was considerable supportive and maybe insight psychotherapy. At least it was obvious that there was considerable self-analysis during the eight months of hospitalization and that Munch's doctor, Daniel Jacobson, was an extremely charismatic individual. It is also obvious that Munch recovered from the florid psychoses rather quickly after entering the clinic, at least, if recovery is measured by his productivity. Munch said, "a strange calm came over me while I was working on this series (Alpha and Omega)—it was as if all malice let go of me."[8] It is this kind of dramatic remission which so often characterizes the episodic disorder.

MUNCH'S CURE

At the time of his hospitalization Munch was very concerned about what treatment would do to his creativity and, in fact, many art critics have suggested that it took away this creativity. Even in the hospital Munch was quite productive, particularly painting or etching a number of portraits of those about him, including

Dr. Jacobson and his nurse. It is said that these portraits are more finished than the work before and there is more contact between the subject of the portrait and the viewer, less of the element of being overwhelmed. On leaving the hospital in May of 1909, Munch returned to Oslo and settled for good in Norway. He gave up alcohol, although some say there were rare relapses. Munch himself in 1938 said: "I enjoy alcohol only in its most distilled form—watching my friends drinking."[8] It is often asked what would have happened to van Gogh if he had been successfully treated and had not committed suicide at age thirty-nine, the implication being that treatment would have ruined his creativity. We might look at Munch's paintings as reflecting what effect successful therapy might have had on van Gogh.

Munch's paintings became his love and he could not bear to be without them. He treated them much as if they were children and when he did sell one he would often paint another with the same motif. However, he did this throughout his life, obviously reworking the same subject many times, but now it seemed more like replacing a lost child. Instead of overpowering and over-whelming, the pictures draw one by their soft mood. They were brightly colored and decorative with a lyrical tone. The highlight of Munch's life immediately upon his return was to win the commission for painting the murals of the festive hall at the University of Oslo. Although some would consider this mural banal or boring, for me, personally, to view it standing in the center of the hall was a moving experience. As Stange, one of his biographers said: "He did not use traditional symbols nor did he fall back on allegories or ancient Norse mythology or history which so many makers of monumental art have done before him. His stroke of genius was to paint the daily occurrences that he saw around him in the little coastal town of Kragero. He painted a seaman telling a little fellow about his life of fantastic adventure. They are under a large oak in an ice blue landscape and the marvelous thing is that Munch is able to lift the entire scene from the level of the everyday."[8] Munch also painted several other monumental projects, probably an inspiration that lingered from many years before when he visited Florence. Many of these paintings were of workmen shoveling snow or returning from a factory—everyday scenes, but with a deeper symbolic meaning as when a heavy dark mass of workers moves slowly towards us like a force of nature. Perhaps Munch wanted to tell us something more important than the fact that tired workers are returning home.[8] His paintings please and entice rather than overpower as before. Obviously, Munch had given up his earlier philosophy that the viewer should be cowered by the artist into seeing art as a reflection of the existential tragedy of personal human existence. Certainly his paintings became less blatantly autobiographical. Does this mean that his art after his illness was less creative or does it just mean creative in a different way? Although Munch stood on the periphery of new trends in art, he was still influenced by the endeavors of the younger generation and his paintings, while retaining his own special style, constantly reflected and condensed impressions from contemporary art.[10]

Munch displayed, in common with van Gogh and Virginia Woolf, episodic aggressive acts—officially designated in the psychiatric nomenclature "Intermittent Explosive Disorder." We will see that he also shared this with Mary Lamb and August Strindberg. It is not clear whether he shared with these creative artists and writers their episodic psychotic reactions, although he may have had episodic paranoia. What Munch did experience was an episodic panic reaction—which the others to some degree also experienced. Munch's episodic disorders may well have been precipitated at least on some occasions by alcohol and this was also true in the case of van Gogh and Strindberg. What makes Munch's story interesting is that he (and to some extend Strindberg) recovered from their episodic disorder—and continued their creative output for many years after they were "cured."

Chapter 4

August Strindberg—Another "Cure"

There is no doubt that Strindberg represents a classic example of the episodic disorder. He provides us with extensive data to support this claim. He wrote eight volumes of self-analysis saying, "I determined to examine my life . . . to make use of all of the resources of psychology . . . to probe the deepest depths . . . I appeal to the reader for a verdict after a careful study of my confession. Perhaps he will find in it elements of the psychology of love, some light on the pathology of the soul, or even some fragment of the philosophy of crime."[1]

Strindberg studied the psychiatric and psychological literature and endeavored a systematic self-analysis like Munch even before Freud proposed such an enterprise, saying, ". . . what is necessary for me is to know how things are related; that is why I want to make a deep, careful and scientific examination of my life."[2] However, it must be remembered that Strindberg was not so much a scientist as a novelist, poet, dramatist and actor—so that one wonders how much he wrote was poetry and how much accurate self-evaluation.[3] At least he did not openly express such a caveat as Munch did.

It is difficult for the psychiatrist to make an evaluation of the pathography of Strindberg utilizing primary sources because there are over sixty volumes of his writings, including 5,600 letters, much of this still untranslated and others "sealed" until the Year 2000.[4] A definitive psychological analysis of Strindberg must wait the scholars of the next century.

LIFE HISTORY

Strindberg was born on the 22nd of January, 1849, in Stockholm.[5] His father, Karl, was a steamship agent and in turn was the son of a clergyman who had some intellectual interests as well as an aristocratic background. Strindberg's father, however, was a stern tyrannical man who did everything according to set rules and punished his children severely. August's mother was a woman of humble origin who had been a domestic servant. She was of limited intelligence with violent emotions and a primitive, narrow religious outlook.[4] She died during Strindberg's adolescence, having borne twelve children, five of whom died in infancy. An elder brother of Strindberg's was described as "hysteric" and "melancholic," while a younger sister developed a chronic mental illness at age forty and died in a mental hospital. Also, Strindberg's daughter Kerstin was admitted to a psychiatric hospital with the diagnosis "paranoid disorder." Soon after Strindberg's birth his father went bankrupt this, plus the fact that he had married below his class, left the family socially isolated. In describing his childhood in the third person, Strindberg says, "He was fifteen years old when he left the penitentiary which every community keeps for children who commit the outrageous crime of being born and where the innocent little ones are made to atone for their parents' fall from grace—for which it otherwise becomes a society." He speaks of "the tyranny of the family from which no revolution can deliver us. There is more need for foundation societies for the protection of children than for the societies for the protection of animals."[2] In a classic double bind (a "no-win" interaction) he remembers being accused of drinking his aunt's wine and being punished for lying when he denied this. His mother asked him to beg his father for forgiveness, but when he did then was thrashed for his admission of guilt. Later the parents heard that he still denied any wrongdoing; he received another beating for lying. It is not surprising then that Strindberg early developed an underlying distrust of authority and paranoid attitude towards "justice."[2]

There was a definite pietism during Strindberg's adolscence, probably related to masturbation guilt; hence, his fears that his spine would disintegrate and his nose fall away. Obviously, his view of Christianity at that time was colored by a certain pessimism with little hope that one could find grace. Strindberg's schooling was marked by rebelliousness and an indifferent academic record, so that even though he entered the University of Upsala in 1867, he left several years later without a degree. He continued this impetuous, rebellious behavior toward authority, not only toward his professors, but also drama critics, his king, and his church. This rebelliousness was usually unnecessary and in the long run only self-defeating. He became in turn a journalist, actor, medical student, and finally, until age thrity-three, through the patronage of the king, an assistant librarian.

Even before Strindberg's twenty-second birthday, there were ominous signs of both dyscontrol behavior and impending "madness." Because of critical rejection of his writing, he turned to painting but then had a "dreadful suspicion" that he'd gone mad, and in fact wrote to a private sanitarium asking to be admitted for treatment. When one of his plays was turned down by the Swedish Royal Theatre it was said that Strindberg escaped to an island where he attempted to drown himself because he could not pay his debts, but then had a love affair instead.[5] After living for several days with a women who left him for another man, he went into a frenzy dashing headlong through the woods "trampling upon nature and beating upon trees which he envisioned as his enemies."[1] During this period he published some plays, but his most successful publication was "The Red Room."[5]

Blatant deviant behavior, serious enough to be considered "mental illness," made its appearance during his first marriage, which occurred in 1877. Strindberg was befriended by the Baron and Baroness (Siri) Wrangel; in fact, he moved in to live with them and soon was erotically attracted to Siri. This attraction to a woman who "belonged" to another man was a repetition of his oedipal conflict which occurred several times during Strindberg's life. He was consciously aware of his early erotic attraction towards his mother and recognized this as a source of guilt and expiation before Freud established the oedipal conflict as the cornerstone of neurotic behavior.

Encouraged by the infidelity of the Wrangels, a *ménage à trois* was established, which only intensified Strindberg's guilt as it ultimately evolved into a divorce, Siri's impregnation by Strindberg, and then the marriage of the two. Following this, there occurred the first flare-up of his "paranoid mania" in the form of pathological jealousy, when Strindberg became convinced that he was not the father of his child—a delusion that was reinforced when Siri admitted occasional infidelities.[5]

On one occasion, before his marriage, Strindberg announced his intention to abandon Siri and go to Paris. He no sooner had embarked on the boat than he changed his mind and arranged for the pilot's cutter to return him to dry land, at which time he decided that he must make a grand renunciation. If he could not live with Siri he would die but he wanted her to see him pass away. The fantasy was that he would die of pneumonia but would linger long enough so that she could come to his bedside. After a cigar, a drink of absinthe, and booking a room in a local hotel so he could die in comfort, he swam into the cold sea and then sat on the shore shivering. This not being enough, he left his clothes on the ground and he climbed a tree to continue his exposure to the October weather. He then wired to Siri about his illness, but in deference to his comfort he then took sleeping medicine. The next morning the Baron and Baroness rushed to his side where Strindberg received them in good health. The sleeping potion had given him a good night's rest and his exposure to the elements a ravenous appetite.

Throughout the next fifteen to twenty years, Strindberg attempted to assuage his guilt by projecting fault and responsibility on to others. Sometimes this was on a segment of society and had some basis in reality: for example, the feeling that he was persecuted by the Swedish Feminists after he had written his conviction that women were naturally inferior, not only mentally and morally, but also biologically. At other times he blamed God and his God was the vengeful God of the Old Testament. When he gave up God the blame was projected onto the Fates which led him to his studies of mysticism and the occult. In his home country, his rebellion against the establishment made him the darling of the socialist movement.[5]

His grandiosity regarding his literary talents, while justified, extended beyond this talent into science, driving him into a misguided effort to seek the transmutation of baser metals into gold. This work was more philosophical and lyric than scientific and he said of his experiments, "what awakened my disgust for modern science was the way in which many small minds have elevated the gathering of data to a position above that of the philosophy of natural science,"[6] and told his wife that he wanted to give a lecture in Berlin about the "philosophy of chemistry." A monistic view of the organic and inorganic led him to see the various elements copulating with a process of natural selection existing in the copulations. Platinum, he stated, "is the most perfect because it protects its individualities better than other elements which means it does not readily copulate."[6]

MUNCH AND STRINDBERG

In 1893 Strindberg, living in Berlin, located a small tavern which he named The Black Pig (Zum Schwarzen Ferkel) and under that name it became famous in German and Scandinavian cultural history. Making it his headquarters, he drew together a group of Bohemians which included the art critic Julius Meier-Grafe, an enthusiastic supporter of Munch (and also van Gogh and Monticelli); the Polish writer, Przybyszewski; the doctors

Asch and Schleich, the latter the first physician to use a local anesthetic; the Norwegian artist Krogh and his pupil Munch, among others.[7] All were driven by sex, art, and alcohol. It was here that Munch introduced in March of 1893 his new mistress Dagny Juel. The cultural significance of The Black Pig was that ideas changed hands faster than mistresses but what was culturally important is that this period bridged the gap between naturalism and expressionism among the creative artists and writers in attendance. In Munch's case, paintings like "The Sick Child," "Day After," and "Puberty" represented the change to expressionism. Munch immortalized Dagny in such oils as "Madonna," "Woman in Love," "Conception," and "Woman in Three Stages" (the nude in the center of the canvas). Dagny rapidly passed from Munch to Strindberg to another colleague, Lidforss, and finally to "Przy" who ultimately married her, even though Dagny continued her seductive teasing ways. By 1894, the backbiting among its habituates had become so bad that one by one they departed, leading to the demise of Zum Schwarzen Ferkel. Strindberg disparaged Dagny and went on to marry Frieda Uhl, the daughter of a Viennese newspaper editor. Throughout this period, Strindberg's friends reported that he had the paranoid delusion that he was constantly being followed or persecuted. One of his most outstanding character traits was Strindberg's hypersensitivity and a tendency to mood swings between a sickly tenderness on one hand and ruthless violence on the other. By the Berlin period, Strindberg's behavior showed extreme suspiciousness regarding all of his friends, who he did not hesitate to slander behind their backs and then imagined their vengeance. All of his life he retained something of a child's candor and we have noted this is an attribute of many geniuses. Guilt, desire for punishment, and a tendency toward self-punishment or self-destructive behavior appeared early in childhood and persisted throughout Strindberg's life just as it did with van.Gogh.[3]

At first glance the similarities between Strindberg and Munch are startling, but with a moment's reflection this should not be surprising. First, they were virtually contemporaries, Strindberg only thirteen years older than Munch. In fact their lives did cross. They shared the common Scandinavian culture and had many of the same intellectual mentors, including Hamsun (see pp148). Both, for instance, admired Nietzsche and Kierkegaard and were part of the same clique of Scandinavian and Northern European intellectuals who in the 1890's gathered in Berlin. In fact, they probably shared the same mistress, Dagny Juel (Dacha to Munch and Aphasia to Strindberg), if not simultaneously at least in rapid sequence. Munch made three portraits of Strindberg and Strindberg in turn dreamed of some of Munch's art (a beheaded Przybyszewski—or Popoffsky as Strindberg called him in The Inferno).[5]

There were also common features in the childhood of both so that to the psychoanalyst it is again not surprising that they developed similar neurotic and characterological traits. Both were reared in families of genteel poverty. Their fathers were powerful, domineering, religious fanatics and their mothers died before either reached maturity. Each developed an extreme ambivalence toward females, seeing them either as the Madonna, virginal mother on one hand, or the harlot on the other. Thus, they could not get along with women but had equal difficulty getting along without them. (Note such themes in Strindbergs plays [8] and Munch's art). Here they differed. Strindberg sampled (unsuccessfully) marriage on three occasions while Munch at the last moment avoided such a fate.

There are many other similarities. Munch was an artist who at times aspired to be a writer—and Strindberg a writer who at times aspired to be a painter. Both had talent in their secondary creative aspirations. It is alleged that Strindberg commented to Munch, "I'm the greatest painter in Scandinavia" and Munch replied, "Sure, sure and I'm greatest poet in Scandinavia."[7] Both were rebels against society but had a small coterie of ardent admirers and a larger population who considered them heretics. Both experienced periods of popular acclaim as well as episodes when they were pariahs. Not surprisingly, then, both had periods of economic success but often suffered abject poverty while pursuing their creative efforts. Both were recognized as true geniuses even within their lifetime. They profoundly influenced Western culture far beyond their Scandinavian homeland. Not surprisingly, they both had paranoid character traits based to some extent on reality and they both had grandiose appraisal of their talent, again based on reality although this grandiosity often extended beyond their area of talent and expertise.

Even the life style and the life pattern of Munch and Strindberg had a number of parallels. Early in their careers they were considered to have been "hysterical personalities." This meant that they were impulsive, emotionally unstable, self-dramatizers who lived a life of excesses both in terms of alcohol abuse and sexual promiscuity.[3] In mid-life each suffered a period of psychotic disorganization but recovered from this disorganization into a period of "schizoid" autistic withdrawal that seemed to preserve their sanity without interfering with their prodigious creativity, which persisted throughout their lives, despite the ups and downs in their mental states. Until this ultimate period of tranquility both manifested a number of dyscontrol acts and experienced florid psychotic symptoms with hallucinations and delusions which both interfered with and contributed to their creativity. The fact that they had episodic disorders makes them particularly appropriate case studies for understanding the relationship between creativity and madness.

STRINDBERG'S ILLNESS AND CURE

August Strindberg had a number of episodic illnesses, usually of a psychotic nature (as is true of our other subjects).[6] This was particularly so during the years 1894–1897 and is commonly referred to by the title of his publication on the subject *The Inferno.*"[7] During these thirty-three months he had five episodes.[3,6] Often they lasted less than a month, at the longest three to four months. The most common characteristic of these episodes was restless agitation with paranoid panics, fleeing until he could feel safe. The first occurred in Austria when he developed a pain in his neck and thought his wife was spying on his scientific experiments. He toyed with the idea of taking his life by poison. He described the tension within him as so great that he was afraid he would ''burst.'' He also reported spurts of energy and then inertia.

The second occurred in Paris when he was suffering severe eczema of his hands from his chemical experiments. He became preoccupied with his state of poverty and accusations that he was not supporting his children. He had somatic delusions, feeling a cold air stream passing over his face. (The early Greeks noted such a sensation was a premonitory experience of epilepsy, hence we now refer to all prodromal epileptic experience as an ''aura,'' meaning a light wind).[9] He bolted the door against persecutors but recovered quickly when he was hospitalized for his eczema. During both of these episodes, it was reported that he had been drinking absinthe the day before he became mentally ill.

The third also occurred in Paris when he feared the ''evil one'' which he visually hallucinated. He thought that there was a plot against him and fled to the safety of a local hotel. He indulged in black magic hoping to make his daughter sick so that his wife Frieda would have to invite him home.

The fourth was preceded by nightmares and then marked referential ideas with somatic delusions of an electric current in his body and feeling that he was paralyzed from hips down. He fled from Paris to Dieppe and from there to Sweden where he was treated by his friend Dr. Eliasson.

The fifth ocurred when he was again in Austria visiting his daughter. He had a return of the electrical sensations in his body with illusory distortions, such as viewing a broomstick which he misinterpreted as a witch who was after him. Buying a dagger, he stabbed at the broomstick—his illusory tormentor.

A plethora of psychiatric diagnoses have been proposed by diverse psychiatric experts. The report of Anderson[3] on the matter can be summarized as follows. The bizarreness of the symptoms frequently led to the diagnosis of schizophrenia and such a diagnosis was applied to Strindberg in 1921 by A. Storch and in 1922 by Karl Jaspers. Storch noted the atypical features but Jaspers, as well as Storch, emphasized a state of deterioration which allegedly took place after Strindberg's "inferno crisis." Anderson, I believe, quite correctly points out that there probably was no lack of a creative output following the inferno crisis; in fact, the autistic schizoid withdrawal so often attributed to Strindberg's later life was not a fair appraisal because of his active involvement with the "intimate theatre" in Stockholm, the dinner parties he gave and the enthusiasm he showed for developing his young actors. W. Hirsch in 1894 proposed a diagnosis of a chronic paranoia and paranoid traits with episodic paranoid panics as characterizing both the personalitty and the acute episodes of Strindberg. Birnbaum in 1920 uses the ambiguous label hallucinatory delusional psychosis and Rahmer in 1907 proposes that Strindberg was suffering from melancholia. The pervasive sense of guilt that characterized Strindberg's life and recurring suicidal trends would support such a diagnosis and Lange in 1908 identifies what he thought were hypomanic periods with increased eroticism and productivity. Anderson notes the toxic psychotic features with numerous visual hallucinations and illusionary misinterpretations of his surroundings, as well as the panic and precordial tension, all suggestive of a toxic delirium of a mixed form intermediate between delirium tremens and alcohol hallucinosis. Anderson also questions whether Strindberg's sensorium was entirely clear during most of these episodes and feels strongly that absinthe may have played a role in his illness, finally coming to the conclusion that Strindberg suffered from "episodic acute mental illness." Harding,[4] in commenting on Lidz's presentation, mentions Marcel Reja, a French doctor, who felt that Strindberg, while suffering from a persecution mania, was "looked down on" by his inferiors, and had some reason for being paranoid. He felt that Strindberg was not insane nor schizophrenic, but nervous and hysterical. This mixture of symptoms as well as the atypical aspects of his illness is precisely what characterizes the episodic psychosis resulting from a limbic ictus and I have already discussed that alcohol, particularly absinthe, can precipitate such episodic disorders in predisposed individuals (pp.36). Strindberg's symptoms, then, are similar to those of the episodic disorders which afflicted Vincent van Gogh, Virginia Woolf, and Edvard Munch. We will look at these symptoms in more detail in Chapter 11 to see the similarities in symptoms between all of these creative individuals during their episodic disorders. Again, the similarities between Strindberg and Munch should be stressed. Both of them struggled desperately to solve their psychological problems by a systematic self-analysis and to a great extent both of them in this way accomplished a "cure."

All of Strindberg's attacks sound similar to the "bad trips" that can be induced by psychedelic drugs. In studies that I conducted these bad trips were related to bursts of electrical activity in the limbic system deep in the brain. I have also demonstrated that thujone, the toxic element in absinthe, can induce a similar electrographic pattern. The precipitous onset of these experiences, the short duration, and apparently equally abrupt remission, all suggest an ictal (epileptoid) phenomenon. This theory does not rule out the possibility of precipitating events other than alcohol or absinthe, such as the stress Strindberg was experiencing because of his poverty, divorce from his second wife, and demands from his first wife for support of his child.

What is striking about Strindberg's case history is that subsequent to this "crisis of the inferno" he recovered and had no serious episodic disturbances in the fifteen years remaining in his life. Anderson,[3] however, does report that he had three minor crises in 1904, 1907, and 1910. Without giving details, these were less severe than earlier ones, but still characterized by jealousy, some grandiose and persecutory ideas, and once again, Strindberg imagined portents in everyday happenings. During these years, his creativity continued (e.g. "To Damascus" and other so-called "dream" plays). Was his relative health following the episodes due to the fact that he gave up or reduced his alcoholic or absinthe intake? Psychologically there seemed to be a constructive reparative process because Strindberg came under the influence of Swedenborg's writings and turned back to religion.[2] What may be even more important is that Strindberg came to see that the causes of his miseries were within himself and that he alone was responsible and not others.

There is considerable evidence that Strindberg was susceptible to limbic seizures and there are characteristic behavioral
concomitants of this early in his life. It was reported that the first
time he got drunk "he felt blissful, gloriously happy, strong,
kind, and gentle, but later insane."[3] He said foolish things and
saw visions in the dishware. He also felt a sudden desire to mimic
his older brother. In 1872 (age 23), seeing himself a failure as
a playwright, he locked himself in his room and turned to painting, mostly gloomy seascapes. This was the time he was assailed
by the terror of going mad and asked for therapy. In 1873 he
apparently suffered auditory hallucinations of an accusatory nature and, as already mentioned, went into a frenzy dashing
through the woods beating upon trees. In 1875 he tried to induce
pneumonia in a bizarre attempt at suicide. This is an example of
what I will later describe as a hysteroid or manipulative dyscontrol
act. His behavior in this instance was obviously a conscious
attempt to manipulate others. In 1890, after Nietzsche and de
Maupassant were both committed to asylums, he felt that this
was the fate of all geniuses and that he would be next, so he
sought for himself a "certificate of sanity" to prevent such persecution. While in Berlin, shortly before his inferno crisis, he
described what sounds like a fugue state or perhaps alcoholic
blackout, i.e., being mysteriously transported from one restaurant
to another. During the inferno crisis, he describes a psychedelic-
like experience very similar to what one might have under the
influence of LSD or Mescaline. Looking over to the Orangerie,
he saw "mysterious forces above the arches radiating like an
aurora borealis."[6]

There seems to be little doubt that Strindberg had at least
a dozen psychotic episodes of the type associated with storms of
electrical activity deep in the brain (limbic system) that could
have been precipitated by alcohol, particularly absinthe, but at
other times might be precipitated by psychological stress. These
were intense, emotional experiences that in his autobiographical
writings were utilized in imaginative ways. An illustration of this
is Strindberg's memory of visiting the Palace of Versailles where
he was possessed by sudden panic, with a feeling that the great

buildings seem to draw him as great bodies draw small bodies. He says:

> I rebel against this blind, brutal power and to be able to fight it better I personify it and make it God. Of course, I wish to reach my goal the Palace, but at the same time I wish to defy this superior force. My brain splits into two and joins battle with myself. I expect to see half my body walking across the Place d'Armes and the other half clinging to the lamp-post. In vain, I seek to join the two parts of the machine together; I struggle to find an ego which is above myself, when suddenly by an involuntary but unerring chance, my hands meet around the iron pillar with the immediate result that the psychic currents are joined in the iron and closing circuit, thus, forming a psychomagnet which acts on my immediately restored nervous system . . . Uneasily, I glance around to see if I can catch sight of a vessel which can rescue me from this desolate rock and from old habit, I raise my eyes to the blue heavens, through which rays of warmth and light percolate down . . . Just then white clouds cover the sun and cast their great moving shadows on the Place d'Armes.[6]

These shadows then represented boats to Strindberg and riding on one of the shadows he attained his goal—The Palace.

Strindberg gives some interesting clues as to his version of creativity in a written introduction to the Gauguin exhibit where he says, "he is Gauguin the savage who hates a bothersome civilization, something of a titan, who jealous of the Creator makes his own little creation in his free moments, the child who takes his toys to pieces in order to make other toys from them. One who denies and defies, would rather see the heaven red than, like ordinary people, blue. A contemporary writer has been reproached for not depicting real people; he has they say quite simply constructed his figures. *Quite simply!*"[7] In another comment on creativity, Strindberg suggests that the artist be on the lookout for the "fortunate accidents which may occur while one is creating and that one follow the suggestion of his artifacts as they take shape in his hands instead of sticking to his own pre-determined plans.''[7] Again, is the shaping power of this imag-ination ''quite simple?'' Hemingway, as we will see, was not sure whether such experiences enhanced creativity or interfered with it, but van Gogh described similar feelings when he was painting in a ''frenzy,'' as did Virginia in describing her ''racing words.'' I will also report how frequently institutionalized psy-chiatric patients who create deny authorship, seeing it as a product of some mystical force outside of themselves (See Chapter 9).

Chapter 5

Mary Lamb—Matricide and No "Cure"

Mary Lamb was born December 3, 1764 and died in her eighty-third year on May 20, 1847. Mary then lived a century earlier and lived longer than our other subjects. She also had more illness episodes, at least thirty-seven following her first attack at age thirty. On the average, she had an attack every seventeen months.[1]

All our subjects were highly creative to the point of being considered at least "minor" geniuses. If there is an exception, I am sure that most would identify Mary Lamb as something less than this. Mary Lamb's creative writing extended a mere four years from 1805–1809, during her fortieth to forty-fourth year of life. She published with Charles, *Tales of Shakespeare, Mrs. Leiscester's School* and *Poetry for Children: By "the author of Mrs. Leiscester's School."* In *Tales of Shakespeare,* fourteen chapters were written by Mary and six (the tragedies) by Charles. In *Mrs. Leiscester's School*, seven chapters were written by Mary and three by Charles. The only other significant publication by Mary was in 1817 when she published an article on embroidery in *British Ladies Magazine*, which may have been the most creative effort of all of her writings as it is considered to be one of the earliest articles on the subject of women's liberation. In comparison with our other artists hers might seem to be a meager effort, but one must consider Mary's total situation: her abject poverty, commitment to the care of others, lack of education, as well as her frequent recurrent psychosis. In view of this, her literary contribution was no small accomplishment, particularly when one considers the status of the ''independent'' woman of her era. For example, her joint authorship with Charles of *Tales of Shakespeare* and *Mrs. Leiscesters School* was not even acknowledged in the early editions and the children's poems were written by ''the author of *Mrs. Leiscester's School*'' rather than by Mary Lamb.

EARLY ILLNESSES

Mary was one of three surviving children, with an older brother, one year her senior, and Charles, ten years her junior, born to John and Elizabeth Lamb. There probably were five other siblings who died at birth or early infancy. John Lamb was the valet to Mr. Samuel Salt, a typical member of the legal fraternity, who possessed considerable social and political prominence and served several terms as a member of Parliament. Despite the master-servant relationship, Samuel Salt and John Lamb were genuine friends. Actually, Lamb functioned as much as a lawyer's clerk as he did a valet. Mr. Lamb's wife, Elizabeth, was the daughter of a country housekeeper. The Lambs then were ''lowly born.'' Mr. Salt's quarters were in the Temple Chambers in London and these were expanded to include the Lamb household. Unfortunately, the household also included John Lamb's elder sister ''Aunt Heddy.'' Aunt Heddy and her sister-in-law habitually disagreed and this led to constant domestic friction. Through the support of Mr. Salt, the children had good elementary school education and his extensive library was freely accessible to all the children including Mary. Through Salt's political influence, Charles Lamb and his brother John were enrolled in ''Christ's

Hospital" where they received a scholarship for their education, Charles being a contemporary of Coleridge at the school. Mary, as she grew up, was trained as a seamstress and in this way could contribute to the meager family income, a role that became essential with Mr. Salt's death. During childhood, both Mary and Charles had episodes labeled as "a nervous breakdown" centered around guilt, anxiety, and religious delusional ideas. Both apparently recovered by being sent off on a vacation with relatives.

Following his schooling, Charles Lamb became a clerk in the East India Company and served in this capacity for the next thirty-three years. This was not a taxing assignment so that while it provided modest financial security it also left significant time for his creative writing. As apparent with all of our subjects, the Lambs seem to have established a relationship with their outstanding artistic contemporaries, including Coleridge and Wordsworth.

For a six week period at the end of 1795 and the beginning of 1796, Charles Lamb had an acute psychotic episode which required institutionalization in an asylum. In writing to Coleridge regarding this breakdown he said, "I look back on it at times with a gloomy kind of envy; for while it lasted I had many hours of pure happiness, dream not, Coleridge, of having tasted all of the grandeur and wildness of fancy, till you have gone mad."[1] Although this was the only time that Charles was hospitalized, "nervous breakdowns" supposedly occurred at other times in his life, including the six weeks after his retirement, March 29, 1825 when he "fell into a state of sleepless, irritable depression"[1] and again in the winter of 1827–1828 when he was again nervous and sleepless. At that time he said, "We (he and Mary) seem doomed not to be well together."[1] He also drank excessively throughout his life.

Mary's second and most dramatic outbreak occurred September 22, 1796 when she was thirty-two. While setting the dinner table, she suddenly and inexplicably became irate with her young apprentice dressmaker, throwing forks about the room, one wounding her father in the forehead. She began chasing her apprentice, shrieking. Her mother, admonishing Mary to subsist, was suddenly turned upon and stabbed in the heart. At this point, Aunt Heddy had fainted on the floor and Charles entered the room to take the bloody knife from his sister's hand. Charles had written to Coleridge that day saying Mary had been acting strange for a day or two, "talking, laughing and crying with exaggerated gestures and mounting excitement."[1] These were symptoms Charles recognized as characteristic of Mary's previous illness as well as prodromal symptoms of his own breakdown. On the morning of the day of the matricide, Charles had left the house to find Dr. Pitcairn who was not available but whom he sought to provide medical attention regarding Mary's condition.

The day folowing this event, Mary was taken to the asylum in Islington and eleven days later Charles wrote to Coleridge saying that Mary was already "restored to her senses."[2] He added, "A dreadful sense and recollection of what has past" and then added ". . . knows how to distinguish between a deed committed in a transient fit of frenzy and the terrible guilt of a mother's murder."[2] He commented that "Mary was now calm and serene but very far from an indecent forgetful serenity. She has a most affectionate, tender concern for what has happened."[2]

Although the precipitating cause for this event is unclear, many predisposing elements can be identified. Mary's mother doted on the oldest sibling, John, neglecting Mary, who despite her mother's attitude was always obsequious and loving. However, Mary's mother thought that Mary was somewhat crazy and said that she never understood her daughter, pushing her away whenever Mary attempted to show any filial affection. There were other predisposing factors. Mary's father, following Mr. Salt's death, had rapidly deteriorated into a senile dementia and her mother was invalided by arthritis. Not only was Mary then taking care of both father and mother, earning her way by being a seamstress, but immediately prior to this episode, had nursed both brothers, first Charles, who had been hospitalized because of his mental breakdown, and then John, who had the misfortune to be the recipient of an injury to his leg which was serious enough so they thought it might result in an amputation. For a person as sensitive and as intelligent as Mary, this house-bound existence must have been a severe stress, but as Charles said within ten days she was not delusional nor did she appear unusually guilty, "She remained strangely free from the agonies of remorse."[2]

In an enlightened decision, considering the era, Mary was judged not responsible for her behavior by reason of insanity and she was allowed her freedom as long as her brother Charles was responsible for her. This started a symbiotic dependency between the two which persisted throughout the rest of their lives.

SYMBIOSIS WITH CHARLES

This was just the beginning of a series of attacks as within the year Mary had a relapse and Charles wrote to Coleridge, "I consider Mary as perpetually on the brink of madness."[2] A third attack in the same year elicited a comment from Charles, "My heart is quite sunk and I don't know where to look for relief. Mary will get better again, but her constantly being liable to such relapses is dreadful; nor is it the least of our evils that her case and all our story is so well known around us . . . I almost wish that Mary was dead."[2]

The popular diagnosis for Mary's illness is manic-depressive psychosis because these episodes include periods of extreme depression as well as other periods of excessive excitement, with complete recovery between acute episodes. William Hazlitt said that "he" had met with only one thoroughly reasonable woman in his whole life and that woman was Mary Lamb."[3]

However, Mary's episodic illness, although in some ways similar, was in other ways different from the typical manic-depressive psychosis as experienced by Robert Lowell (see Chapter 6). First of all her, illnesses were dramatically precipitous, coming on in a matter of a few hours or at most a few days. Second, the agitated episodes were generally ones of violence rather than euphoric disinhibited behavior. On occasions, the remission of the illness was equally dramatic.[4] For instance, Mary describes an episode when her nurse friend Mrs. Waldon drank a toast of wine with Mary on the wedding date of a mutual acquaintance. Mary said, ''It restored me from that moment as if by an electrical stroke to the entire possession of my senses. I never felt so calm and so quiet . . . as I do now. I feel as if all tears were wiped from my eyes and all care from my heart.''[2] This description is quite similar to what Munch described during his hospitalization (pp.96).

Charles made a number of observations regarding Mary's illness which reflect the confusion and disorganization of her thinking that is extreme for a typical manic-depressive patient. For instance, he said, ''When she is not violent her rambling chat is better to me than the sense and sanity of this world. Her heart is obscured not buried, it breaks out occasionally and one can discern the strong mind struggling with the billows that have gone over it . . . her memory is naturally strong and from ages past, if we may so call the earliest records of a poor life, she fetches thousands of names and things that never would have dawned upon me again and thousands from the ten years she lived before me. What took place from early childhood to her coming of age principally lives again (every important thing and every trifle) in her brain with a vividness of real presence. For twelve hours incessantly she will pour out without intermission all her past life, forgetting nothing, pouring out name after name . . . as a dream; sense and nonsense; truth and error huddled together; a medley between inspiration and possession.''[3] Talfourd, Lamb's biographer, says of Mary, ''She would fancy herself in the days of Queen Ann or George the First and describe the brocaded dames in courtly manners as though she had been bred among them in the best style . . . it was all broken and disjointed so that the hearer could remember little of her discourse but the fragments were like jewels . . . only shaken from their settings. There were sometimes even a vein of crazy logic running through them, associating things essentially most dissimilar but connecting them by a verbal association in a strange order; it was as if the finest elements of her mind had been shaken into fantastic combinations like those of a kaleidoscope."[3] These grandiose delusions sound more typical of the euphoric manic patient but again the looseness of her thought process is not typical of the rigorously defined syndrome of manic-depressive disorder as I feel it should be defined.

The precipitous attack is noted in the following comments of the events which preceded her fourth attack in 1800. May 25th, Coleridge noted that she smiled ominously. May 27th, she herself reported she was falling ill. May 29th, she grabbed Coleridge and began raving, and was escorted back to the asylum. She was violent at the onset of her seventh attack in 1807, so that Charles had to borrow a bystanders waistcoat to tie her arms behind her back. In her ninth attack on March 8, 1811, she had a "distressing manner of conversation" and had to be taken to the asylum the next day, but she was home again within two months. The violence, suddenness, and unexpectedness of the attacks and the unpredictability of when the attacks would occur always startled Charles. Sometimes she seemed to be in a stupor and not in contact with what was going on around her. Other times, she was sadly rambling and showed no pleasure or interest in anything. Apparently, the most common premonitory symptoms were restlessness, insomnia, and "low fever."

The violence of Mary's behavior was as dominant as depression and her illnesses were referred to by Charles as "temporary frenzy." In describing his own illness he said, "I am got somewhat rationale now and don't bite anymore but mad I was."[2] Their brother John apparently never was overtly psychotic, but in one of Charles' essays he refers to his brother who as a youth was "fiery, glowing and tempestuous." It was said that the siblings inherited "a taint of mania from the father's side" but documentation for this statement is lacking. When John Lamb, Mary and Charles' brother, died it was said that Mary was "in a melancholic stupor only half sensible regarding the news of John's death."

During the period 1794 through 1804, Mary's attacks were generally of one month or less duration. From 1804 through 1826 the attacks were most often of two months duration. Following

MARY LAMB

PERIODS OF ILLNESS: OCCURRENCE AND DURATION

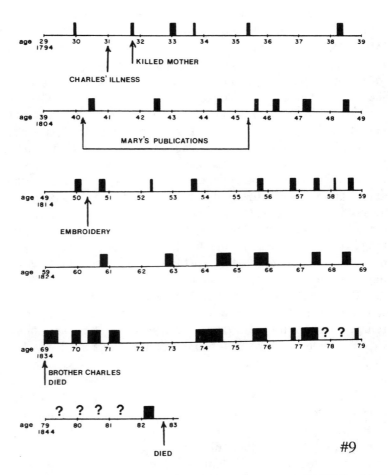

#9

MARY LAMB'S ILLNESSES: OCCURRENCE AND DURATION—this is adapted from C. P. Richter, *Biological Clocks in Medicine,* page 92. Springfield, Illinois: Charles C. Thomas, 1965. Note that Mary's creative period was only a 5 year span, except for her most creafive effort an essay on embroidery. This was a protest against women being relegated to creative needlework.

this, some of the attacks were as long as six months and in 1838 after a period of 2-½ years without symptoms, she had a ten month relapse.[5] At that time her doctor revealed that she was being treated with leeches applied to the top of her head which "died from the effects of the heat." The doctor, therefore, reduced the fever by using "lowering" medicine and cooling applications. With this kind of medical care, it is perhaps astounding that she recovered at all.[6] The last two extant letters of Mary Lamb were written in 1842 and until her death in 1847, it is not clear whether she had any significant lucid periods, nor can we determine whether her incapacity was due to chronic psychosis or senility. During these years she showed certain childish traits typical of the patient with senile dementia. For instance, when she would visit friends she would carry several empty snuff boxes with her to fill up from her friends' supply. At other times, if she took a liking to trinkets lying on the table she would stuff these into her pocket. Her nurse-housekeeper, finding these items at home, would return any trinkets of value to the appropriate friend. (Illustration # 9)

As we see in the episodic disorders of Vincent van Gogh and Virginia Woolf, Mary Lamb, like the others, developed a close symbiotic relationship with a sibling or a spouse. Although the close relationship was dictated initially by legal considerations, it is undoubtedly true that the forty-two year living arrangement must have been of mutual benefit: Charles closely monitoring Mary's behavior to see that she was isolated at the first sign of psychotic behavior, and Mary nursing Charles through his agitations, depression, and alcoholic binges. During the four year period when Mary and Charles worked together in publishing the *Tales of Shakespeare* and *Mrs. Leiscester's School,* the symbiosis included their creative efforts and there is some evidence that Mary, not Charles, took the initiative in this endeavor. Mary's independence and self-assertive act in publishing her essay on needlework, expressing a philosophy so contrary to Charles' attitude regarding the place of women in society was followed ten years later by Charles expressing his first self-assertive, independent philosophy of life in response to Southey's criticism of his Elia.[3] Anthony notes that Charles Lamb's only evangelical publication lagged far behind Mary's similar publication ten years earlier.[1]

In considering the closeness between brother and sister, one can be only amazed that so little jealousy was in evidence despite the fact that Charles had several emotional involvements and talked occasionally of marriage. There was resentment on Mary's part when their "adopted" daughter approached womanhood and Charles spent increasingly more time on long walks with her. One can speculate on the possible erotic element in the attachment between brother and sister, but whatever erotic element entered into this symbiosis must have been sublimated.

Reviewing the typical manic-depressive episodes of Robert Lowell, one will perceive an entirely different flavor in the agitated, depressed swings characteristic of Mary Lamb and Virginia Woolf and the exuberant behavior of Lowell. We do not have details regarding the symptoms of the florid psychotic episodes of Mary Lamb that we possess in the case of Virginia Woolf, so we do not know whether she suffered the bizarre hallucinations or delusions of Virginia. What is reported for Mary is the melancholic stupor or the agitated violence that also characterized Virginia Woolf. Both experienced the extreme disorganization in thinking that is unusual for the more typical manic-depressive patient, but quite typical of the episodic disorders. The precipitous onset and occasionally equally abrupt remission also is more characteristic of the episodic psychotic reaction rather than the more insidious onset of symptoms seen in the typical manic-depressive patient, such as Lowell. What Mary's life history reveals, and this is confirmed by modern observation, is that individuals with intermittent psychoses, whether a manic-depressive psychosis or an episodic psychosis, do not have residual impairment between attacks, but if the attacks are frequent enough they become longer in duration. The psychiatric literature indicates that about 50% of such individuals become chronically impaired as Mary did. Unlike the data on Virginia Woolf and Edvard Munch, it is not clear whether Mary utilized her psychotic experience in her creative writing. It may be that the frequency of her episodic psychoses resulted in an intellectual inertia which interfered with the full development of Mary's creative potential. We must remember, however, that Mary's background and culture did little to encourage the flowering of creativity, so if her creativity was limited it must have resulted from a combination of factors, particularly her frequent episodic illness and her extreme social-cultural deprivation.

Section II

Artists and Writers With A Different Affliction

Chapter 6

Robert Lowell and Ernest Hemingway —Mania and Depression

ROBERT LOWELL

As we've seen, a common diagnosis for the creative artist who goes "mad" has been manic-depressive psychosis. This label has certainly been given to Mary Lamb, Virginia Woolf, August Strindberg, and even Vincent van Gogh. The reasoning behind such a diagnosis is the intermittent and recurrent course of their psychoses, without residual impairment during the many extended periods of rationality. This differentiates the manic-depressive from schizophrenia, the latter illness being character-ized by an insidious early onset with a gradually increasing deficit no matter how often the florid psychotic systems wax and wane. Nevertheless, it has been my thesis that in each of the previously examined pathographies there are sufficient atypical features to warrant a diagnosis other than a manic-depressive or schizo-phrenic psychosis. Robert Lowell, who had a typical manic-de-pressive illness, provides an interesting contrast to those individuals who suffer from the episodic psychosis.

Robert Lowell was renowned for his recurrent psychotic episodes. He had at least fourteen attacks between his first psychosis in March, 1949, when he was thirty-three years old until his death at age sixty from a heart attack. During the intervals between attacks Lowell was exceptionally productive. It was obvious that many of his poems were autobiographical and included his psychotic experiences.[1]*

The most striking difference between Lowell's illness and the others was that his hyperactive periods were characterized by a sense of euphoric grandiosity or as he labeled them, "periods of exuberances." Early in his episodes Lowell would display an optimistically playful life style. This is in marked contrast to the others who had hyper-active agitated episodes but the accompanying mood was most often painful dysphoria.

A second difference between Lowell and the others is the manner in which such episodes developed. As we have seen in Mary Lamb, Virginia Woolf, and van Gogh, the onset was quite rapid, although there were minor prodromal symptoms several days before which alerted close friends that an episode was going to occur. Sometimes it was a matter of mere hours between the prodromal symptoms and the break with reality. While it might seem to casual observers that this was true of Lowell, his friends and relatives could recognize early symptoms appearing weeks, even months, before his final break with reality. Furthermore, even when ill some casual acquaintances would think he was sane, while this was not true of the others.

Finally, we have seen that all our subjects have manifest dyscontrol acts, i.e., sudden, explosive outbursts of rage or panic occurring either during the periods of psychosis or between psychotic episodes. This was also true of Lowell, but I will show such outbursts were both quantitatively and qualitatively different. Lowell's behavior, as is true of most typical manic-depressive patients, was often quite frightening to people in his immediate environment. His size, physical strength, and blazing eyes alerted one to the dangers in crossing him. However, again like most of the typical manic-depressives, it is surprising how seldom he

*All quotes from reference 1.

really did explode into a physical attack and that firm limit-setting was often enough to dampen his exuberant manic behavior.

Lowell was marked as a "wild man" and was noted for his intermittent fits of rage. However, as one friend noted these were cautious rages, not really "mad challenging rages." Because of his wildness as an adolescent school boy he was called Caligula by his classmates and his nickname "Cal" stuck with him throughout his life.

There were two episodes that sound like typical dyscontrol acts. One is described by Carley Dawson, a Georgetown neighbor with whom Lowell had a six month affair.

> . . . I had argued something—just really for the sake of discussion, because I don't really know anything about Shakespeare's play particularly. And all of a sudden Robert—who was sitting on my right—swung around and took my neck in his hands and swung me down onto the floor. And I looked at his face and it was completely white, completely blank. I can't describe it. The person inside was not there. And I have marvelous Guardian Angels. I think that if I had struggled at that time I wouldn't be here. But I said, Robert it is rather uncomfortable like this. Do you mind if I get back on the sofa? And then he came back to himself, he was back in his body, and we sat down and continued our conversation. I didn't argue anymore.

Lowell's marriage to Jean Stafford was always stormy, but particularly after Lowell converted to Catholicism. As she says, "Once Cal went for Romanism he was all Roman," and although she was Catholic she had minor lapses from full piety which would enrage Lowell. One time he tried to strangle her and then hit her on the nose, badly fracturing it. This was particularly ironic because several years earlier he had crashed his car into a wall and Stafford, his passenger, had severe facial injuries with a fractured skull, nose, and jaw. At the time of his car accident, his friends never thought of Robert as crazy, just a "violent man doing his own thing."

These are the only two explosive uncontrollable violent acts by Lowell that I have uncovered, otherwise his violence was either a threat, sublimated physical violence on the playing fields, or verbal violence in the parlor. Lowell did knock his father to the floor one time, although there was considerable provocation because his father had called his current girl friend "no better than a whore."

Current diagnostic procedures now refer to manic-depressive disorders as a bipolar affective disorder. By the label bipolar one infers that the individual is likely to swing from manic periods into depression with or without a period of normal mood in between. The patient manifests extreme emotional states, from grandiose euphoria in the mania to self-derogatory painful sadness during the depression. Another recurrent affective disorder is referred to as a unipolar affective disorder characterized by recurrent and intermittent depressions without significant periods of mania. Theoretically, there is a possibility of a unipolar manic disorder but this has been reported rarely in the psychiatric literature. In the case of Lowell, mania was the outstanding feature because of the dramatic problems this mania presented for the patient, family, and society. Ernest Hemingway may have been an example of a unipolar depression, i.e., a recurrent depressive disorder, but Robert Lowell's was close to being a unipolar manic disorder as his depressions were usually but not always short-lived, a matter of a few days immediately following "coming down" from a manic episode. One characteristic of the typical manic-depressive disorder (which differentiates it from atypical episodic psychosis) is that both euphoric and depressed periods are prolonged—lasting weeks or months. There is not the rapid mixture of agitation and hyperactivity and then a lack of energy and immobility that one sees in the atypical disorders, which can switch from hour-to-hour and day-to-day as exemplified by Leonard Woolf's description of one of Virginia's psychotic episodes (pp.58).

Lowell's first attack occurred in March of 1949. After attending Mass with a friend he announced that he'd returned to the church that morning having received an incredible outpouring of grace. He was described as, "shooting sparks in every direction." But this was not recognized as the onset of illness. His friend reports, "The change taking place in him was like the process which sometimes occurs at a late stage in the formation of a work of art where everything begins to coalesce, to flow together into patterns that had not been foreseen. It is a stage of inspiration that is well beyond the deliberative." This is much the way that Barker defines "brain-storms" (pp.219). But other friends recognized this as the beginning of "one of his manic phases" which suggests that they had observed minor manic episodes previously, even though Lowell had not been previously hospitalized. His mania vacillated but some days later he provided Carolyn Tate with a list of her husband's lovers and then implored him to repent. Needless to say, the Tates were less than pleased with this incident. The next event was for him to open a window and begin shouting obscenities. Soon a crowd gathered and he was handcuffed by the police, but friends talked them into releasing Lowell to their custody. The following day he was off to Bloomington, Indiana, where it is said that Lowell's psychosis first went public. Lowell describes the attack as "pathological enthusiasm." He was running up and down the streets crying out against the devil and homosexuals. He recalled later, "I believed I could stop cars and paralyze their forces by merely standing in the middle of the highway with my arms outspread. Each car carried a long rod above its tail light and the rods were adorned with diabolic Indian or voodoo signs." He goes on, "I suspected I was the reincarnation of the Holy Ghost and had become homicidally hallucinated. To have known the glory, violence and banality of such an experience is corrupting . . ." This led to his first hospitalization and first consultation with a psychiatrist, Merrill Moore, who was also a poet. He reported that Lowell was "having considerable conflict between religion and sexuality" and this led to "a brainstorm which he will in time ride out." I wonder whether Moore in describing the episode as a brainstorm was thinking of the storms of electrical activity that I have proposed leads to the episodic disorders when it involves deeper areas of the brain, particularly the limbic system?

After his mania subsided, he began to slip into a depression. "No one can care for me, I've ruined my life, I'll always be mad." And so in September, 1949, he was readmitted to a hospital and at that time first considered as suffering from a manic-depressive disorder. Lowell said, "I seem to be in the other half, the down half of what you saw in Bloomington." It was reported that he was well by Christmas so we see that this first attack was a true bipolar illness with a period of mania starting in March, at which time he was treated with electroconvulsive therapy, being discharged in mid-June only to be hospitalized for his depression September 5th. During the interval between swings he was engaged and then married to Elizabeth Hardwick. Thus,he had an illness with a three month manic period, terminated by electric shock treatment and then a brief interlude followed by a depression that lasted three to four months. The onset of both the mania and the depression were insidious and not recognized by friends and acquaintances until they became severe.

The next episode 3-½ years later occurred in Salzburg, Austria, in July, 1952. Lowell was presenting a seminar to a group of twenty European poets and, as one observer said, "He developed an extraordinary following. There was a series of very intense seminars, people were almost passionately involved with him—with his ideas." However, his wife looked on apprehensively as she was beginning to realize that these creative bursts also might be a prelude to a manic attack. In this attack, one of the early symptoms of an impending disorder, which was repeated frequently in the future, was "falling in love," on this occasion with a young music student, Giovanna Madonia. Toward the end of August, Lowell disappeared and then the next night was found wandering alone near the border between Austria and Germany. Having been brought back by the police, he barricaded himself in his room and only after great effort was hospitalized. He felt all of the people in one country were good and all of those in the other evil. He said that he was having fun and when he arrived at the hospital simulated a limp claiming this was the reason for hospitalization. When his wife asked the doctor how he was doing the doctor said, I hope facetiously, "He's fine, he's left the

Church and wants to join the army.'' There was a rapid remission and according to Lowell, ''In a period of twenty days I went through the three stages of exuberance, confusion and depression and can now safely say its all definitely over.'' This episode then was somewhat similar to the rapid cycling that we see in the episodic psychotic reactions.

His next attack occurred in 1953 when his mother, who had been traveling in Europe, suddenly died. On his flight over he stopped off in Paris to visit a friend who said, ''I knew that he was in the early stages of illness because he couldn't sleep, sat up all night talking and drinking. Everything was racing.'' Following his return to work after his mother's burial, he again became enamored of his old girl friend, Giovanna Madonia, and his wife, Elizabeth Hardwick, correctly perceived this as an early symptom of his mania. Nevertheless, she was in a bad position, as others saw her as an interfering rejected spouse so, while friends thought he was ill, his peers at Cincinnati, where he was teaching, thought ''that the great poet was better, if anything, than he had been before.'' His tireless energy and his eloquence were taken as signs of a newly liberated spirit. At this time he was writing to and lecturing about Ezra Pound. On the 25th of March he announced his separation from his wife, but by Arpil 8th was committed to a hospital where he again received electric shock therapy with only temporary remission. By June there was a new surge of elation. At that time the diagnosis of acute schizophrenia was entertained and so, for the first time, Lowell was treated with what was the newly discovered major tranquilizer, chlorpromazine (Thorazine). Lowell's account of events for the period June-July 1954 describes what could be considered the devastating effects of a tranquilizer. ''My blood became like melted lead . . . I wallowed through badminton games . . . I sat gaping through *Scrabble* games unable to form the simplest words . . . I watched the Giants play the Dodgers . . . I couldn't keep count of the balls and strikes for longer than a single flash on the screen.'' His wife was encouraged by what she considered his extraordinary response to the new drug. By September, he was out of the hospital and living in Boston. She said, ''Together we have managed so far to keep the depression from becoming incapacitating—it comes down upon us like a cloud but always lifts in a day or two.'' This trend of minimal depression following a rather severe manic episode is the most frequent pattern of Lowell's illness.

The next attack developed insidiously in 1957. It is amazing how often people refused to admit that Lowell was sick. For example, his hostess at a Washington party said, ''There was a table covered in glasses and Cal came up to this corner where a number of us were circulating, including Lizzie, and he sat down in the chair and dashed the glasses off the table with his feet and sat there with his feet on the drinks table surrounded by broken glass and shouted 'Lizzie, Hiss wasn't guilty.' Dorothea and Iver Richards were sitting on the sofa and Dorothea said to me, 'What a lovely party, everybody's such fun.' There were punch ups, there were insults and Cal was just going around like the devil pitting people against each other. It was the most extraordinary party, an absolute triumph for Cal . . . the extraordinary thing was that nobody seemed to realize that he was mad.'' Again, Lowell was hospitalized and again he fell in love with another young girl, a psychiatric field worker from Bennington College. The next year he was high again, ''active as electricity,'' and the doctors pronounced him ''truly under the complete domination of childhood fantasies.'' He was released from the hospital the weekend of his forty-fifty birthday (March 1958) after three months hospitalization.

In February, 1961, Lowell again showed signs of speeding up and again there was a girl, a young New York poet named Sandra Hockman. On March 3, 1961, his ''elation'' reached its climax. Friends reported Cal was in terrible physical shape, shaking and panicky. ''God knows what he was taking in the way of drugs. He was sweating, talking non-stop. They both stayed overnight at my house. I locked my door and in the middle of the dark night she (Cal's wife) started beating on it. I think it was not so much that he was attacking her but that she was so worried about him because he was breathing badly and drinking so I spent the rest of the night trying to calm everything down, trying to get him to sleep and I think the next day I took him to the hospital.'' Although Lowell left his wife and set up an apartment with his girl friend, as he became depressed he repeated the familiar pattern of renouncing his girl friend. His wife said: "He came home very low and sad, just shattered."

In talking about his treatment with a New York psychoanalyst, Lowell said, "Dr. Bernard has decided my dreams are more rewarding than my actuality. This adds great plot, color and imagery to our sessions and seems to remove them for me to the safe and detached world of fiction—my disease in life is something like this."

The next attack, in the summer of 1962, occurred on a trip to South America. Again, it is amazing how bizarre Lowell's behavior could be before people were willing to admit that he was sick. For instance, the description of his behavior was: "After lunch, Cal started his tour of equestrian statues, undressing and climbing the statues. He insisted on being taken to every statue in Buenos Aires—well, we didn't do every one, thank God. And he'd stop the car and start clambering up and sit next to the general on top of the statue." In the hospital, it was said that he received 2,000 milligrams of chlorpromazine four times a day—a massive dose—but was still violent underneath it. When they finally got him on the plane to fly back to New York he, of course, fell madly in love with the stewardess and tried to leave the plane so he could marry her and start a new life in South America. By January 1963 he wrote that he had been writing for the last four months and that this was the best way "to get out of the slump that usually follows my attacks." However, one year later, at the end of November, 1963, he was telling people that Lyndon Johnson had asked him to join his cabinet and so was returned to the hospital, but by February, 1964, was himself again, although following this he reported there was a "dark, post manic pathological self-abasement."

In the fall of 1964 the insidious onset of Lowell's symptoms were described as follows: "It was all very subliminal, you only gradually noticed." He was becoming "tenacious of schemes and ideas." "He would want you to sit up a little bit later at night and then later and later and then would become hectic and impatient if he was refused.'' In January, 1965, it was noted that Lowell had ''gone over'' and again he had a new girl friend, this time a Latvian dancer who he shortly began introducing as his future wife. In February, 1965, Lowell in his depression again wanted to give up his new girl friend and return to his wife. In October of 1965, Lowell again collapsed, his ninth episode since 1949. There was always in Lowell's illnesses ''an element of simple mischief of sly, childishly perverse outrageousness.'' On Christmas Eve, 1966, it was necessary to call the police and put him into the hospital.

In 1967, Lowell, who had previously been treated with electro-convulsive therapy (ECT) or the phenothiazines was now being treated with a new drug, lithium carbonate. When he did not relapse (these manic episodes had been occurring at least yearly,) he and his friends were praising this new medication. Some people thought they recognized a change in his personality and creativity describing a low key agreeableness (passivity or receptivity) in most of his sonnets. They also noted a slackening of the grandeur and of the ferocity. During 1968 there were a number of Harvard girls for whom Lowell had an attachment, but not the kind of attachment that usually accompanied his insidiously developing manic state.

Again, in July 1970, Lowell had to be hospitalized, this time in England, and it was at this time that his second marriage was breaking up and his courtship of Lady Caroline Blackwood evolving. Recognizing his own propensity to fall in love when manic he says, ''I fell in love part manic, was sick in hospital a good part of the summer, got well, stayed in love. There was great joy in it all, great harm to everyone. I have been vacillating. I think Lizzie (his wife) and I will come back together if that can be done. Anyway, I'll be home in New York during Christmas.'' However, this reconciliation did not take place and he then married Lady Caroline, returning to England to live.

In the spring of 1971, Lowell had a hypomanic attack which it is said he was able to fight off (lithium probably helped) although he became possessed with dolphins, buying up all of the antique dolphins that he could find. For a period of four years, lithium seems to have prevented a full blown manic attack although there were a number of times when friends felt that he was on the brink. However, in November of 1975, he was again admitted to a hospital in England. He said to his new (third) wife Carolyn Blackwood, "Honey, Christ, I'm going to have an attack. I can feel it in the spine, its a funny creeping feeling. Its coming up the spine from the lower back up." He felt a massive Valium injection might stop it and indeed it might have if this was caused by a limbic seizure. The description of his illness sounds like it could have been or, perhaps, some of these episodes were associated with a seizure, but even though he received massive doses of Valium, which has anticonvulsant action, it had little effect on him and he was still constantly walking about, talking and waving his arms. The fact that Valium didn't calm him down suggests that the episode was not a seizural phenomenon.

Lowell's treatment reflects the fact that psychiatric labels become more important as our therapeutic interventions become more precise. He was treated with Electroconvulsive Treatment (ECT), which we now know is useful in treating depression although currently the newer antidepressants would be tried first. He was also treated with chlorpromazine (Thorazine), which we now realize is most effective in treating schizophrenics. Finally, he was treated with Lithium, which is most useful in treating mania and prophylactically in preventing both manic and depressive attacks. In a non-specific manner ECT also suppresses manic hyperactivity and often induces a temporary remission of schizophrenic psychoses, while chlorpromazine suppresses a wide range of psychotic behavior by "tranquilizing" patients, making them more tractable, as Lowell so aptly described. When one or two procedures were somewhat helpful in a multitude of disorders, and there were no effective alternatives, precise labels were unnecessary. As our therapeutic armamentarium becomes more specific, so must our diagnoses be more precise. No longer is rest, and removal from stressful situations, as used in the case of Mary Lamb and Virginia Woolf, sufficient. Also one of the main theses in this book is that we should add the anticonvulsants to our potentialy useful drugs for those individuals who have episodic disorders due to limbic seizures.

ERNEST HEMINGWAY

Ernest Hemingway had only two hospitalizations and these were both late in his life. These occurred in November, 1960, and in April, 1961, when he was 61 years old. Both times he was hospitalized for severe depression with suicidal impulses and treated, as Lowell, with ECT. However, Hemingway did have mood swings from hypomania to depression throughout his life, but not serious enough to lead to hospitalization. In current diagnostic nomenclature, he would probably be labeled as a Dysthymic disorder or what we previously referred to as a cyclothymic personality, or a neurotic depressive reaction.

Scott Fitzgerald says, "His (Hemingway's) inclination is towards megalomania, mine towards melancholia," but Ernest probably concealed from Scott and most of his other friends that the pendulum in his emotions swung periodically the full arc from megalomania to melancholia. The diagnosis, Dysthymic, is a more characterologic description rather than an illness. Baker[2]* says of Hemingway, "He was proud of his manhood, his literary and athletic skills, his staying and recuperative powers, his reputation, his capacity for drink, his prowess as a fisherman and "wing" shot, his earnings, his self-reliance, his wit, his poetry, his medical and military knowledge, his skill in map reading, and navigation. There is the temperamental manic-depressive, the inveterate hypochondriac and valetudinarian who spoke seriously of suicide at intervals throughout his life, yet, possessed enormous powers of resilience and recuperation that could bring him back from the brink to the peak within days and sometimes within

*All quotes from reference 2.

hours. He was a persistent warrior who wryly cautioned others against this pernicious habit. He was plagued all of his adult life by insomnia, and in sleep, by nightmares.'' At another point Baker says, ''In his treatment of those he liked or loved there was often something of chivalric; once he had turned on them he could be excessively cruel and abusive. When drunk or sufficiently provoked, he sometimes slapped or cuffed them,'' (women).

Throughout his life Hemingway often talked about death and various ways of dying, saying, ''. . . I think about probably the best way unless you could arrange to die some way while asleep would be to go off a liner at night.'' Even as early as 1925 he had resolved to kill himself if his current love affair were not settled by Christmas, but then added it was foolish to want to die. Nonetheless, many times at evening around five o'clock, depression would come on him like a fog. As Baker says, ''The underside of Ernest's spiritual world was a nightmare of nothingness by which he was occasionally haunted.'' In January, 1936, Hemingway went through a spell of insomnia and melancholia. It lasted only for a period of three weeks and disappeared when he decided that it was caused by insufficient exercise. Considering Hemingway's literary output, it is startling to realize that he probably had a greater facility for action than he did for writing. Although one could consider that Hemingway's life was a struggle for the ''macho'' image, his attitudes and aspirations were only moderately megalomaniac, that is to say he managed to obtain most of the goals he set for himself, whether this was the critical or financial success of his writings or his capacity as a fisherman and hunter. His depression seemed more pervasive, but he once wrote to Archibald MacLeish that he loved life so much that it would be ''a big disgust'' when the time came for him to shoot himself.

He did show certain paranoid personality traits, which toward the end of his life, particularly during his final months, reached psychotic delusional proportions, but this was a minor character trait based on considerable reality. He often said that the reviewers hated him and would like to put him out of business, although he admitted that it was no doubt partly his own fault, as he had been pretty "snotty" sometimes in the past and his victims held this against him.

His psychological state reached pathological proportions late in his life. In May, 1960, he wrote that the forced labor of writing a bullfight article for *Life* magazine had confused his brain if not something more serious, and this is one of the earliest hints that he had some awareness that his mind was deteriorating. The loss of his mental functions is not surprising because throughout his life Hemingway drank a fabulous amount, although he would cut down his daily intake at those times when he was energetically pursuing his writing. Pertinent to our discussion is the fact that Hemingway did like and frequently drank absinthe. It is not clear whether such intake precipitated explosive outbursts, but it is recorded that one night, drunk on absinthe, he threw knives at his wife's piano. It was also reported that he would frequently go into "black rages" which overcame his judgment and then he would give individuals bitter tongue lashings. He did this to Donald Ogden Stewart, John Dos Passos, and Archibald MacLeish.

In his last years, Hemingway was in bad physical condition, partly as a result of his two airplane crashes in Africa, which had seriously damaged both his kidneys and his spleen, and also what must have been considerable damage to his liver from drinking. It was said that Ernest Hemingway's protagonist was his "poor long-suffering liver." Considering this, as well as his alcoholic intake, it would not be surprising if Hemingway had some brain damage and he apparently was aware of this, saying quite pitifully between his hospitalizations that he could not write—"it just wouldn't come anymore" as tears were rolling down his cheeks.

Hemingway expressed during his war years a contemptuous attitude toward the psychiatric patient and the psychiatrist's view that every individual had a breaking point and could just take so much for so long. He rejected the idea that there should be no more criticism of a mental breaking point than a physical one. So it must have been a real blow to him when he was hospitalized.

In July 1960, after his sixty-first birthday, he became seriously depressed. His symptoms were fear, lonliness, ennui, suspicion of the motives of others, insomnia, guilt, remorse, and failure of his memory. He had a number of physical complaints and nightmares and expressed the fear that he was having a complete physical and nervous crackup. The only optimistic note was that he remembered similar attacks in the past when he had gotten out of the slumps.

At this time he began developing true paranoid delusions and bizarre ideas. For instance, one time backing up and lightly scratching another car, he became fearful that the sheriff might arrest him and expressed the conviction that the ''Feds'' were on his trail.* So, on November 30, 1960, he was flown with the utmost secrecy to the Mayo Clinic and put under the care of a psychiatrist. After being treated with ECT he was discharged from the hospital on January 22, 1961. Upon his return home, the tension steadily increased until one April morning his wife, Mary, caught him standing with his hands on a shotgun and two shells resting on the adjacent widow sill. In the struggle to get him to the hospital, he threatened a second suicide attempt with the shotgun but was thwarted after a wrestling match with his friend Don Anderson. On his flight to the clinic, when the private plane stopped to refuel, he was obviously looking for a gun and it was thought that he wanted to walk toward the whirling propeller of an incoming plane.

He was again treated with ECT and was discharged from the hospital on June 26th, although is wife felt that he was far from well and protested the early discharge. On the way home he kept worrying that state troopers would arrest them because he was carrying alcoholic beverages in the car. They arrived at his home in Ketchum, Idaho, Friday, June 30, 1961. On Sunday morning, Ernest Hemingway arose early, found the key to the locked gun closet, opened it, took out a double barreled Boss shotgun with a tight choke, loaded it with two shells, put it to his forehead and pulled both triggers simultaneously. Ironically,

*An article in the Washington Post dated Monday, October 10, 1983, indicated that there was no love lost between Hemingway and J. Edgar Hoover. F.B.I. files reveal that Hoover was suspicious of Hemingway's anti-facist proclivities and had Hemingway followed probably up to the time of Hemingway's death in 1961.

in 1940 he carefully explained to his third wife, Martha, the technique of using a shotgun to commit suicide by springing the trigger with a bare toe. Also, he once said, "Living is much more difficult and complicated than dying."

Both Lowell and Hemingway were "mood swingers," but Hemingway's mood swings were attentuated compared to Lowell's. These mood swings were recognized by both as pathological and the depressive phases as uncomfortable. Perhaps, because of Hemingway's disdain for psychiatry, he did not see this as signaling a need for psychiatric intervention. Lowell did, but one wonders how seriously Lowell took this. He at least acquiesced to hospital care and even during intervals between psychotic episodes accepted, with some derogation, psychoanalysis.

In common with our subjects suffering from episodic disorders, Lowell's and Hemingway's manic-depressive swings were episodic with significant periods of normalcy between attacks. However, the attacks of Lowell, and (when they could be discerned as attacks) also in Hemingway, developed insidiously over a period of weeks or months, not hours or days as in the episodic disorders. Lowell and Hemingway had uncontrolled rages like the episodic group, but they were less frequent—less primitive, although at times there was a remarkable similarity with the rages of the individuals suffering from the episodic disorder. This suggests that in some aspects the differentiation between episodic disorders and the manic-depressive disorders may not be clear cut and that there may be some underlying neurophysiologic deviation shared by both. The most distinctive difference is the sustained euphoric periods with hyperactivity in the manic phase of the manic-depressive disorder, while the hyperactivity in the episodic disorder is most often associated with painful feeling, including mixtures of fear, rage, dread, and depression, even though there may be momentary ecstatic feelings as well.

Another distinctive characteristic which differentiates the manic-depressive from the episodic disorder is that the swings from hyper to hypomotility, and from rage to melancholia, persists for significant periods (e.g. weeks to months) in the former while it changes from hour-to-hour, or at least day-to-day, in the latter. But again, there are exceptions in both groups suggesting the possibility of some common underlying neurophysiologic mechanism.

There are significant clinical symptoms characteristic of both syndromes and these are severe insomnia, nightmares when they do sleep, and a multitude of physical complaints including headaches, fainting spells, tremulousness, swings in eating habits, or dramatic changes in body weight. In both there is usually an excessive dependency on nicotine and/or alcohol. Nevertheless, current clinical observations suggest important differences between the two disorders in that there is a unique responsivity to anticonvulsant medication in the episodic disorders. This suggests that the differences are important in planning a medical regimen, even though there are perplexing exceptions which suggest either a failure in our symptomatic differentiation of the two disorders or a varying degree of commonality in the underlying neurophysiology.

From the standpoint of creativity the shared aspect of manic-depressive and episodic disorders are the long periods of quiescence between attacks which allow creative effort.The memory of this psychotic experience leads to new insights which is incorporated in the individual's art or writing. During the "before" and "after" periods there is a frenzy of creativity that enhances the artistic output. The process underlying these disorders at both the physiologic and the psychologic levels results in a fitting together of concepts or percepts, which because of these individuals' innate abilities and learned skills, can be conveyed meaningfully to the public. Their inner world thereby becomes an outer world that is shared for the benefit of all. We must remember, however, that to the individuals afflicted, their madness is not a myth.

Chapter 7

Ezra Pound and Adolph Monticelli—Paranoia –Or Was It Feigned?

EZRA POUND

There is one form of chronic psychosis that would not preclude creative activity and that is paranoia, a condition that gradually develops in the fourth or fifth decade and includes an intricate, complex, and elaborate delusional system based on or proceeding logically from misinterpretation of actual events. These individuals consider themselves endowed with a unique and superior ability, and in spite of the chronic course of the condition it does not seem to interfere with the rest of the patient's thinking and personality. We have already seen that there were sustained periods in the life of both Edvard Munch and August Strindberg characterized by such paranoid behavior, and in fact, all of the rest showed some transitory paranoid ideation or minor paranoid character traits. The unanimous opinion of four psychiatrists (Joseph L. Gilbert, Marion R. King, Wendell Muncie, and Winfred Overholser) who examined Ezra Pound was summarized as follows: "In our opinion, with advancing years his

(Pound) personality for many years abnormal has undergone further distortion to the extent that he is now suffering from a paranoid state . . ."[3] They characterized his thinking as abnormally grandiose, expansive, and exuberant in manner, with pressure of speech, discursiveness, and distractibility. They said he exhibited extremely poor judgment and indicated that his activities in question were part of his mission to "save the constitution." The abnormal personality was described as eccentric, querulous, and egocentric. This report was submitted in December, 1945, at a hearing to determine whether Pound could stand trial on an indictment by a grand jury in October, 1945, that "Pound as an American citizen owing allegiance to the United States had committed the crime of treason by adhering to the enemies of the United States, namely, the Kingdom of Italy and its military allies, giving them aid and comfort by making propaganda speeches over Rome radio during the years when the United States was at war with Italy."[3,4]

As mentioned before, the eccentricity of geniuses, their new or unusual perspective of reality, an inner conviction of their own uniqueness, borders on psychotic paranoid grandiosity, just as the zeal and intensity with which geniuses pursue their creative activities may be difficult to differentiate from the manic patient. However, we have also noted that the core creative individuals studied in Section I had an intermittent psychosis that was not only easily recognized by others, but also by the individuals themselves. These creative individuals viewed their psychosis as both a threat as well as a possible asset to their creativity. This is quite different from the chronic paranoid state where the borderline between creativity and madness may be obscure and external observers argue as to whether the individual is a genius or merely mad. Also the individuals themselves are seldom willing to concede their "madness." This is certainly true of Ezra Pound at the time of his indictment, for he not only denied that he was insane, but also could not understand the seriousness of the charges against him as he did not perceive that his behavior could be interpreted as treasonable. It was this lack of judgment which led psychiatrists for both the government and the defense to consider him mentally unfit to advise properly with counsel or to participate intelligently and reasonably in his own defense. Thus, he was considered unfit for trial and in need of care in a mental hospital.

Pound, sixty years of age at the time of his indictment was an American born poet who had been a voluntary expatriot for nearly forty years, living in England and France, and for the previous twenty-one years in Italy. Pound was generally considered to be the greatest English language poet of the 20th Century and also possessed an outstanding capacity to recognize latent creative talent in others, not only among writers but musicians and artists as well.[5] It is not surprising that the lives of almost all the subjects discussed in this volume (with the exception of Mary Lamb and Vincent van.Gogh who lived in a different era) crossed paths with Pound and that many of them had been encouraged in their creative efforts by this man who they recognized as a mentor. Hemingway said: "Any poet born in this century or in the last ten years of the preceding century who can honestly say that he has not been influenced by or learned greatly from the work of Ezra Pound deserves to be pitied rather than rebuked. It is as if a prose writer born in that time should not have learned from or been influenced by James Joyce . . . the best of Pound's writings—and it is in the Cantos—will last as long as there is any literature."[5]

On April 19, 1958, after twelve years incarceration at St. Elizabeth's, the federal mental hospital in Washington D.C., this indictment was dismissed by the District Court for the District of Columbia. Thus, at the age of seventy-two he was released and allowed to return with his wife to his home overlooking Rapallo on the Italian Riviera.

The handling of Pound pinpoints serious legal, constitutional, and social questions that were never decided and in fact are still unresolved. There was never a court trial so that guilt of treason was never established. The supposition was that his chronic psychosis, which prevented him from aiding in his legal defense at one time in his life, continued unabated throughout his twelve years of incarceration in a mental hospital. On the other hand, it was admitted that hospitalization was no treatment for his psychosis and that the prognosis was quite poor, namely, that he would never recover. Furthermore, it was conceded that Pound was not a danger to himself and others so that while he might be chronically psychotic, and unable to aid his legal defense, he did not need continued hospitalization. However, if Pound had been tried and found guilty of treason he could have been punished by death.

Opinions regarding Pound's status were intense. On one hand, a vociferous segment of the population believed Pound was a malicious anti-Semite feigning his illness who should be tried and found guilty.* On the other hand, there was an equally vociferous group who felt he was a misunderstood, if perhaps somewhat naive, "ivory tower" genius whose deviations from the norm were really quite harmless and should be overlooked. The end result was that the government relied on expert opinions to equivocate on any decision. It would seem that justice in this equivocation would not satisfy anybody—except that during twelve years of equivocation tempers could cool so that it would be possible to dismiss the indictment. Such a dilemma is still current in the treatment of political dissent in the Soviet Union, as reflected in the renowned hospitalization of such dissidents as Medvedv, Gorbanevskaya, and Plyushch. Such a situation was handled with dispatch regarding Knut Hamsun, the Norwegian novelist who, we have noted, was a mentor of both Munch and Strindberg and who was accused of treason in 1945 for having become a member of the Quisling Party during the German occupation of Norway. He carried on intensive propaganda for this party as well as the German invaders against the legal Norwegian government. Hamsun was eighty-six at the time. The experts agreed that he was not insane even though there were senile changes which accounted for his poor judgment. Nevertheless,

*E. Fuller Torrey, a psychiatrist, in his recent book, *The Roots of Treason* (McGraw Hill, 1983), presents the point of view that Pound committed treason and should have been executed but this was prevented by the deliberate perjury of Dr. Winfred Overholser, Superintendent of St. Elizabeth's Hospital. A critique of Torrey's thesis is presented by the Pound scholar Carroll F. Terrell in his book review in the Washington Post, Sunday, October 9, 1983.

under the more lenient treason laws of Norway he could be found guilty and fined without incarceration. The leniency of this sentence must surely have been influenced by not only Hamsun's age but also his mental condition.[6] Thus, the stance taken by Thomas Szasz (see pp.229) that every individual should be considered responsible for their behavior, led to a more appropriate and humane solution with regard to Hamsun as opposed to the procrastination regarding Pound. The ultimate leniency towards Pound was to a large extent the initiative of Robert Frost but was also helped by support from Archibald MacLeish, Ernest Hemingway, T.S. Eliot, W.H. Auden, Carl Sandberg, Marianne Moore, Allen Tate, John Dos Passos, and others.

For our purposes, we are interested in whether Pound did or did not slip from genius to psychosis and if he did, how this affected his creativity. The first question we have to ask is whether he ever was psychotic and then, if we decide this in the affirmative, how this affected his poetry.

In a letter written to Pound's wife Dorothy, dated January 25, 1946, Pound's lawyer, Julian Cornell, writes, "While the doctors are agreed that he is to this extent mentally abnormal, I feel quite sure that you will find, when you see him again, that he is his usual self and the mental aberration which the doctors have found are not anything new or unusual but are chronic and would pass entirely unnoticed by one like yourself who has lived close to him for a number of years. In fact, I think it may be fairly said that any man of his genius would be regarded by a psychiatrist as abnormal."[3] This was written after Pound was judged insane and unable to aid in his defense. I am uncertain whether Cornell was writing these words because he believed them or because he wanted to reassure Mrs. Pound as he says, "You need not be alarmed by the report on your husband's mental condition."[3] However, on July 14, 1946, Mrs. Pound wrote to Mr. Cornell: "I have now seen Ezra three times. The first time for an hour. I find him very nervous and jumpy I believe his wits are really very scattered and he has difficulty in concentrating for more than a few minutes." In a letter to Cornell dated July 17th she says, "He is certainly very nervous and worried." After a

writ of habeas corpus had been filed and turned down, the possibility of an appeal was considered but Mrs. Pound demurred,
"My husband is not fit to appear in court and must still be kept
as quiet as possible; the least thing shakes his nerves up terribly.''[3] One cannot be sure what were her motives behind such
comments, but at face value they suggest that Mrs. Pound did
find him different than before. Certainly Pound was maltreated
for a man of his age at the military prison at Pisa, where he was
confined in a solitary steel cage in the hot sun of the Italian
summer, unable to communicate with any other prisoners or
guards. It was reported that he was "stricken with violent and
hysterical terror." He became desperately thin and weak and was
finally rescued by the prison doctor. This act restored to some
level his physical health but his recurrent terror continued until
he was flown to the United States on November 18, 1945.[4]

In 1927, Wyndham Lewis, in a critique of Pound, maintained that there was a gap between Pound's feeling for the past
and his fire-eating utterances of contemporary affairs, saying that
Pound was, "A sort of revolutionary simpleton." At this early
date, when Pound was just over forty, he was becoming interested
in history, politics, and economic affairs. He wrote that it was
the responsibility of the literary man to present ideas clearly and
concisely so the leaders could perceive the problems of the world
and act accordingly. Pound's father, who was living with Ezra
at the time, said to a visitor, "You know, there isn't a damn
thing that boy of mine don't know." This was apparently the
way Pound felt and acted. During the 1930's, Pound began for-
mulating ideas far beyond his knowledge and if what he said at
times was sound, this seemed to be true of no more than a few
sentences before he went off half-cocked. He wrote a book entitled *The ABC's of Economics,* became active in the social credit
movement, and became particularly enraged at what he called the
usurocracy, which he then used to support his anit-Semitic tirades.
He was enthralled by the concept of the corporate state, thereby
becoming an early supporter of Mussolini, and later, Hitler. The
language he used was at least inflammatory, usually vitriolic, and
at times his editors thought libelous. In 1934, he began circulating

questionnaires to bankers, politicians, and writers in the United States and England. Joyce was convinced that Pound was "mad" saying he was "genuinely frightened of him." At the same time Hemingway remarked that Pound spoke "very erratically." He began to have grand activist fantasies of trying to influence the leaders in the American government, including Roosevelt. In 1939, he visited the States and had correspondence or interviews with Henry Wallace, Byrd, Bankhead, and many others. At the same time he was described by William Carlos Williams as depressed and fearful. Pound felt that he was carrying out a mission as a man of truth and later in 1944 described his ideas as "guided by an interior light above warring factions."[7]

During the decades before World War II, Pound had published forty volumes of verse, criticisms, history, and economic theory. He translated and published Chinese and Japanese poetry and drama. He had even composed a musical score for an opera, "Villon," which was sung in Paris, and in 1924, after reitring to Rapallo, he started work on his monumental *Cantos* and continued writing these through the period he was incarcerated in the military prison at Pisa. His divergence into economics and politics, while it must have interfered with his poetic output, did not terminate such efforts. Toward the end of this period, i.e., the pre-1945 era, his wife did mention to him that both what he wrote and what he said often made jumps in content that left them hard to follow. Those cantos written in the prison seemed confused and fragmentary and did not bear much relation structurally to the earlier ones but they still are considered good poetry. Noel Stock, his biographer, says, "If at times the verse is silly, it is because in himself Pound was often silly; if at times it is firm, dignified and intelligent, it is because in himself Pound was often firm, dignified and intelligent; if it is fragmentary and confused, it is because Pound was never able to think out his position and did not know how the matters with which he dealt were related; and if often lines and passages have a beauty seldom equaled in the poetry of the 20th Century, it is because Pound had a true lyric gift."[7] It seems that Ezra Pound will always be an enigma. When does creative imagination cease and craziness begin? But

Ezra's perception of himself is quite different than that of most of our core subjects, who were first to admit that they had episodes of craziness that were both a source of inspiration and a source of terror.

Kapp believes[5] that the best diagnosis for Ezra Pound would be a cyclothymic personality, i.e., an individual who had mood swings, both depressions and manic states, most of which did not reach psychotic proportions—the diagnosis that I propose as appropriate for Hemingway. The description by the examining psychiatrist at the time of Pound's indictment in 1945 would suggest some symptoms characteristic of the cyclothymic personality including the expansiveness, exuberance, pressure of speech, discursiveness, and distractibility. Kapp identifies a period of depression when he (Pound) dropped out of the University of Pennsylvania; another in 1936 when his mother died and he was described as moody and agitated; another when he had the so-called "nervous breakdown" in the prison at Pisa characterized by mutism, agitation, hypochondriasis, and dejection. Another example would have been in 1959 when it is said that he (Pound) lost his creative drive and Pound himself reports, "I have lived all my life believing that I knew something. And then a strange day came and I realized that I knew nothing, that I knew nothing at all. And so words have become empty of meaning. I have come of late to a state of total uncertainty, where I am conscious only of doubt. I do not work anymore, I do nothing. I've fallen to lethargy and I contemplate. Everything that I touch I spoil. I have blundered always."[7]

Stock reports that in 1960 Pound ate little and had to be taken to a private clinic for treatment. Again he was treated in a clinic in Rome during 1961, complaining not only of difficulty in concentrating, but also a urinary infection which left him bedridden for some time. However, he continued for the next ten years to receive awards, attended Eliot's funeral in London, occasionally gave public readings and even, in June of 1969, again visited the United States. As we mentioned, Hemingway, who had minor mood swings as Stock proposes for Pound, nevertheless recognized such swings as pathological. I find no evidence that Pound had similar insight and believe it more likely he suffered from paranoia; it seems there were early symptoms (long before his association with fascism) which suggested such a diagnosis. This interfered with his creativity, but his brilliance was so intense that it showed through his psychotic disorganization. It seems unlikely that Pound feigned his illness. His doctors could have consciously or unconsciously "feigned his illness," but the early opinion of devoted friends that Pound was mad suggests the doctors' diagnosis was correct. Pound's anti-Semitism may have been part of delusional paranoia, but think what a catastrophe it would be if society considered all anti-Semitism as madness and then held such people not responsible for their behavior because of madness. If the literary critics are correct, Pound's thinking and style deteriorated in his later years and within a biopsychosocial perspective, this deterioration reflected a process which included more than just social factors but also psychologic, as well as biologic, changes.

As we saw in the case of Robert Lowell, psychiatric labels are important—if they indicate a specific therapeutic intervention (in his case treatment with lithium). Psychiatric labeling in the case of Pound was important because it had both social and prognostic significance. If the labels are used appropriately and the implications properly explained to society then society can decide whether individuals should be held responsible for their behavior.

ADOLPH MONTICELLI

Monticelli, a French artist born October 14, 1824, dying in 1886, spent most of his life in Marseilles. Aaron Sheon, the American art historian, recognized Monticelli's genius and arranged for an exhibit of his work to be shown at the Museum of Art, Carnegie Institute, October 27, 1978 to January 7, 1979. Sheon's book, *Monticelli: His Contemporaries and His Influence,* published at that time, is the definitive work in English on this artist.[8]* Monticelli's art and his life style were much admired by Vincent van Gogh. His art was far advanced over his contemporaries and like van Gogh, he was addicted to absinthe and also considered to be psychotic, although many believe that most of his psychotic symptoms were feigned. Unfortunately, Monticelli wrote few letters and had only a small group of close friends and even with these, he seldom discussed either his work or his goals. He was viewed as a bon vivant with an unhurried provincial appreciation for life's pleasures, but Sheon says that his character was more meditative, poetic, and intense and that history would ultimately judge him as a major artist. He was totally immersed in his art and detached himself from everything mundane, having no home or family obligations. He also possessed a total disregard for success or honors and kept himself aloof from any artistic movements. It is reported that he used bizarre phrases or words which had only a special personal meaning for him so that he was difficult to understand and for that reason people thought he was mad. In fact, this description of his language sounds like the idiosyncratic speech characteristic of chronic schizophrenics. However, others felt that he had a special skill in language and enjoyed misleading people about himself because when he wanted to, he could make himself perfectly clear. He also expressed ideas which sound like the grandiose delusions of a paranoid as he conversed regularly with God, and claimed reincarnation from prominent Italina renaissance artists. These certainly sound like delusions, but again other observers thought that he mischievously exaggerated his peculiarities. This impression was not helped by his later paintings which were almost abstract in style so that it was not surprising that many, even though sympathetic towards him, felt that he was insane toward the end of his life. The van Gogh brothers published a text and lithographs of Monticelli's painting, allegedly to save at least one ''alienated genius'' for posterity, and to prove that he was not mad when he painted, but worked carefully to produce each picture. It is apparent that van Gogh identified with Monticelli and had very personal reasons

*All quotes from refereence #8.

to save Monticelli from oblivion. Not only did Monticelli have a fondness for alcohol and absinthe, but he adopted colorful, bizarre dress. He was described by Cezanne as a master of improvisation and it was stated that he painted in an excited state of mind. Thus, one Paris critic said he was a strange person whose art seemed to derive from his madness and reported incorrectly that Monticelli had been in and out of asylums.

Adolph Monticelli was born illegitimately. His father was an obscure civil servant and his mother the daughter of a military officer. Monticelli's father's family disapproved of the marriage and refused permission; however, they did finally wed in 1835, almost ten years after Adolph was born. As was characteristic of the provincial artists, Monticelli used a vigorous but a less finished technique than his contemporaries in Paris, although on several occasions he traveled to Paris for study. Unlike the impressionists of this period, Monticelli could totally let himself go and covered his surfaces with jewel-like crustaceans of color. As Sheon said, "By creating forms that functioned as color and surface reflections, he worked at the threshold of modern art." Verlaine, whom we have referred to several times as an absinthe addict (pp.36), much admired Monticelli; in fact, he bought some paintings for his own collection. He felt that Monticelli's paintings were the visual equivalent of his poetry and indeed there was an element of expressionism in Monticelli's art.

Monticelli was much influenced by the painter Watteau and Rococo art. He was most productive during the years from 1871 until his death in 1886. During this period he underwent a dramatic transformation in his art style that was different from almost all 19th Century painting. His work became freer and simultaneously his coloring brighter. The surfaces were thick impasto and during the final few years of his life his technique was rich, creamy, and briliant so that it was only rivaled by van Gogh and Matisse. However, his work was not understood by either the layman or most of his peers. In 1880, the brushwork in his landscapes became more animated than ever. Much like van Gogh, his subject matter was loaded with colors that seemed to pulsate and flicker, which I have mentioned is a perception that

#10

DON QUIXOTE—Adolph Monticelli's most creative period was during the 1870's and 80's. At that time he worked at the threshold of modern art.

occurs under the psychedelic drugs lysergic acid and mescaline, and such perceptions may have been induced by Monticelli's use of absinthe. In these paintings the figures were almost obliterated by his brushwork. (See Illustration # 10) Monticelli wrote, "I can tell you that I do not only paint for my pleasure and that from time to time I make one of these pictures that creates a certain dream or feeling . . . seriously speaking I don't conjure up my pictures from thin air and they cause me more trouble than you can believe;" a statement that reminds one of Edvard Munch. His painting of vases with flowers must have been an inspiration for some of van Gogh's paintings on the same subject. One such painting purchased by the van Goghs is now in the Vincent van Gogh Museum in Amsterdam. Also, the marine series by Monticelli must have inspired similar paintings by van Gogh. Sheon attributes van Gogh's broad, flowing brushwork to the influence of Monticelli, but van Gogh showed such brushwork early in his painting career, long before he knew of Monticelli's portraits. As Sheon says, ". . . with the common facial distortions to Soutine-like hands and angled eyebrows but the most common characteristic between the two was the fluid brush strokes."

Van Gogh described Monticelli in his letters to his brother in such a way that they sounded almost like self-descriptions. He wrote, "Monticelli was a melancholic, somewhat resigned man, an unhappy person who saw the wedding party of the world pass by, he was the one who had been left out of things."[626a]* Later he wrote, "I think of Monticelli terribly often here. He was a strong man, a little cracked, or rather very much so . . . always harassed by poverty, of an extremely refined taste as a colorist . . . He died at Marseille in rather sad circumstances . . . after passing through a regular Gethsemane. Now listen, for myself I am sure that I am continuing his work here, as if I were his son or his brother." Van Gogh even fantasized "going to Marseille dressed as Monticelli to prove to the people that he did not die sprawled over the café tables as it was thought."* At another time van Gogh wrote about a conversation with Dr. Peyron, the

*3 digit # refers to a letter # in reference 1, chapter 1.
*See reference 1, chapter 1.

physician who took care of van Gogh at the asylum at St. Remy, "The doctor said to me about Monticelli that he always thought him an eccentric but as for madness he had only been a little that way towards the end. Considering all of the misery of Monticelli's last years is there any reason to be surprised that he gave way under too heavy a load, and has one any right to deduce from this artistically speaking that he fell short in his work? I do not believe it, he had such a power of logical calculation and orig-inality as a painter that it is still regrettable that he hadn't the stamina to make its flowering more complete."[(602)] Dr. Gachet, Vincent's last doctor, also admired Monticelli and collected his pictures and Vincent hoped that the doctor would print a second album on Monticelli like the one printed by the van Goghs. Actually, Monticelli's paintings had more influence over British than French artists and this may have been due to the avid col-lection of Monticelli's paintings by Alexander Reed, the son of a Glasgow art dealer, who, as a friend of van Gogh, called van Gogh's attention to his work, giving him two paintings of Mon-ticelli; in turn, van Gogh painted two portraits of Reed. Monticelli was put down as a crazy artist and absinthe addict who ultimately had a stroke and a serious paralysis. On the other hand, his friends and supporters seemed to go to extremes in trying to prove that Monticelli was perfectly normal. This seemed to reflect the at-titude of the time that if an artist was crazy then his art was not worthwhile, very few being willing to accept that "craziness" might enhance creativity. One physician wrote that Monticelli had a visual defect and thought this visual defect led Monticelli to seek colors too intensely. Another person called Monticelli "fada" a provincial term applied to someone who is slightly crazy or out of touch with reality with the implication that he painted with insufficient intellectual effort. Another critic claimed that he was essentially demented during his last five years and in his painting during these years he exaggerated without any control over his style so that his work became a grotesque parody of his early work, a terrible caricature of the early fine qualities, adding that in his madness he tried to diminish his likely chances for later recognition and success. However, it is these very pictures that to me are the most creative and exciting. this is particularly evident in a room in the Lyons Museum devoted to Monticelli's paintings which were collected with the advice of Jean Garibaldi for the Charbonniers. As Sheon says, "Like Pollack and DeKooning, technique became more important to Monticelli than representation."

Monticelli then was considered by many, including his admirer van Gogh, to be "a little cracked." Whether he was or not is unclear, but I propose that the experiences induced by his addiction to absinthe influenced his artistic creativity much the way that absinthe influenced van Gogh and that many of the similarities of the two could be accounted for in this way. However, Monticelli as far as we know, was never put away in an asylum and despite his eccentricities, was consistently productive throughout his life. Many of his symptoms, particularly his grandiosity which we have seen characterized many creative artists and writers, is also typical of paranoia. The speech disorder described of Monticelli is typical of chronic schizophrenics and supposedly reflects an underlying thought disorder that is a consequence of chronic psychosis. This thought disorder, if it existed, vacillated in its intensity and the reported frenzy in his artistic efforts suggests common characteristics with the illness of van Gogh. Whatever Monticelli's mental condition, we have no record that it bothered him or that it interfered with his creativity. The only possibility is that whatever mental aberrations he possessed may have enhanced his creativity. In this instance a psychiatric label has no meaning except that it can be used by critics and a disapproving public to put down the artistic creation of an individual who was fifty years ahead of his time. In such instances, of course, psychiatric labeling is destructive. For Pound, one can argue whether labeling was constructive or destructive—but it did have an important implication for society, as well as for Pound.

Chapter 8

Emily Dickinson— Borderline Insanity

Emily Dickinson was born in Amherst, Massachusetts, December 10, 1830, and died fifty-five years later. During Emily's adolescence, when attending Mt. Holyoke Female Seminary, she was frequently, if not continuously, depressed and in poor health, but also rebellious because despite her family's religious revivalism into the Congregational Church, Emily managed to resist the family pressures to join. From the time the Dickinson's children's education ceased, all of them, including Emily's older brother Austin and younger sister Lavinia, either lived in or lived within a stone's throw of the house in which they were born. Emily, who had a wry sense of humor and a youthful friendliness, gradually became strange and incomprehensible so that by the time she was thirty years old she had become a recluse within her parent's house, eventually she retreated not only indoors altogether, but upstairs, so that neighbors and visiting friends never saw her during the last fifteen years of her life. Peers who had some contact with her during earlier periods found her very difficult and referred to her as ''partially cracked.'' Despite her extreme eccentricities, most biographers, when confronted with the question as to whether she was insane, come to the conclusion that she was not. This was summed up by Theodorea Ward who

said, "The insane cannot explain themselves and Emily could."
John Cody, a psychoanalyst who wrote a psycho-history of Emily,
points out that although it was not unusual for a spinster to live
in her parent's home, the fact was neighbors considered her out-
standingly odd and her closest friend, her sister-in-law Susan,
said that Emily herself, "hated her peculiarities and . . . longed
for a normal life."[9]

CREATIVITY AND NORMALCY

Why do biographers of creative artists strive so hard to prove
the normalcy of their subjects? Why can't creative people be
crazy and the craziness even help in their creativity? What is so
important in making them all normal? Of course, one of the
reasons is that if they have the reputation for being crazy then
their artistic accomplishment is derogated, as we saw was true
in the case of Monticelli. However, Emily even refers to her
breakdown saying, "and then a plank in reason broke." Why
must we think in all or none terms, i.e., of sanity versus insanity?
As Cody says, "Why must we think her poems are descriptions
of normal feelings only if she is sane, considering that if she is
insane then both her life and her poetry are meaningless." The
clear demarcation between sane and insane was characteristic of
our subjects with episodic disorders and during their episodic
psychotic reactions creative activity usually ceased, although
viewing these psychotic episodes in retrospect, they often incorporated their psychotic experiences into their works. Cody points
out, however, that writers about madness and genius are always
grappling with the apparent paradox of a mad artist and sane art.
I will propose that Emily suffered from a borderline state where
minor breaks with reality could take place and yet her creativity
continue. Cody's statement, "But we know from many first hand
accounts how eloquently gifted patients have been able to convey
the thoughts and terrors of a psychosis, sometimes even from the

midst of the state itself,'' applies only to those individuals with relatively minor breaks. One point we will consider is whether Emily's extreme neuroticism superimposed on her borderline psychosis was necessary for, or did it inhibit, her creativity? Cody believes the former and proposes that the "psychological calamities, decades of frustration, isolation and loneliness, all created a void that Emily Dickinson's talent rushed in to fill. Without this void there might well have been no poet.'' The author's implication is that with a different mother who had provided a better model, Emily Dickinson may well have been married and had children, and pursued a conventional existence living in uninterrupted ignorance of her latent artistic gifts. However, we must remember that Emily Dickinson did not believe her seclusive way of life was normal or appropriate. She considered herself the victim of an irrational and inflexible aberration. I suspect that, given her talent with meter and rhyme, she would have been far more productive if anxieties had not confined her to isolation within the parental home. Given the fact that she was isolated, her artistic preoccupation with her inner life, particularly during her pre-psychotic periods, was a prime source of poetic inspiration. Thus, her incipient psychosis may have saved her from the compulsive rigidities of chronic neuroticism and its inhibiting influence on creative work as described by Kubie.[10] Furthermore, as we have seen in our other subjects, creative effort was often therapeutic and this seems to have been true for Emily Dickinson. Thus, her illness both provided the material and the motivation for her outstanding poetic efforts. However, I do not believe that even in the early Victorian era a talented woman would have failed to recognize her underlying talent and, I believe, she would have resisted any life style that seriously compromised the expression of that talent, even to the point of eschewing marriage and motherhood. At least it's hard to imagine anything more confining than Emily's chronic neurosis, which left her too fearful to leave the house at age twenty-four; by age twenty-nine, it was too much of an ordeal for her to meet even friends within the house.

Because of or despite this isolation, she developed an all

consuming dependency on family members. In writing to her sister-in-law Sue she says, "Your absence insanes me so—I do not feel so peaceful when you are gone from me—all life looks differently." In writing to other friends, the Bowleses, she says, "I'm sorry you came because you went away. Hereafter I will pick no rose, lest it fade or prick me." Such a dependency must have been a heavy burden to put on family and friends.

Cody's scholarly and penetrating psycho-history of Emily Dickinson entitled, *"After Great Pain—The Inner Life of Emily Dickinson"*[9] demonstrates all of the richness as well as the hazards of a psychoanalytic interpretation of biographical material. The primary source of his data is Emily's poems. The poems present a double hazard for interpretation because not only does one have to make the usual clinical translation from verbalized introspection that converts the primitive primary process of the unconscious with its idiosyncratic symbolism into the logical thought processes of everyday life, but in the case of Emily, one is faced with a further interpretation of the poet's metaphorical language. Not to do both leaves one with only half a picture; a view of only one side of the coin. The psychiatrist is an expert for one side of the coin based on his experience with his patients while the literary critic is the expert on interpreting the metaphorical side. Each is a layman in the other's field of expertise so it is not surprising they often disagree. Cody does not have the help that is available while analyzing our patients, in that Emily did not discuss her symptoms, nor did her family and friends. Thus, he is forced to construct a "plausible" case history by reading between the lines of her letters and poems, and analogizing from his considerable clinical experience and knowledge about patients with similar life patterns. He proposes that even in Emily's active, vivacious childhood and adolescence there were ominous signs of aberrations; one was her unusual and sometimes inappropriate preoccupation with death and dying. By inappropriate Cody means that she had an "avid interest in death scenes and thirsted for details; it was important to learn just how the dying felt in the face of imminent dissolution."

Another early characterisitc was Emily's masochism: that

is, suffering herself to protect others from pain and unhappiness. Like all masochists there was a suppressed streak of sadism which was reflected in a letter she wrote to her brother Austin after he had written home regarding his "savage" discipline within his classroom of young Boston Irish boys. She wrote, "So far as I am concerned I should like to have you kill some—there is so many now there is no room for the Americans . . . Won't you please too state the name of the boy that turned the faintest . . . I don't think deaths or murders can ever come amiss in a young woman's journal."

In Emily's early letters there was a persisting sadness and fear of losing loved ones and increasing themes of suicide repeated both in poems and letters. There was evidence for intense, underlying rage, and frustrated erotic feelings and a constant fear that these would explode into action. This, in part, was the basis for her fears in meeting strangers, because she believed that her feelings might explode uncontrollably into words that would hurt others or reveal her unaceptable impulses. An example is her mock anger in a letter written to her uncle when he failed to reply to a previous letter, "I call upon all nature to lay hold of you, let fire burn—and water drown—and light put out—and tempest tear—and hungry wolves eat up—and lightening strike—and thunder stun—let friends desert—and enemies draw neigh and gibbets *shake* but never *hang* the house you walk about in! My benison not touch—my malison pursue the body that hold your spirits! . . . Had you a pallid hand—or a blind eye - we would talk about coming to terms but you have sent my father a letter . . . at any rate I shall kill you . . . You can take chloroform if like—and I will put you beyond the reach of pain a twinkling." Later in the letter she goes back to this theme, ". . . Now when I walk into your room and pluck your heart out that you die—I kill you . . . but if I stab you while sleeping, etc." This was written when she was nineteen and certainly represents a perverted sense of humor. By early adulthood depression, guilty feelings, and a widening range of incapacitating phobias dominated her life.

For the psychoanalyst our character and even our neurotic

symptoms are a product of our life history—and Cody feels that the crucial ingredient in Emily's past which led to such aberrations was the inability of her mother to love her child—a "withholding mother." Emily's mother has been described as shallow, self-centered, ineffectual, conventional, timid, submissive and not very bright. Further adjectives levelled at her were that she was obsequious, self-abnegating, plaintive, and dependent. She was described as uninterested in ideas or art. Biographers see her as a nonentity, but as Cody points out, to a child, mother is never a nonentity. It is certain that she didn't present a good model for the role of wife and mother so it is not surprising that Emily and her sister, who was unencumbered by Emily's neurosis, remained spinsters. In fact, mother abdicated her role of housekeeper as soon as the younger daughter, Vinnie, was old enough to assume such responsibilities. It is felt that the mother's cool aloofness is enough to explain the recurrent theme in Emily's writing of hunger for love. This demand on others for love was so intense, and Emily seemed so insatiable, that it was frightening to those whom Emily latched onto. In our study of previous subjects, we have seen how often the psychobiographer sees an absent or unloving mother as a prime factor in adult mental problems. There was the depressed mother (van Gogh), absent mother (Virginia Woolf), controlling mother (Robert Lowell), disapproving mother (Ernest Hemingway), a mother who died when her child was young (Edvard Munch), or an adolescent (August Strindberg). The description of Emily's mother as cold and distant is similar to that applied to Mary Lamb's mother. Mothers carry a heavy burden and may, in fact, be unfairly blamed for adult mental disabilities. What may be important in Emily's case is that her mother did have recurrent depressive episodes; the most severe occurring during postpartum (at the birth of her younger sister) and then during the involutional period. A depressed mother, of course, can have a devastating effect on children, but also there may be a strong genetic transfer of this propensity from mother to some children, and this may in some sense explain the severity of Emily's disorder compared to her sister and brother.

Following her father's death, when Emily was forty-three,

her behavior changed dramatically, to the point where she expressed tender maternal feelings towards her second nephew—feelings Emily did not display for the first nephew who was born while her father was still alive. Furthermore, Emily could openly express love for her mother, although this was a time when her mother had become an invalid from a stroke, developing a child-like dependency on her two daughters. In any case, this suggests that Emily's father may have been as important, or even more important, than Emily's mother in terms of Emily's ultimate development.

Her father was described as the absolute head of the house, aloof, and one whose inherent tenderness was skillfully concealed. It was said that he never played and that he was estranged from his own contemporaries. He believed that women were distinctly inferior. Within the home he was irascible and occasionally exploded into violence that terrorized the family. Emily once characterized him as a "Roman general upon a triumph day." At least it's noteworthy how often in our other subjects we saw a release of creativity when a stern, authoritarian father died. This seems to have been true of van Gogh, Munch, and Woolf.

QUESTION OF PSYCHOSIS

It is Cody's contention that sometime during the years 1857–64 Emily suffered a major psychotic break; this would have occurred between the ages of twenty-seven and thirty-four. He does not indicate whether this was one psychotic break or many repeated ones nor noes he indicate the probable duration. He interprets Emily's poetry of that time as confirming his belief, even though unlike our other subjects, this was a period of peak creative effort for Emily as she wrote at least half her poems during these seven years. Because of this, many biographers deny that she was ever psychotic, but Cody says that she describes psychosis so well one can only conclude that she had experienced it herself. He says that the simplest explanation for continued productivity during this period would be that she had intermittent, recurrent, psychotic episodes and produced her poems during lucid intervals, much as I found true for our core subjects. Without any clear justification, he rejects this possibility, but at another point, when describing her catatonic symptoms, says that Emily must have written her poems about psychotic experiences in retrospect, but he finds no logical sequence in her psychotic imagery which would identify this retrospective reminiscing about psychotic episodes. In Emily's poems, Cody believes, she uses imagery of morning, night, and next day in alluding to psychotic and lucid periods, but he feels that this is poetic license having nothing to do with real time. I think one must take seriously, however, that she may be referring to real time, and her psychotic episodes might have been extremely brief, although perhaps quite intense. If this was the case, then Emily too would fit the pattern we've seen in our core subjects of immobility and apathy during the psychotic episodes, at least with regard to her creative efforts, and a frenzy of creative activity in periods immediately preceding and following such episodes. Emily's letters do not prove helpful in deciding this. During the mid-1850's there are no extant letters but during the latter years of her alleged psychosis there is no clean break in her letter writing, as we saw in the case of Mary Lamb, Virginia Woolf, and Vincent van Gogh.

One outstanding difference between Emily and our other subjects with episodic psychosis was that Emily never had to be institutionalized because of her agitated violent behavior. Apparently, she was not dangerous to herself or others. She did not go public with her psychosis because of the isolation afforded by her parental home. However, we have already seen that Emily had violent impulses and was afraid of losing control, and did so, but only with words. Another difference between Emily's psychosis and those of our subjects with episodic disorders was the gradual onset of the psychosis with insidiously developing prodromal symptoms appearing years before the alleged overt psychotic symptoms. According to Cody, she only had one break and this was of several years duration, with a gradual return to her pre-psychotic, chronic, neurotic state. However, his data to support such a contention is sparse. This is certainly in direct contrast with the very short prodromals, precipitous onset of symptoms occurring in a matter of hours (or at most, a few days), the short duration of the illness, and the abrupt remission of symptoms with long periods of relative normalcy that character-ized the episodic-psychotic spells which could be pinpointed chronologically in our core subjects. If Cody is right, Emily's illness was more like that of Ezra Pound and Adolph Monticelli than the others, and just as was true of Pound and Monticelli, many experts would argue that Emily was never psychotic.

As already mentioned, Cody reconstructed Emily's psy-chosis from her poems and, to a lesser extent, her letters. He admits that this is circumstantial and complicated evidence be-cause of the metaphorical obscurities in Emily's writing. He es-chews labels although he refers to her depression, mania or a borderline condition, he is not referring to disease entities as defined in the official Diagnostic and Statistical Manual of the American Psychiatric Association. He explains this in a long footnote in his book (p. 291–292) wherein he follows a concept popularized by his mentor, Karl Menninger, who proposed a continuity of mental disorders from the mildest neurosis through more severe episodic disorders into the chronic unremitting psy-chosis. The labels when utilized are non-specific, such as second order (mild symptoms), third order (episodic severe symptoms), and fourth order (chronic psychoses), mental deviations repre-senting the extent of the patient's failure to cope with the vicis-situdes of life. Menninger also describes a first order representing the psychopathology of everyday life and a fifth order repre-senting mute immobility or coma. In contrast, it is my thesis that the two major psychoses, manic-depressive disorders and schiz-ophrenia, can be rigorously defined and at least tentatively con-sidered discrete illness within the medical model. That is, there seems to be a different inheritable factor, distinctive course of illness, and a different response to pharmacologic therapy in these two disorders. Admittedly, this leaves a large group of atypical

psychoses that are difficult to assign to one of the other of these
two major illnesses, but many could, as I propose, be assigned
to a third psychosis which designates an episodic disorder as
characterized by Vincent van Gogh as a prototype. There may
also be a fourth psychosis: the paranoid disorder as represented
in the volume by Ezra Pound.

Where does Emily Dickinson fit into this scheme based on
Cody's "plausible" construction of her illness? He summarizes
the development of Emily's psychiatric disorder as follow: "Evidence for a severe aberration did not appear until Emily's early
twenties when she began a disconcerting withdrawal from family
and friends and appeared unable to cope with even the most
mundane household activities." This was attributed to her phobia
and melancholia, but such social withdrawal is often a characteristic, "deficit" symptom in patients with a chronic schizophrenic illness. However, Emily's fixed and pervasive neurotic
symptoms were much better documented than any psychotic ones,
but in her twenties there were ominous disturbances suggesting
a loss of "ego boundaries," or what I have called in this volume,
a disintegration of the "self," that were not unlike some of the
severe psychotic symptoms experienced by Virginia Woolf.
These were a sense of estrangement from the world ("everything
looks so strange"), derealization (dream-like states), and depersonalization (a loss of self-identity). The combination of these
prodromal psychotic symptoms and the fixed neurosis in the past
has been called "pseudo-neurotic schizophrenia." This term
evolved from the fact that even though the early symptoms were
typically neurotic, in later life the patient developed overt schizophrenic symptoms.

What are the overt psychotic symptoms that Cody infers
from Emily's writings? He asserts such postive schizophrenic
symptoms as hallucinations, delusions, catatonic disturbances of
motility, as well as the so called deficit, or negative, symptoms
of emotional flatness, thought disorder,and social incompetence
and isolation. In the usual schizophrenic, the positive symptoms
tend to wax and wane while the negative ones become increasingly more prominent. What is atypical about Emily Dickinson's

disorder as constructed by Cody is that towards the end of Emily's life she seemed to get better, in that, following her father's death, and with the appearance of her mother's terminal but chronic disability, she developed a new-found filial love and sense of responsibility in caring for her mother, as well as maternal instincts towards her younger nephew Gilbert. For a schizophrenic to demonstrate this later flowering of such instincts would be unusual to say the least.

We've discussed the characteristic childishness of many of our subjects and it has been said that many creative individuals carry a sense of childishness with its unique imaginative capacity into adulthood, which sustains their creative efforts. Such childish dependency is also characteristic of the schizophrenic, the difference being that when the creative individual establishes such a dependency, it seems to be a symbiotic one, i.e., the rewards of creativity are shared with the person upon whom the genius is dependent. This is true as we have noted in Virginia's relationship with her husband Leonard, Vincent's relationship with his brother Theo, and Mary's relationship with her brother Charles. On the other hand, the schizophrenic dependency is a parasitic one, the patient extracting from the person depended upon without reciprocal giving, and it seems, to a large extent, that this characterized Emily's relationship with her family. However, in the sense that we use the word, Emily's relationship does become symbiotic after her death when one considers that her sister Lavinia was dedicated to publishing Emily's manuscripts which, during Emily's life, Lavinia did not even know existed. It is likely that if it had not been for Lavinia, Emily might have remained an unknown genius.

METAPHOR AND PSYCHOTIC ASSOCIATIONS

What is there in Emily's writings that Cody uses as data for Emily's prodromal and overt psychotic symptoms? With regard to the estrangement, Emily says in a letter to her brother Austin, "I hardly know what to do everything looks so strangely." With regard to the derealization, an example would be a letter she had addressed to Mrs. Holland syaing, ". . . and sometimes I wonder if I ever dreamed—then if I'm dreaming now, then if I always dreamed and there is not a world." The loss of ego boundaries is reflected in one of her love letters, "Incarcerate me in thyself." Of her fear of psychotically losing control over her violent emotions, she writers to her sister-in-law Sue during a period when she was angry over Sue's supposed rejection, "In thinking about those I love my reason is all gone from me, and I do fear sometimes that I must make a hospital for the hopelessly insane, and chain me up there such times, so I won't injure you."

In what way does Emily imply more overt psychotic symptoms, as deciphered by Cody? In Poem 937 she says,

I felt a Cleaving in my Mind—
As if my Brain had split—
I tried to match it—Seam by Seam—
But could not make them fit.

The thought behind, I strove to join
Unto the thought before—
But Sequence ravelled out of Sound
Like Balls—upon a Floor.

This seems to express Emily's awareness of her own thinking disorder, but the last two lines are obscure enough so that it may actually reflect the thinking disorder of a schizophrenic patient. Such obscure metaphors that could have reflected a thinking disorder are frequent in Emily's poems. In poem 282, written around 1861, she says, "I felt a funeral in my brain," and later in the same poem, "and then the plank of reason broke." At another point in the same poem, "I thought—/my mind was going numb." In Poem 410 she writes:

My Brain—begun to laugh—/

I mumbled—like a fool—/
And tho' 'tis Years ago—that Day—/
My Brain keeps giggling—still.

The thought disorder of the schizophrenic is revealed by the cryptic disconnected speech that is filled with metaphors with only private meaning and their speech includes new words, or strange combinations of words referred to as neologism. In one of Emily's letters she seems to be referring to this when she said, "My words put all their feathers on and fluttered here and there." In fact, some of her poems, notably No. 42, written in 1858, are so obscure that many critics believe this poem represents Emily's thought disorder. According to Cody, under the pressure of her anxiety, depression, fear of losing control over unacceptable impulses, a breaking point was reached and one of the more severe schizophrenic symptoms developed—that is, catatonic motor behavior—as a defense against all of the inner turmoil and fear of becoming violent. This, he believes, is illustrated by Poem 396 part of which reads: "There is a languor of the Life/More imminent than pain/—Tis Pains—Successor—When the Soul/Has suffered all it can."

At another time she said, "Dimness like a fog/envelopes consciousness." Other evidence Cody utilizes is Poem 761, "from Blank to Blank— a thread-less way / I pushed Mechanic feet"—and Poem 1046, "I've dropped my brain—my soul is numb—/ the Veins that used to run/ Stays Palsied—Tis Paralysis." Other evidence is in Poem 341, "A wooden way" and "a quartz contentment, like a stone—" and again in the same poem, "first—chill—then stupor—the letting go."

Other defenses against more psychotic behavior must have been obsessive compulsive activity which seems to be reflected in Poem 317, "We do life's labor . . . with scrupulous exactness to hold our senses on."

Apparently, reasoning by analogy with other similar patient, Cody's "plausible" reconstruction of Emily's illness includes hallucinations, but there is not direct evidence for this. Certainly, if, as is highly likely, her love affair with the unnamed man was a delusion of loving and being loved, by either an imaginary person or someone she knew only at a distance, this would suggest a delusion indicating overt psychosis. In Emily's metaphorical poems, Cody also notes the similarities between the communication of the poet and the schizophrenic. Both require intense concentration by the listener before they make sense. What originally appeared as illogical and disconected, and filled with idiosyncratic and private symbolism, then becomes intelligible. This is an essential ingredient of the psychiatrist's expertise—that is, understanding both poetic and schizophrenic communication. If one assumes that clinical experience helps in distinguishing the metaphors of the poet from schizophrenic verbal nonsense, one must take Cody's conclusions seriously, and from one psychiatrist to another he makes sense. Emily's insatiable need for love, fear of abandonment, inhibition in taking risks or striking out on her own, must have been a consequence of early interactions within the Dickinson family because it is apparent, at least to some extent, that both her older brother, Austin, and younger sister, Lavinia, had similar attitudes. They too were aware of their mother's inability to love and their father's stern aloofness. Nevertheless, Emily's life was filled with turmoil both quantitatively and qualitatively different from that of her siblings. Of course, Emily came into this world with a different innate potential (and also different liabilities) than either her brother or sister. She was probably the most intelligent of a highly intelligent family. Certainly, she had a rare gift for language and creative imagery—and not surprisingly, as we have seen with our other creative subjects, a psychologic perspicacity which made her particularly sensitive to the vicissitudes of life.

Emily inherited, probably through her mother, a propensity for mental illness. Her genius could be expressed in many ways despite this propensity and in some ways, perhaps, because of it. At least writing poetry seems to have been therapeutic for Emily, and this may be why her peak creativity occurred at the same time of or, perhaps, immediately folowing her psychosis. A psychoanalyst, Lawrence Kubie, in writing about creativity and mental illness, says that the rigidities of chronic neurosis preclude creative efforts.[10] Emily Dickinson would seem to be an exception, and it may well have been that the onset of her pre-psychotic, and even psychotic symptoms with her autistic turning inward, corrected what otherwise could have been a disastrous inhibition in her creativity. This provided Emily with the inspiration for her unique poems—poems that without an intervening psychosis would not have been written, although it is likely her innate talents would have found some expression in poetry that would reflect her skill with rhyme and meter, but which might have been much more superficial, even saccharine, given her restricted life style. Thus, as with most of our subjects, their psychoses were part of their creativity.

EMILY'S ILLNESS

What was Emily's illness? I use the word illness advisedly, realizing that it represents bias in favor of the medical model, and, I must admit, there are no biologic markers which identify a specific illness within the genre of the group of behavioral disorders referred to as major psychoses. With regard to the episodic disorders, I have presented a hypothesis which includes a neurophysiologic mechanism, that is, a limbic seizure or ictus, even though direct data in support of this is limited to studies on a few hundred patients, but which is supported by considerable circumstantial evidence. (See Chapter 11). Data for such underlying neurophysiologic or biochemical mechanisms for the two classical major psychoses, schizophrenia and manic-depressive disorders, are less certain, although there are indications that within the near future such biologic markers may be discovered. The lack of these markers is why I must refer to my conviction regarding the value of the medical model as a bias. Only further data will convert this bias to a fact.

Emily's illness, whatever it was, is in marked contrast to the episodic disorders and it is precisely because of this contrast that a study of her life is included in this volume. Her neurosis had an insidious onset, gradually becoming more severe, persisting unremittingly from at least age twenty-five until her death at age fifty-five. As we have seen, Cody presents a compelling interpretation of Emily's writings which indicate pre-psychotic symptomatology such as estrangement, depersonalization, and derealization. Her poems also suggest periods of more overt psychosis including the motor and emotional inhibition characteristic of the catatonic state, which must certainly have interfered with her writing. Furthermore, she showed a thinking disorder characteristic of the schizophrenic patient, a disability that probably would have been severely incapacitating if Emily was a novelist such as Virginia Woolf but, perhaps, being a poet, and only at times mad, the metaphorical thinking of the psychotic could be used creatively in her poems, and only occasionally were the poems nonsensical. Emily might have developed a delusional love relationship. This is probably the best explanation for her love letters and love poems, but the data is not conclusive on this subject either. Viewing these episodes in retrospect, these experiences provided Emily's inspiration for her poetry. Had she not had such a rich inner world to supplement the constrictions she put on her outer world, her poetry might have been quite banal.

Another difference between Emily's illness and our other subjects with episodic disorders is the lack of explosive violence against others or towards her self that characterized the episodic disorders, although we have seen that in Emily's fantasy life she was at times quite violent and, perhaps, some of her symptoms were defensive moves to control such violence. She certainly made reference in her poems suggesting that she felt like a volcano that was about to erupt. Fortunately for Emily, if this violence did erupt it did so only in words.

One aspect of Emily's mental aberration is shared by most of the subjects with episodic disorders. It seems that the "angst" of psychic turmoil leads to a pervasive concern as to the meaning of life and love, as well as the finality of death, i.e., "the riddle of existence." This existential preoccupation dominated the thoughts of not only Emily, but as we have seen Munch, Strindberg and Virginia Woolf. Emily shared another common experience with our subjects suffering from an episodic disorder, inasmuch as all of them, for significant periods of their life, withdrew from the usual social intercourse, leading an isolated, almost schizoid existence. This too seemed to be an attempt, apparently successful, to protect their sanity. Such withdrawal was dramatically illustrated by Munch and to a lesser extend by Strindberg and van Gogh, and it may have also been true of the Lambs, although in this instance it may have been the increasing length of Mary's psychosis rather than an attempt to protect against psychosis.

What then is Emily's diagnosis? For the reasons stated above, it seems unlikely that she had an episodic disorder as I operationally or neurophysiologically define it. Many would consider that Emily suffered from a recurrent, depressive disorder or what is technically called a unipolar affective disorder, meaning that she had recurrent depressions without intervening periods of mania. If labeled thus today, she would receive antidepressant drugs or, perhaps, like Lowell, electroconvulsive treatment. On the other hand, depressive episodes do occur in other disorders, even schizophrenia, while the thought disorder and catatonia supposedly suffered by Emily are characteristic of the schizophrenic syndrome. If labeled as schizophrenic today, she would receive antipsychotic drugs (in the past referred to as major tranquilizers), again, just as Lowell did. The fact that Emily had a rich and intense emotional life up to her death, and did not show a gradual intellectual deterioration, mitigates against a schizophrenic diagnosis, at least, as schizophrenia is now defined. Currently, if the psychiatrist is unwilling to assign a patient to one of these major psychoses, but recognizes symptoms characteristic of both of them, he has an alternative diagnosis, i.e., schizo-affective psychoses. This, of course, leaves the medical regimen ambiguous and, in fact, a number of psychiatrists do not feel such a mixed illness exists. Such ambiguities within the medical model are the reason why some psychiatrists, like Cody, prefer a continuum in mental deviancy which is defined as to the degree of social incompetency, as previously discussed on page 169. Or, a more extreme view is that the whole concept of mental disorder is a myth (see pp 64). I have proposed in other sections of this volume that part of this ambiguity can be solved by considering that there exists a third major psychosis associated with limbic epileptoid phenomenon which I have labeled episodic disorders, and if one is labeled thusly, then a pharmacologic regimen which includes anticonvulsant medications, i.e., drugs which raise the seizural thresholds, is the treatment of choice. One characteristic of these episodic disorders is that during the intervals between episodes the individual is relatively normal, and this was certainly not true in Emily's case. For these reasons a diagnosis of an episodic psychosis is also rejected.

There are other diagnostic possibilities that seem to fit Emily's behavior better than any of the alternatives mentioned above. There has been an unofficial and now largely discarded diagnosis of "pseudo-neurotic" schizophrenia which is defined symptomatically as a syndrome characterized by pan-anxiety—that is, a pervasive anxiety that intrudes into all aspects of the individual's life; a pan-neurosis—which means a varied and shifting neurotic picture including phobias, compulsions, depression, and physical complaints, and a chaotic or severely inihibited sexual life. Other symptoms in this disorder include the pre-psychotic conditions of depersonalization as well as a transient overt psychotic episode. The implication of this label is that the patient needs psychotherapy, but may also benefit from the simultaneous use of antipsychotic medication, at least when he/she decompensates into the psychotic stage. Thus defined, this diagnosis would seem particularly apt for Emily Dickinson.

Under the recent influence of interpersonal and social theories of mental aberration, the "pseudo-neurotic-schizophrenic" label has been replaced by the label "borderline syndrome." What is added to the old pseudo-neurotic syndrome is a sense of loneliness, emptiness, and hopelessness that pervades the life of these individuals as well as their dramatic failures in relating to others. Emily expresses this so well when she said in one of her letters, ''I who run from so many cannot brook that one turn from me.'' This too would certainly be an appropriate comment from a patient with a borderline syndrome. As this diagnosis also includes transient psychotic breaks, this might explain why her psychosis did not stifle her creative productivity, although as already mentioned, it might have interfered if her creative work had been writing novels rather than poems. Likewise, the fluctuations of the borderline state protected her from the equally stifling rigidities of chronic neurosis and, as we will see in some of the geniuses to be discussed later (Chapter 13), may have provided the impetus and time for her creative effort. Labeled a borderline personality, the primary mode of therapy for Emily would be psychotherapy, and there is some indication that her opthalmologist intuitively used such a technique with great success when he treated Emily's photophobia and pain in her eyes. The implication is that he saw her regularly over a several month period focusing less on her eyes and more on her depression and anxiety. So, we see again that labeling can have some importance for the individual with mental aberrations.

Whether antipsychotic medication during periods of psychotic decompensation would have been beneficial or not remains a moot point. From Lowell's description of his treatment with chlorpromazine (Thorazine), it might well have dampened her creativity, but some of the newer antipsychotics with less sedative effects might not have done this. One can only conjecture about such an outcome. I suspect that the creative genius would jealously guard his/her creativity and assertively terminate a regimen that impairs this creativity even though the inner torment might be lessened. However, it seems appropriate for the creative individuals themselves to make such a decision, and I suspect that both the individual and society would prosper if a medical regimen were offered, with the decision as to whether it be continued left to the afflicted.

Chapter 9

L'Art Brut—Creative Outcasts

I mentioned earlier that it would be highly unlikely that a schizophrenic as now rigorously defined in the American Psychiatric Association Diagnostic Manual (DSM III) could also be productively creative. On the other hand, the literature is replete with references to schizophrenic artists and writers. However, Pickering makes the dogmatic statement that psychosis (which includes schizophrenia) is incompatible with creativity. How can we untangle these inconsistent points of view?[14] As mentioned, the new definition of schizophrenia requires that the patient manifests certain characteristic symptoms, particularly hallucinations and delusion, but also that these symptoms must persist for more than six months. If such symptoms are transient then another diagnosis is indicated (schizophreniform, reactive, or atypical psychosis). This seemingly arbitrary emphasis on the length of illness is justified by the fact that an illness with residual symptoms lasting more than six months—even though the florid symptoms have remitted—should be separated from the transient psychoses. These residuals are referred to as the negative or deficit symptoms of schizophrenia, such as a flatness or inappropriateness of emotions, an apathy or a lack of initiative, and impaired social adjustment. None of our subjects discussed thus far, no matter how sick or how chronically ill, showed these negative symptoms. If they had, their fate would more likely have been similar to the German poet Hölderlin or the dancer-choreographer Nijinsky, whose creative lives ceased when their illnesses began (Chapter 10). Such patients, unless they have strong social or family support, will spend the rest of their lives in mental institutions of one kind or another. Thus, such facilities become inhabited by individuals who, although they may not be dangerous to themselves and others, need institutional support in order to survive, much as van Gogh did when he voluntarily admitted himself to the asylum at St. Remy. Van Gogh probably would not have done this if either his brother or his mother and sister could have offered their homes as an alternative to the asylum. So van Gogh had the initiative to seek institutional care and likewise, the same initiative in terminating it one year later. Schizophrenics with residual symptoms either do not have the initiative or the support systems necesary for such action and are thus often forced to accept the deprivations of insititutional life.

Although the residual schizophrenics are also characterized by a social ineptness that precludes independent coping behavior, we have seen that such social ineptness is present in many of the individuals we have studied who developed a symbiotic dependency on spouse, family or friends. Van Gogh, throughout his life, had strong emotional and financial ties to his brother Theo, and at times had to return to the parental home when coping with the ordinary demands of life became too much for him. It is not surprising that some inhabitants of asylums, even though not suffering from a persisting psychosis, become institutional inhabitants without a major illness.

One of the simplest recreational activities provided in the mental hospital is offering paint and brushes, clay, or other artistic accouterments. It is a joy to see some patients' eyes light up as they zestfully initiate a communication in form and color which may be quite difficult with words. This is why the specialty of art therapy has developed. Furthermore, what is most surprising is that occasionally individuals will demonstrate real creativity and ingenuity years after they have entered such institutions as either psychotically or socially inept. Thus, in simple terms there seem to be three possible outcomes in this complex interaction between creativity and madness: (1) an individual may be episodically mad and creative during lucid intervals, (2) one may be creative and when madness descends the creativity ceases (Chapter 10), or (3) one becomes mad and in some manner this sooner or later opens the person to creative effort.

In 1945 the French artist Jean Dubuffet began to seriously pursue the art of those he describes as "dwellers on the fringe of society." These individuals were working outside the system of art schools, galleries, and art dealers. The creations were not done to appeal to the public or to appease the critics but to please only the creators themselves. These individuals were not culturally indoctrinated nor for that matter were they socially conditioned inasmuch as they required institutional (hospital or prison) care. Many of them were diagnosed as schizophrenic. It was unusual for an internationally renowned artist to approach the creative efforts of such individuals with respect. Upon investigation Dubuffet found that others, particularly doctors, had quietly collected the works of patients. In 1948, sixty individuals formed the Compagnie de l'Art Brut and by 1962 twelve hundred works by over 100 "creators" had been assembled. These found a permanent home when the Collection de l'Art Brut opened to the public at the Chateau de Beaulieu, 11 Ave. Des Bergieres, Lausanne, Switzerland.[11]

SCHIZOPHRENICS

Vignettes of some of these creators reveals the diversity among the outcast.

Aloise (1886–1964) finished her education preparatory for entering the University but remained single, assuming various posts as a governess. After the outbreak of World War I, she proclaimed pacifist and humanitarian ideas in such an exalted manner that she was confined at age thirty-two to an asylum in Switzerland and continued as an inmate for the rest of her life. In 1941, at the age of fifty-five she suddenly began to assiduously draw and continued so until her death twenty-three years later.

Carlo was born in 1916. He had to leave school at nine and subsequently worked as a laborer. He preferred the company of his dog to people and after being inducted into the Army during World War II he suffered an immediate breakdown described as visionary terrors and persecutory delirium, being hospitalized at age thirty-one for the rest of his life. Ten years later he set up a small studio in the hospital and began painting.

Gaston Duff was born in 1920 and had a miserable childhood, growing up sickly and almost illiterate. He drank heavily, was suicidal, and could not permanently hold a job so that he was confined to an institution at age twenty. One day his doctor noticed that he was hiding strange drawings in his clothes. Encouraged by the doctor, who gave him pencil and paper, he drew copiously for six years and then suddenly stopped.

Jules Doudin (1884–1964), with a family history of mental illness, worked for a short time as a laborer. He began to drink heavily, felt that he was being spied upon, and manifested violent rages which led to confinement at age twenty-six with the diagnosis of schizophrenia. One of his peculiarities was to make and then strip his bed all day long. He scratched his head until it bled and then developed the delusion that teeth and eyes grew in these abrasions. After fifteen years of this he suddenly became quiet and two years later began to make pencil drawings in little books and this continued sporadically over the next ten years of his institutionalization.

Clement, born in 1901, was hospitalized at age twenty-four, when in a fit of rage he tried to set fire to the family house. At the asylum his violent and rebellious behavior required seclusion in a narrow cell. Utilizing a handle broken off his chamber pot, he carved intricate designs in the wooden walls of this cell. Later he was allowed to perform various manual jobs within the institution and his behavior became so reasonable that he was considered cured, and given his liberty. He spend the rest of his life as a shepherd.

These individuals were considered chronic schizophrenics, although we've seen that in some their dyscontrol behavior suggests that they might be an example of our episodic psychosis. What is surprising is the sudden appearance of their creative activity and sometimes the equally sudden cessation of such activity.

MYSTICS

There was another group of individuals who, in a delusional way, denied "authorship" of their creative effort.

Madge Gill (1882–1961) who was never institutionalized, began to draw at age thirty-seven saying, "I felt that I was very certainly guided by an invisible force without being able to say what its real nature was." In time it became obvious that Madge felt she was a medium guided by an outside spirit. Under the spirit's influence she knitted, produced inspirational writings, and huge drawings in India ink, some on rolls of material eleven meters long.

Augustin Lesage (1876–1954), at age thirty-five heard a voice ordering him to paint. At age thirty-seven he completed a large painting which took two years and continued painting until his death. He said, "It never happened, before painting a canvas, that I had any idea of what it would be; I never knew what the picture would be like no matter what stage I was at. A picture is made detail by detail without my ever having a mental view of what was coming. My guides told me: don't try to know what you are doing; I give myself up to their influence; I draw the figures they impose on me." This is suggestive of what Mozart described in the spontaneity of his creation and Strindberg as the fortunate accident (pp220).

Raphael Lonne, born in 1910, worked as a postman. He never was hospitalized, but became convinced that he was gifted with supernatural faculties and a "drawing medium." He had the feeling that his hand was directed so that he was not really the author of what he drew. Some of the writing on his pictures he attributes to reminiscences of former lives, which reminds one of Monticelli, who claimed that he was the reincarnation of renaissance Florentine painters.

Pascal-Desire Maisonneuve (1863–1914) was a secondhand dealer with anarchist and anticlerical views. At age sixty-four he began making shell effigies of sovereigns and leading politicians in order to ridicule them. This is reminiscent of Munch's poem with which he ridiculed his friends. It is interesting that later Maisonneuve turned from derision to philosophy and began to inquire into the nature of facial expressions, an enterprise that also interested Darwin.

A visit to the museum of L'Art Brut is an eye-opening experience. One sees mosaics and paintings reminiscent of modern Mexican art, figures floating in the air (Chagall); distortions in the body presenting profile and full-face in one figure (Picasso); and distortion in perspectives (van Gogh); pictures that look like paper cutouts (Matisse). In fact, one is reminded repeatedly of elements that have been portrayed by the accepted creative geniuses in the art world, including the current American artists such as Rauschenberg, Warhol, Motherwell, Lichtenstein, and others, Furthermore, the deprivations of institutional life led to amazing ingenuity regarding the materials utilized for artistic expression. Some might consider these materials unusually bizarre and, I believe, in some instances they were, but by and large they reflect the combinations of materials seen in modern art museums. One, who worked in his institution's storehouse and kitchen, made dolls and various articles coarsely put together with pieces of boxes, which he sculptured with a cobbler's paring knife, adding fragments and scraps picked up in the rubbish bin, and painstakingly collected over the years. Another, who had previously been a pastry cook, resorted to mixtures of gum and powdered eggshells spread with a rolling pin which he then dusted over with covers of jujubes. Others saw the artistry of the gnarled olive branches or rocks and designed their sculpting to fit the natural form. One exploited his mechanical and carpentry skills by designing machine-like moving statues, while another assembled wooden boxes and pieces of lumber into a sculptured piece (like Nevelson). Most would utilize whatever resources were at hand, sometimes sewing the paper sheets together to provide a larger format. Again, pieces of cloth, sticks, as well as paper and paint were utilized in the artistic creation (Carboni). This was long before most professionals resorted to such artifacts in their professional creations.

Perhaps it was this that led Dubuffet to question who stood on what side of the bars of the asylum; that is, who had the right to interpret who was creative and who was mad. He admits that these works are sometimes rudimentary and then quickly adds, "but who is going to decide what is rudimentary after all." How can one establish absolute criteria of the difference between mad art and sane art? Michael Thevos says, "At all events aesthetically speaking the concept of mental illness is impertinent and irrelevant," which is exactly the opposite of the thesis of this book which proposes that investigating both mental illness and creativity furthers our understanding of creativity as well as mental illness. On the other hand, I agree that it is impertinent to stand in front of a painting and say he (the painter) must be crazy; or to say, "My children could paint that well." Don't make the mistake I once did when first viewing a Mondrian with its lattice of colored blocks by suggesting to my wife, "I could do that." The next day she presented me with paints and brush; I sat in front of the easel for many hours but nothing came and I didn't even have the inspiration to paint white on white. If the painting is not understandable to you, don't dismiss it as psychotic art; it may be understandable to others now or in the future and it may even be understandable to you in time. If you like what you see and then discover that the artist was crazy, don't apologize or lose interest. We all have some capacity, particularly with extra concentration and effort, to understand the psychotics, and when we do, we usually learn something new about ourselves and our world. (See Illustration # 11)

Is it easier for the overtly psychotic to communicate through his art rather than through words? A number of the creative

#11 A and B

A and B—L'ART BRUT—two examples of art completed by "outcasts"—that is, people without formal training who were institutionalized. Note the change in technique in the lower left hand corner of 11A and the pleasing flow in the painting 11B.

outcasts who contributed to L'Art Brut were reported as writing as well as painting during their creative bursts, but I have no access to what they wrote even if it has been preserved and I suspect that most of the writing was not. The schizophrenic, over time, may deteriorate in his thinking and speaking until his words become gibberish like a mixed salad; before that his speech may be blocked or his thoughts disconnected or so idiosyncratically metaphorical that only he can explain what he means and this he often refuses to do or does so with difficulty. But the poet speaks in metaphors which often are obscure and understanding depends upon the reader's knowledge of literacy and historical allusions and an intimate knowledge of the poet's personal history. As we saw in the case of Emily Dickinson, incipient or early psychosis might have facilitated new insights which have a universal meaning that conveys a message to all of us if we work at it. But just as it is impossible to decide where the boundary is between sane and insane art, it is perhaps especially difficult in the case of poetry. Even Dickinson scholars have difficulty in deciphering some of her metaphors and they cannot agree whether some of the poems may not represent true psychotic dis-organization in her thinking. We also saw that Pound's wife complained that his thoughts were difficult to follow during the last years of his life, but even the last of his *Cantos,* however disconnected, showed flashes of his poetic genius which could be appreciated by the reader. It seems unlikely that the novelist who is overtly psychotic would have the organizational capacity and perseverance to produce a universally acclaimed work, yet Marcel Proust and James Joyce must have approached the borderline of psychoses, but in a manner that was immediately perceived as highly innovative and full of meaning, and in the process, discovered new literary techniques. Perhaps we should be less concerned about this borderline, but it is important to be concerned about mental processes that stifle inherent genius or which could cut short productive, creative careers (Chapter 10).

Chapter 10

Chronic Aberrations and Creativity

HÖLDERLIN

J.K. Wing, in his book *Reasoning About Madness* called my attention to the sad stories of two creative geniuses whose onset of psychosis terminated their creative work.[6] Both apparently suffered from schizophrenia and their residual symptoms precluded further artistic output. Hölderlin, a German romantic poet, was born in 1770 and died in 1843.[12] His most famous poem was "Hyperion" published in two volumes in the year 1799. This poem was considered a forerunner of Ezra Pound's poetry and was all the more remarkable because it was published over 100 years earlier. Hölderlin began to show signs of psychosis, particularly paranoid delusions and disorganization in his thinking, as early as 1802, but he continued to publish until 1804. Family and friends at first denied that he was ill and, because they gave considerable social support, he managed to stay out of the hospital until 1806, but from then on he was irretrievably ill. The chronicity of his illness cannot be attributed to the devastating effect of long term institutionalization because one year after admission he was discharged and lived for the rest of his life with a carpenter who provided food, shelter, and some supervision. During the last thirty-six years of his life, he occasionally showed brief glimpses of his talent, but he only managed to write a dozen or so six line poems. He had a habit of addressing people as, "Your Highness" or "Your Majesty," but the apathy and loss of initiative, referred to as abulia by the famous psychiatrist Bleuler who wrote the classic monograph on the "Group of schizophrenias," stifled any creative effort. Another German psychiatrist, Kretschmer, said of Hölderlin that his pre-psychotic personality was an hyperesthetic autism meaning that he was excessively sensitive (this characterized many of our core subjects) and because of this sensitivity retreated into an inner fantasy world (this likewise occurred in some of our subjects). Hölderlin was different, however, in that the first episode persisted through his life. From the data I could uncover on his illness he would now be diagnosed as Schizophrenia—Paranoid type.

NIJINSKY

The other example was Vaslov Nijinsky the famous Russian dancer and choreographer who was born in 1890 and died in 1950.[13] He made his first dance presentation in Paris in the year 1909 and was immediately proclaimed the premiere dancer of all time. Furthermore, his originality in the choreography of what became modern dance was an even more creative product of his genius. However, his career was terminated at age twenty-seven by insanity. The first ominous sign of illness was when he began to imitate Tolstoy. This was followed by hallucinations, violence, and refusal of food. The family reqested a consultation with Bleuler (mentioned above), who confirmed the diagnosis of schizophrenia and proclaimed a poor prognosis. Apparently, Bleuler was correct in that, although not institutionalized but cared for by a devoted wife, he rapidly deteriorated, becoming mute, emotionally flat, and quite uncharacteristically stiff and immobile in his motor movements. Not surprisingly, this devastated his career as a dancer and choreographer. He seemed powerless to do anything and became what is often referred to as a "burned out" schizophrenic. During the years between world wars, he was tenderly nourished by his wife Romala who was also rearing their two children. In 1938 she took him to Vienna for a consultation with Dr. Sakel, who had discovered insulin coma therapy, a new treatment for schizophrenia. It is surprising considering the length of his illness, but he did respond to this treatment, showing brief flashes of his old personality and at times demonstrating the grace of movement in his hands and body that characterized his dancing. The family survived the rigors of occupations by the Nazis and then by the Russians, ultimately settling in London where he died. From the data available I would suspect that today he would be diagnosed as Schizophrenia, Catatonic type.

These are two examples of the outcome I would expect in creative individuals who develop schizophrenia as it is now rigorously defined. In the past, this diagnosis has been applied to a much broader group of patients. We saw in studying our core subjects that at one time or another almost all were diagnosed as schizophrenic, even though by current standards none would be so labeled.

The outcome in these two tragic instances seems somewhat at odds with what we saw of the creators of l'Art Brut (Chapter 9), as many of those individuals were institutionalized for years with a diagnosis of schizophrenia yet they suddenly became artistically productive. Unfortunately, some just as suddenly ceased such activity. How could this happen? Some were probably misdiagnosed by present day standards and from the sparse data provided might have been examples of the episodic disorders that characterized our core subjects. Certainly, they demonstrated dyscontrol acts which often accompany the episodic disorders. Others may not have been mentally ill at all, but incarcerated because of their obstreperous, rebellious behavior, and still others had probably recovered, remaining in asylums because they had nowhere else to go. Motivation for these sudden bursts of creative activity may have been to relieve the boredom of living within an institution. There was certainly one outstanding difference between these individuals and the more famous artists we studied. Our artist subjects had a burning passion to contribute something to the world; the artists in the asylum by most accounts were creating for their own pleasure alone. If someone had not recognized their talent and preserved their work they would be completely unknown—but this would also apply to Emily Dickinson. It was only because her sister discovered her manuscripts and persevered in seeing that they were published that she is now recognized as a great poet. Perhaps much of van Gogh's art would have been lost if his brother Theo had not recognized his genius and carefully preserved his artistic works.

The weight of evidence supports the hypothesis that psychotic individuals either are not creative or lose their creativity with the onset of psychosis, recovering their creativity only if the psychosis remits. These episodic psychotic individuals, as we have noted, had the capacity to incorporate their psychotic experiences as well as the promontory or prodromal psychotic symptoms into their creative works and this seems to give a special quality to their efforts (see next chapter).

As this is a study of madness and genius, an in-depth study of chronic mental aberrations other than psychosis is beyond the scope of this book, but a few salient points should be mentioned. It is common belief that all geniuses are eccentric, but I doubt this, and even when it is true, it has little impact on their creativity. All geniuses seem to pursue their creative efforts with a passion and in this sense are strong personalities with prominent character traits which may complicate their lives. The passion is essential to both their personality and their creativity and influences the manner in which they create, but again probably has little influence on the quality of their work per se. Some have had a history of chronic neurosis and this inevitably influenced their creativity, so this must be discussed briefly if only to contrast this with madness and genius.

George Pickering in his book, *Creative Maladies,* presents the thesis that an illness which is not debilitating or disabling or threatening to life may provide the ideal circumstances for creative work.[14] Such an illness is usually a chronic neurosis and he illustrates his point by discussing the life and illnesses of Charles Darwin, Florence Nightingale, Jeanne d'Arc, Mary Baker Eddy, Sigmund Freud, Marcel Proust, and Elizabeth Barrett Browning. On the other hand, the late Lawrence Kubie, a psychoanalyst who probably has treated as many creative artists as any modern therapist, expresses the belief that neurosis (as well as psychosis) stifles creativity.[10] Kubie utilizes in his explanations Freud's topographic schema of the mind which identifies three functions: the unconscious, the conscious, and the preconscious. The unconscious is that part of the mind which is not available to awareness except under unusual circumstances; most often this is through interpretations of the uncensored thoughts or the reported dreams of patients on the psychoanalyst's couch. The conscious aspect of the mind is that part of our thinking which immediately and appropriately comes into our awareness when we are alert and focus our attention. The preconscious is free of the rigidities of the unconscious symbolism and also free of the constraints of our rational conscious thought processes, but the preconscious does not lose touch with either. Put another way, the preconscious is in touch with, but not anchored to, the pedestrian realities of our conscious symbolic process and the rigid primitive symbolism of the unconscious. It is, according to Kubie, the preconscious mind that functions effectively in the creative process. He says that neurosis, and by implication psychosis, corrupts, mars, distorts, and block the creative function of the preconscious mind. Thus, he concludes that psychotherapy, which removes the blocks in the functioning of the preconscious, opens one to creativity rather than, as some suppose, impedes creative efforts. Pickering's thesis is at odds with this in that he believes neurosis may actually help the creative process. His appraisal is both more superficial and more comprehensive than Kubie's.

Pickering identifies several ways neurosis contributes to creativity.[14] One way is that neurosis serves a secondary purpose in allowing freedom from mundane activities so that the creative process can take place. As an example he cites Darwin's illness, which provided him with the solitude and leisure needed to develop and support his revolutionary concepts of evolution, while the neuroses of Florence Nightingale broke the stranglehold that her exploitive mother and sister were trying to place on her life which, had they succeeded, would have seriously curtailed, if not stifled, her efforts at reform of the British War Office. Another way that neurosis influences creativity is that the neurosis is an integral part of the creative process itself, as Pickering believes was evident in the lives of Jeanne d'Arc, Mary Baker Eddy, Sigmund Freud, and Marcel Proust. He believed that in the last two their creative output had a common source in the mental torment of their neurosis. His opinions deserve some attention.

DARWIN

Charles Darwin was born in 1809 and lived to age seventy-three. During his youth his intellectual accomplishments were at best mediocre and his goals were vague. He didn't follow through with his family's aspirations for him to be either a doctor or a minister. He did have one pertinent interest and that was collecting. However, he was mostly preoccupied with riding, hunting, and carousing with his young rich friends. Because of his interest in collecting, he was asked to sail as an unpaid naturalist on the H.M.S. *Beagle,* which was about to embark on a hydrographic investigation for the navy. The boat left England in December, 1831, not to return until 1836. During this trip he avidly and energetically collected non-organic specimens as well as organic specimens of current species and fossil evidence for extinct ones. Periodically he sent these back to Cambridge for safekeeping and later examination and categorizing. There is no evidence from his diary or notes that he conceived of the theory of evolution during the course of his voyage. On this trip he suffered from one severe illness, probably typhoid fever. Upon his return he did not immediately plunge into his scientific work, but married in 1839, and by 1842 had retired to a country home purchased by his father, living there on an independent income for the rest of his life. He said of his subsequent years, "Few persons have lived a more retired life than we have done." Already mysteriously ill by the time he retired to the country, this progressed until he established a rigid routine consisting of short periods of work (1-½ hours) interspersed with resting on the couch, reading his mail, or as a diversion being read fiction, or playing backgammon with his wife. He limited after dinner discussions with the family to thirty minutes; otherwise he would become agitated and sleepless. Several times a day he walked in the garden. Total working time then was limited to 4 to 6 hours per day—but no other demands were placed on him.

He first conceived of the origin of the species in 1837, but it was over twenty years before this was published—and then it was probably rushed into print because of the manuscript espousing a similar theory that Alfred Rusell Wallace had submitted to him for comments. During these years and subsequently, however, Darwin was immensely productive, publishing a series of technical volumes which had considerable popular appeal.

What were the symptoms of Darwin's illness? Palpitations occurred even before he left on his voyage in 1831 and this symptom continued for the rest of his life. Upon his return, new symptoms developed including breathlessness, fatigue, and insomnia. Socializing induced violent shivering and vomiting. These symptoms were certainly not specific for any physical illness nor did they particularly shorten Darwin's life. Some thought he was merely hypochondriacal, others believed that he had a psychosomatic disorder; i.e., an illness wherein neurotic conflicts are expressed through physiologic dysfunctions that may or may not ultimately result in physical damage to bodily organs. Others felt that he had a tropical illness called Chaga's disease because it was known that in Argentina he was bitten by the bug that is the vector of the trypanosome which causes this illness, but most experts in tropical medicine feel this is highly unlikely. Furthermore, if the "purpose" of his illness (to relieve him of social and professional obligations that would divert him from his scientific work) was conscious, then his invalidism could be considered malingering. This differential between organic and functional illnesses and neurosis and malingering is one of the most difficult discriminations that a physician faces and a conscientious doctor is never completely comfortable making such decisions. Many have begged the issue, suggesting that he had both an organic illness and a neurosis. The interesting question, yet one that cannot be answered, is whether Darwin's invalidism actually impaired his productivity. Considering the prodigious output and the impact of his writing, it is hard to believe that his efforts were less than maximally effective. It seems unlikely that his illness interfered significantly with his work and may, as Pickering suggests, actually have facilitated it.

NIGHTINGALE

There are some striking similarities between Darwin and Florence Nightingale (1820-1910). Both were high born with good connections and independently wealthy. Both, early in their lives, went through an energetic data gathering phase (nursing in the Crimean War for Florence Nightingale), and both then relapsed into chronic invalidism for the remainder of their lives.[14] Florence Nightingale's illness started in 1857, shortly after her return from Crimea, and by 1862 she was bedridden, remaining this way until she died in 1910 at the age of ninety. During this invalidism she not only established nursing as a respected profession and manipulated reforms in the war office, but also established the importance of the budding science of epidemiology and public health. Her fervor in doing this rests to a large extent on her "maternal devotions" to the lowly soldier when she discovered that 73% of the soldiers who died in Crimea, died from a medical illness and not war wounds.

Florence Nightingale had an additional problem not shared

with Charles Darwin, one that we have seen present in all of our female subjects: namely, they had to initiate a wrenching rebellion against their family's and society's stereotypical expectations that it was the woman's role to attract, and then marry, an acceptable male; thereafter, run his household, as well as give birth to and rear children. Florence Nightingale infuriated her family by her insistence in pursuing a nursing career and was more or less disowned by them. When she became famous and the darling of Queen Victoria they returned to her hoping to bathe in reflected glory. Her illness seems to have been the only way that she could drive them away. Thus, the illness had what the psychiatrists call secondary gains just as did Darwin's. Also, like Darwin, Florence Nightingale suffered physical deprivations and illness during her period of data gathering, the Crimean War, where she probably had typhoid fever or typhus. The question of whether she had a chronic physical illness or a psychosomatic disorder must be considered. Like Darwin, her longevity and productivity suggests a psychosomatic disorder, but surprisingly, Florence Nightingale's sickness has not been subjected to the kind of scrutiny that Darwin's has nor has any significant neurotic conflict been convincingly demonstrated for either. Superficially, both seem to be examples of conflicts with parents, father-son or mother-daughter respectively. It suffices to say that a chronic neurosis did not contribute directly to their creativity, but unlike Kubie's hypotheses,[10] it did not seem to interfere significantly with this creativity. In fact the secondary gains of the illness may have facilitated their productivity.

Pickering's other proposition is that the inner turmoil of an individual's neurosis leads directly to the creative output. Two examples of this are Marcel Proust and Sigmund Freud.

PROUST

Proust, born in 1871 to a well-to-do Paris physician, seems to have had a not too stressful, pampered childhood and to have spent his early adulthood playing the role of the rich, witty, charming gadabout whose life's aim was to impress the literary, artistic, and social world.[14] He did suffer from hay fever and this ultimately evolved into asthma that was worse during the day so he early devised the regimen of sleeping from 8:00 a.m. until 3:00 p.m. and then working during the night. Letters between Proust and his mother when they were separated revealed that he was an extreme momma's boy—in fact, never emancipated from her, even by her death. Any separation was a real calamity for both. It is surprising how often such mother-son relationships are seen in males who sufer from asthma. Before Madame Proust died in September 1905, she said, "My dear boy mustn't be afraid; his momma won't leave him." Proust was thirty-four years old at the time. Over the next few years Proust gradually withdrew from the world. His nocturnal habits became more fixed and his homosexual proclivity obvious. In 1909 his mind turned towards "times past" and his magnum opus grew of its own accord rather than from any initial plan, the first part, *Swanns Way* being published in 1913 when he was forty-two. He finished this one vast work, *Remembrance of Things Past,* just before his death in 1922, at the age of fifty-one. Allegedly the last word he uttered was "Mother." As we have seen in so many of our core subjects, he relentlessly explored his neurotic pain through early childhood recollections. Thus, like Munch and Strindberg, Proust turned inward for much of his creative insight. In Freud's terms, Proust suffered from an unresolved oedipal conflict and was consumed by guilt following his mother's death because he felt that he had killed her. For Pickering, Proust's work represented a mental catharsis recalling a happier period when mother was alive and furthermore, was an attempt to resolve his matricidal guilt. At least we can say that his neurosis was the core of his creativity.

FREUD

Freud discovered many of his most original ideas on the meaning of symptoms through his own self-analysis. The oedipal conflict was a central hypothesis and this suggests that he too had an oepidal conflict (he believed that we all do) and his self-analysis was an attempt to resolve such conflict. He admitted to a neurosis, particularly his phobia of missing trains. He also revealed that a certain level of discomfort was necessary for him to be productive, i.e., if he felt too healthy and euphoric he was not motivated for creative effort. Ernest Jones, Freud's biographer,[15] feels that between 1890 and 1900 Freud suffered from a painful psychoneurosis that motivated this self-analysis which in turn resulted in two of his most creative publications, *The Psychopathology of Everyday Life* and *The Interpretation of Dreams;* thus, again, we see a creative product evolving out of turning inward. If this self-analysis was necessitated by inner turmoil, Freud kept it well hidden from his family, his patients, and even his colleagues. This is quite different from Proust, who never worked, never assumed responsibility for a family, was physically ill, chronically took drugs, and died relatively young because of the abuse of drugs. It seems a travesty to apply the same label "neurosis" to both and to designate the same basic conflict to both. Freud, like all of us, had his minor neurotic traits (the psychopathology of everyday life) and apparently diffuse anxiety (like most of us), but he valued this as he realized it led to creative effort. Proust, on the other hand, had a neurotic illness and this was chronic, so it would seem to contradict Kubie's thesis that the neurotic could not be creative. However, in one sense, Kubie may be right. Could Proust have written anything other than he did, i.e., about what happened or what he wished might have happened in his childhood? Most of our authors were autobiographical to a degree, but each also demonstrated a diversity of themes. I will leave it to the literary critic to settle whether Proust could have written creatively about any subject other than himself.

In discussing the episodic disorders, I repeatedly point out that these episodic disorders could be hysterical,—motivated behavior. Another way of putting it is that the symptoms have meaning (or purpose), albeit such meaning is usually unconscious. We saw this to be particularly true of Munch and Strindberg. It is also characteristic of some of Pickering's subjects. Jeanne d'Arc had visions of God talking to her.[14] She believed this and so did others. Who would have followed an adolescent peasant girl into battle unless they felt she had talked with God, and what excuse would they have had for burning her at the stake unless they also believed that she had such conversations (with the devil). Mary Baker Eddy was diagnosed by her physician as having hysterical seizures. The experience of being cured by Dr. Quimby, who we now recognize used the power of suggestion through hypnosis to cure his patients, convinced Mary Baker Eddy of the power of the mind over the body, the basis of her treatise *Science and Health* which established the most successful new religion in modern times.[14] It seems that in both instances their neurosis was an episodic neurosis and not a chronic one and that these experiences had immense reality for these individuals and for others. The crux of their creativity was that because of their charisma they could present these experiences to society in a way that had particular meaning for many people. Florence Nightingale, whose neurosis was otherwise chronic, on four occasions, was "called" by God to his service; first in 1837 and then again in 1853 before she went to the hospital for invalid gentlewomen; again in 1854 before she left for Crimea, and once again in 1861 after the death of her good friend Sydney Herbert, who was head of the war office and the one most responsive to her demands for reform.[14] Her belief in these events as real must have given her the strength for rebelling against outmoded conventions.

EINSTEIN

Einstein (1879-1955), with Freud and Darwin one of the geniuses who has had the greatest influence over the lives of each of us during the last hundred years, does not seem to have manifested any symptoms that I would consider evidence for mental illness, although his character traits would fit the stereotype of the absent minded professor, obviously a by product of his intellectual preoccupations.[16,17] One can speculate that if he had been independently wealthy—with wealth's inherent social demands—he might have developed a chronic neurosis to free him from mundane responsibility, as did Darwin and Florence Nightingale. He was not; he had to support himself, and perhaps more like Charles Lamb, from 1902 to 1909 Einstein worked in the patent office in Berne while he completed his Ph.D. and published his first great work on the special theory of relativity (1905). This was so impressive that he was offered a series of academic appointments and rapidly obtained that exalted status all academicians yearn for—complete freedom to pursue creative effort unimpeded. He certainly neglected his wife and family, but continued to be creatively productive, publishing his general theory in 1916 and proposing a unified field theory in 1950. Like all geniuses, he was passionate in his views, whether these were scientific, political, or personal, and interestingly rejected some of the consequences of his own theories, e.g., probability theory, saying, "I shall never believe that God plays dice with the world."[17] He was fortunate in that his genius was recognized early in his life, and like all geniuses he had a coterie of devoted students and also scientific dissenters. Einstein and, I believe, Freud proved that one does not need to be mentally ill to be creative. The similarities and differences between the contribution of chronic and episodic aberrations on creativity will become clearer in the next chapter.

Section III

Medicine— Mental Illness —Creativity

Chapter 11

Episodic Aberrations and Creativity

What generalizations can be applied to our core subjects who include Vincent van Gogh, Virginia Woolf, Edvard Munch, August Strindberg, and Mary Lamb? The broadest generalization we can make is that each experienced the precipitous onset of disturbed behavior with an equally abrupt remission that dramatically interrupted the life-style and life-flow of the individual.[1] These "attacks" were recurrent and interspersed with long periods during which these individuals resumed their usual life-style. What was important in terms of their creativity was that the episodic disorders left no residual impairment during these quiescent intervals. The disturbed period could be as short as a few minutes to a few hours, but more often lasted for days, weeks or even several months, and commonly was associated with intense, unpleasant emotions characterized by fear, rage, depression, or a mixture of all of these and only rarely ecstatic feelings. Most commonly these episodic disorders included restlessness, agitation, sleeplessness, and racing thoughts, that is, disinhibited behavior, but on other occasions might have manifested inhibited behavior such as lethargy, apathy, difficulties in thinking or even muscular immobility, and mutism. Other symptoms were quite diverse and varied between subjects and even between episodes in a given subject. These included confusion, psychotic symptoms such as illusions, hallucinations, and delusions, particularly paranoid delusions; bouts of neurotic symptoms such as panic or phobias; as well as physiologic changes, particularly rapid heart or irregular heart beats, tremulouness, headaches, insomnia, weight changes, dizziness, and fainting spells.

Although the episodes were marked by a precipitous onset, sometimes occurring within a matter of minutes, there frequently were prodromal symptoms which alerted the individual or those in their environment that an attack was impending. Most typically, these prodromal symptoms included restlessness, sleeplessness, racing thoughts, and irritability, but the pattern which was usually typical for an individual might also include headaches, dizziness, and fainting spells, symptoms which can be minor manifestations of epileptic attacks. Our patients had some symptoms which were more like epileptic auras; that is, distortions in visual perceptions such as objects changing in shape and size, or auditory changes with noises becoming louder or fainter. Sometimes they complained of flashing lights and at other times momentary loss of consciousness or hypersensitivity to all perceptions. Following an episode there was likely to be a period of calmness and repose which is also a characteristic feeling following more typical epileptic seizures.

These epileptic-like prodromal symptoms and aftermaths have been attributed to focal epileptic discharges deep in the brain (limbic system), which, precisely because such discharges are focal does not lead to epileptic seizures, although some of our subjects were thought to have had typical seizures. Thus, I propose that the mechanism behind at least some of these disorders was focal or partial epilepsy, although it seems clear that at other times such episodic disturbances were a manifestation of hysteria; that is, explained best by psychodynamic factors. Not surprisingly, many of the attacks appeared to be a mixture of epileptoid and hysteroid symptoms. This can be represented pictorially by a line drawn between two poles, an epileptoid pole at one end and a hysteroid pole on the other, with each subject or each episode falling somewhere on the line between the two poles, but rarely being completely at one pole or the other.

If the acute episode is characterized by confusion, disorientation, or a clouding of consciousness and it is associated with a hazy recollection of these acute symptoms, the nearer the disorder is to the epileptoid pole and the closer the behavior approaches a state of delirium, the kind of toxic psychosis induced by drugs or acute physical illness. The symptoms then include not only hallucinations but illusions (perceptual distortions; that is, the mistaken interpretation of a real visual or auditory event such as Virginia Woolf's hearing birds singing in Greek or August Strindberg's misinterpretation of the broom as a witch). This delirious behavior is distinguished from the usual delirium in that there usually is no evidence of an external toxin or severe physical illness; yet, we did see that some individuals might be hypersensitive to alcohol and absinthe.

Many times one could identify the psychological stress that seemed to act as a precipitant for these episodes, but at other times precipitating events are lacking and the individuals describe a compelling force outside themselves that drives them into their illness. Most individuals who become acutely psychotic do not have appropriate judgment or insight regarding their illness. Perhaps because these episodes are precipitous and intermittent, all of our subjects were acutely aware of their "madness," sought medical help to abort or prevent these painful experiences, and over the years feared their recurrence. They often could predict • when such attacks were impending; thus, they had appropriate insight and judgment. Subjectively they would describe a loss of boundaries between the self and the outside world. Such a loss of "self" and the intense dysphoric emotions cause a devastating inner turmoil so that most often these attacks were dreaded. However, this was not always the case. The emotions might be of pleasure or ecstasy as well as dysphoria and the loss of ego boundaries lead to an increased understanding of one's relationship to one's body, one's relationship to the world, and one's relationship to mankind. These are points Brentano addressed in 1874 as important phenomenologic issues. The racing thoughts were not always confusion but sometimes a startling fitting together of ideas that led to a new persepctive so that the individuals might well be ambivalent about their illness, valuing the illness for its contribution to their creativity, while at other times fearing the painful disruption of their creative work.

All of these individuals feared losing control over their emotions and indeed at times during the illness they exploded into aggressive, destructive behavior that was a danger to themselves and to others. It was as if there existed a short circuit in the brain between the incoming stimulus and the act that responded to this stimulus. In such instances there was a failure of the interposition of "thought as trial action" necessary for modulating primitive emotional behavior. Another way to view this was that the emotions were so intense that they overwhelmed normal inhibitory controls. These impulsive acts in some of our subjects occurred in isolation representing an impulsive expression of primitive, fear-flight, or rage-fight emotions; hence, were usually socially or self-destructive. Such acts were carried through to completion and resulted in at least relief of tension if not the immediate gratification of a specific need. This is commonly referred to as the "dyscontrol" syndrome and officially labeled in the American Psychiatric Association Nomenclature as an Intermittent Explosive Disorder, a subclass under disorders of impulse control. As Boss points out, these symptoms should be labeled "fits" of anger because they "assault us, lift us above ourselves in such a way that we are no longer in control of ourselves."[2] During such fits we are blind, in fact in some sense it heightens our perceptions, but also narrows it. It would seem that many of our core subjects had both fits of anger and more chronic hatred, the latter expressed in their paranoia, but even the paranoid hatred had an episodic or remitting pattern and did not permanently interfere with creativity.

PATIENTS WITH PROBES IN THE BRAIN

In the Prologue I proposed the hypothesis that if the focal excessive neuronal discharge in the limbic system is brief, the behavior may be a spontaneous inspirational or visionary thought or act, instead of these impulsive destructive acts, and if the excessive neuronal discharges are more prolonged or rapidly cyclic over many days, then there develops an intermittent psychosis, or at other times an intermittent neurosis or intermittent physical illness. I also mentioned the difficulties in demonstrating such focal, excessive neuronal discharges as a demonstrations requires the drastic procedure of chronically implanting electrodes as the only way to record such neuronal discharges from deep areas of the brain. This procedure is so intrusive it must be limited to a small group of subjects who are chronically and intractably ill so that surgical intervention is justified as the treatment of last resort.[3]

Contrary to what the layman might believe, this procedure, if done right, is not a threat to life and, in fact, very little undesirable sequelae are associated with it. Briefly, it involves an operating room procedure and general anesthesia, during which a small hole is made in the skull about the size of a button, and utilizing a frame fixed on the head that has scales in three dimensions, one can calculate how to introduce a needle through the buttonhole which carries inside electrical wires to be placed in precise areas of the brain. X-rays before the implantation provide the data for calculating the spatial parameters of this precise area of implantation and x-rays during the procedure indicate the accuracy with which the wires are located. The needle is then withdrawn, leaving the wires in place, the hole in the cranium is plugged with a plastic button that is sealed in place with dental cement, and the wires which exit through a small hole in this plastic button are connected to an external plug outside the scalp and can be confortably carried in place by stitching this plug to a stocking cap. This allows recording of spontaneous brain activity or the introduction of minute currents into specific brain areas utilizing a simple non-intrusive procedure of "plugging" the patient into electronic laboratory equipment.[3]

These areas of excessive neuronal discharges can be identified and modified by either precise electrical stimulation or neurosurgical excision of an "irritable" focus. The by-product of such studies was a more meaningful correlation between brain mechanisms and behavior. It was these observations that led to the discovery of a limbic ictus (excessive neuronal discharge) as the mechanism associated with many of these episodic disorders.[1,3] Vignettes of some of the patients studied in this manner follow:

> One such patient (021) was a 27-year-old housewife and mother of two mentally retarded children who came from a deprived family, her father being an irresponsible philandering alcoholic and her mother hostilely restrictive. She developed paranoid personality traits which during her mid-twenties had become fixed delusions of her husband's infidelity, and at times she burst forth with aggressive jealous acts. Like many of our subjects, she had an episodic disorder labeled by her husband as "spells." These were preceded by severe headaches and then followed by a staring, vacant look in her eyes which alerted those around her that she was about to explode. At the same time she had hallucinations, usually of family members appearing at her bedside and admonishing her for her behavior. She would jump from bed, tear off her clothes, break up the furniture and pull her hair "to get the snakes out of it." She would be confused, disoriented and have only a hazy recollection of the events during the attack. Such attacks were followed by intense depression and remorse.
> She said of herself that she was always different from other children and when asked to elaborate, describes shyness and isolation, a quick temper and rebellion against authority. She also had numerous fears and had frequent bodily complaints which led to several operations, although the need for these were doubtful. She remained in the hospital for some months after the electrode implantation and during that period had repeated episodic psychotic reactions.

At the time of these psychotic reactions the recordings from the amygdala and septal regions (limbic system) showed high amplitude bursts of spikes and slow waves characteristic of the excessive neuronal firing that we associate with epilepsy. When the behavioral episodes subsided so did the excessive firing. At the height of her psychoses, if given a sedative drug, the symptoms would ameliorate and likewise, there was a disappearance of the abnormal electrical activity. Thus, this patient showed symptoms similar to, if much simpler than, those of our subjects. The simplicity would be expected in a person of modest intellectual capacity. The following is another patient monitored by subcortical recordings:

Patient (019) was quite different in that she did not show episodic symptoms but had a chronic deteriorating psychosis typical of paranoid schizophrenia. She was extremely suspicious and reluctant to give significant data regarding her symptoms. Although obviously of high intelligence, she never lived up to her potential; was apathetic, totally lacking in initiative, and emotionally flat and withdrawn. After graduating from college she returned to her home, seldom left her room, and never participated even in the simplest household activities. As a child she was also isolated and withdrawn with a haughty superior air that led her classmates to call her "Queenie." As it had been noted in other patients that stimulating some areas of the limbic system with minute currents could lead to a more appropriate emotional expressivity and increasing interaction with the environment, this patient was stimulated daily over a period of several weeks. During the time this took place her mother reported mounting irritability, frequent rageful verbal outbursts, and increasing resentment towards her mother, as well as violent fantasies and hallucinations. There also developed some confusion and disorientation and problems with her recent memory as she had trouble recalling whether she had taken her prescribed medication or not. During the few minutes that the current was introduced, excessive neuronal discharges occurred in the area stimulated. At first these excessive discharges ceased as soon as the current was terminated. With repeated stimulation this continued for increasingly longer periods after the current had been shut off (after-discharges), until on one occasion (the last stimulation) it suddenly spread to parts of the cortex and the patient cried out that she was about to faint. Thus, this is a patient where the repeated stimulation provoked a "kindling" phenomenon with a lowering of seizural threshold and a spread of the abnormal nerve activity.[4] At the same time there was an increase in her irritability, aggressiveness and hallucinations.

As mentioned above, electrical stimulation, particularly in the septal region, usually would elicit a pleasurable response, increased alertness, a new participation with the outside world, and an openness or friendliness with those in the immediate environment. Electrical stimulation in another more primitive area of the brain (mesencephalon) would elicit violent, animal-like, undirected, and nondiscriminating rage toward anybody, usually the person closest at hand. This would be limited to the period of stimulation. This primitive rage reaction was followed by complete amnesia, the patients only aware of feeling exhausted when the procedure was terminated. Stimulation of another area in the limbic system (amygdala) would elicit a dramatic fight or flight respsonse with more discrimination regarding the object towards whom this response was directed, usually somebody who had symbolic connection with the patient's past life, for instance, the attendant who had a southern accent "like my father." It was interesting that introducing this same current in the same location sometimes would elicit rage and at other times panic, and a careful discussion with the patient regarding events that occurred during the preceding day usually indicated whether on that day the electrically elicited emotional response would be one of fear or one of rage. Again, this emphasizes the complementarity between the psychologic and neurophysiologic approach necessary for studying brain mechanisms and behavior. Electrical stimulation of another subcortal area (hypothalamus) elicited physiologic changes such as elevation of blood pressure, increase in heart rate, flushing, sweating—all typical responses to stress, but there would be no appropriate cognitive or emotional concomitants to this physiologic stress response.[5]

It has been demonstrated in both humans and animals that there seem to be two overlapping circuits in the subcortical structures, particularly in the limbic system, that when stimulated induce a pleasurable sensation in one system and an unpleasant or painful sensation in the other. Thus, if in humans the implanted electrodes are connected to a miniature stimulating machine carried on the belt of the individual allowed to select which electrode he wishes to stimulate, after a few preliminary trials he will avoid pushing the button for some areas and repeatedly push the button for other areas.[6] The pleasure button is often one that elicits sexual arousal and indeed it has been shown that orgasm is associated with storms of electrical activity in certain areas of the limbic system.[7] Of interest to us is one patient who repeatedly pushed one button, not because it led to sexual arousal, but because it elicited a feeling that he was about to recall some important memory or discover some valuable insight; a subjective experience similar to an aborted inspirational thought or vision of the type our subjects so often reported. The repetitious self-stimulation in this patient was a futile attempt to overcome a block to the completion of this aborted revelation.[7]

Earlier we have mentioned that individuals experiencing the perceptual distortions induced by the psychedelic drugs such as lysergic acid and mescaline have noted the similarity between these distortions and some of van Gogh's and Munch's paintings It is interesting that several patients with chronically implanted electrodes were given these drugs and such drugs induced a somewhat different but nevertheless a "hypersynchrony" in the electrical activity in the limbic system. (See Illustration # 12) These occurred at the same time that they were reporting vivid visual distortions and, if the effect of these psychedelic drugs was prevented by a pre-treatment with antipsychotic medication, there was no hypersynchrony in the limbic area.[8] Furthermore, we demonstrated that the drug thujone which is the toxic ingredient in absinthe induces (in animals) this same kind of pattern so that

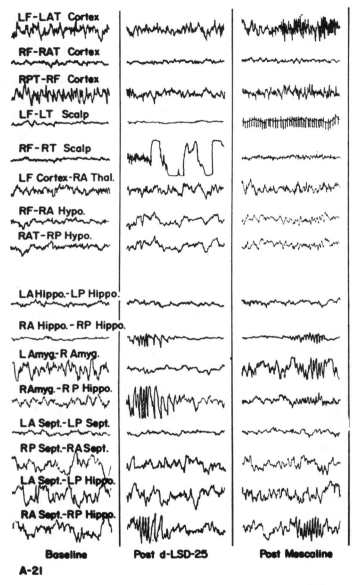

LF-LAT Cortex

RF-RAT Cortex

RPT-RF Cortex

LF-LT Scalp

RF-RT Scalp

LF Cortex-RA Thal.

RF-RA Hypo.

RAT-RP Hypo.

LA Hippo.-LP Hippo.

RA Hippo.-RP Hippo.

L Amyg.-R Amyg.

R Amyg.-R P Hippo.

LA Sept.-LP Sept.

RP Sept.-RA Sept.

LA Sept.-LP Hippo.

RA Sept.-RP Hippo.

#12

Baseline   **Post d-LSD-25**   **Post Mescaline**

A-21

PSYCHEDELIC "BRAINSTORMS"—significant changes occur in the lower
half of the illustration while the apparent changes in the upper half are artifacts.

one can postulate that perhaps van Gogh's experiences with absinthe may have contributed a certain uniqueness to his artistic works and it may well have done the same for Strindberg and Monticelli, both of whom were known to be heavy users of absinthe.[9]

I have also emphasized that sometimes the disordered episodic behavior might be histronic rather than correlated with this excessive neuronal activity in the brain. One report that dramatizes this possiblity is a patient who showed, on some occasions, bursts of excessive neuronal activity in the limbic area associated with confusion and primitive aggressiveness such as driving his fists through a window; whereas on another occasion, when he impulsively ran to the roof of the hospital threatening suicide by jumping off because he was not allowed to leave the hospital, such excessive neuronal discharges were absent.

In studying these patients there was a serendipitous observation that demonstrated how psychological factors alone could alter the neuronal electrical activity in the limbic system. This area of the brain is closely connected to the olfactory system (''smell'' brain) and, not surprisingly then, is highly developed in the evolutionary scale, where smell is a sensory modality with important adaptive value. Questioning what effect odors might have on humans, several subjects with the implanted electrodes were presented with different odors, some highly caustic such as ammonia, others with more pleasant connotations such as perfume, beer, flowers, etc., the expectation being that the more caustic would elicit a more drastic change in neuronal activity. Although this was often true, there were striking exceptions, so that we questioned whether in man it was more the psychological meaning of the odor rather than the caustic quality that determined the extent of the neuronal response. For instance, one subject responded more intensely to the odor of stale beer than anything else. He was asked what came to his mind when smelling the beer, and with some reluctance he began reminiscing about an early adolescent experience. It seems that during one of the first times he visited a bar, an older man made homosexual advances toward him, an act which elicited rageful aggression from the patient. During this recollection there occurred spontaneous hypersynchrony in the limbic region, without the presence of olfactory stimulation. Following this lead, we asked him to reminisce about his war experiences wherein he was the radio operator on a munitions freighter in the Caribbean, a stressful situation to say the least, as only he and the captian were aware of the number of German submarines prowling in the neighborhood which, with one torpedo, could have blown them all to oblivion. Such a recollection elicited dramatic hypersynchrony within the limbic system, but so did pleasant childhood memories such as Christmas morning with an electric train under the tree. Asking him to perform simple mathematical problems immediately terminated this electrical activity. Also, angry memories within the previous few days when he was frustrated by hospital personnel did not induce a change in the electrical activity. Thus, it appeared that certain memories of the distant past that were associated with intense feelings were the prerequisite for this neurophysiologic response.[10] The evidence is far from conclusive, but it does suggest that the recurrent painful memories might provide a "kindling" stimulus which in turn would lower the seizural threshold within the limbic system, making it susceptible not only to psychological stress, but also to psysiologic alterations in the body which would precipitate the limbic ictus that underlies many of these episodic disorders.

I have frequently referred to the hysteroid or motivated pole of the episodic behavior disorders.[1] The characteristic which suggests this hysteroid episodic disorder is the following: a clearly identified external stress which precipitates the attack, although we have seen that many times such an external stress will also precipitate an epileptoid attack. One measure to differentiate a spurious coincidence from a true precipitating event is that this external stress in the hysteroid patients is often one that would affect us all, such as catastrophic floods, hurricanes, fires, and battle experiences. The pattern of response for hysteroid dyscontrol is one of denial of what has happened; thus, a mute catatonic withdrawal from the world or dissociation from events that occurred, both psychological mechanisms that deny the existence of the catastrophic event. Sometimes the precipitating event is an internalized neurotic conflict and then the denial takes the form of an inability to recall who one is, or where one lives; or the patient assumes a new identity, or develop multiple personalities. Such denial is associated with complete amnesia for the behavioral response to the traumatic events, unlike epileptoid episodic disorders wherein the forgetfulness is only partial and recollection, even though at first hazy, can be encouraged by repeated questioning. None of our subjects seemed to have a pure hysteroid episodic disorder, although many had hysteroid elements and this was particularly true of both Munch and Strindberg. Certainly Strindberg's suicidal attempt by inducing pneumonia which would bring his paramour to his side so that she could prove her love was a histrionic conscious manipulation. It is unlikely that there were any concomitant excessive neuronal discharges deep in the brain associated with that event. Undoubtedly, the underlying motivations behind many of these hysteroid experiences are unconscious and in this sense such behavior is truly neurotic. Tennyson (Chapter 12), by repeating his name to himself over and over again, could elicit the paradoxical response of losing his personal identity; thus he was willfully inducing a hypnoidal fugue state.[11] Whether this and the hallucinatory episodes of Nightingale, Jeanne D'Arc, and Mary Baker Eddy were associated with excessive neuronal discharges is a point for debate, but more likely than not these were probably hysterical.

BRAINSTORMS AND CREATIVITY

As I said in the prologue, *Brainstorm* is "a sudden idea or inspiration" that is something we have all experienced. It is "a familiar term for the common experience of being suddenly possessed by a great idea and suddenly moved into spontaneous action."[12] In this context it seem particularly apt as applied to our core subjects, and Barker cites others such as Mozart, Hou-

seman, and Rimbaud as creative geniuses with brainstorms, all
of whom felt that they were not completely responsible for the
creative inspiration just as an epileptic feels his fit is the result
of a compelling force beyond his control. Mozart said of his
creation, "I . . . have nothing to do with it," much as did some
of the creative outcasts (see Chapter 9, ref. 14)). Barker conceives
of this process as consisting of two parts: first, a "whirlwind
fitting together of patterned action" and a second,"automatically
acting out or experiencing the fitted together pattern." "There
is an uncanny quality to the experience as though it is completely
outside the self or without considered intention or volution."[12]
This sense of whirlwind activity is reflected in Vincent's comments about his work, that he painted in one rush as much as
possible. At other times his work seems to be accompanied by
mounting tension, culminating in frenzy which sounds almost
orgastic and indeed it might be close, because in patients with
subcortical electrodes, limbic hypersynchrony does occur during
orgasm.[7] Vincent made such statements as, "ideas come in
swarms," [535]* or "continuous fever of work,"[474] or "extraordinary feverish energy,"[544a] or "terrible lucidity,"[543] and finally, "pictures come as if in a dream."[543] All of these comments
sound very much like what Barker was describing as the creative
spontaneous action that accompanies "mini-fits." Strindberg was
probably experiencing the increasing sense of an outside compelling force when he wrote of the "fortunate accident" that
". . . one follows the suggestion of his artifacts as they take
shape in his hands instead of sticking to his own predetermined
plans."

We have already mentioned that psychedelic drugs induce
changes in neuronal activity within the limbic system suggesting
"fitting" activity, and those who have experienced the pharmacologic effect of these drugs report the sense that suddenly
one's consciousness is raised. There is a sense of terror mixed
with bliss; a sharp awareness of patterns, altered color perceptions, swirling movements and rushing thoughts which seem to
suddenly coalesce into a meaningful whole. This book was first

---

*3 digit # refers to letters in Reference 13.

conceived on a warm summer day more than twenty years ago when a group of my colleagues and myself, monitored by a non-toxic physician, sat down on the shady porch of a small farmhouse overlooking a flower garden and more distant fields to experience a moving florid scene under the influence of the psychedelic drug psilocybin (from Mexican mushrooms). At the height of the effect, I excitedly jumped to my feet and exclaimed, "My God, a van Gogh painting." The bright hues of complementary colors reminded me of "LePont De Langlois." (F397)* The spinning, wavering, glistening lights reminded me of the "Night Cafe." (F436) The voluptuous exaggeration of forms, the shape of one's hand, the beautiful and meaningful caricature of my friends were like van Gogh's painting of "Roulin The Postman." (F532) All gave a heightened sense of reality which has never left me. Even now in the museum I see paintings in a way that I never viewed them before. Without talent, skill, and incentive these reminiscences of mine remain only my private pleasure; however, Vincent, because he had developed these skills and had native talent, could share them with the rest of the world.

Huxley was also struck by the similarities between the psychedelic experience and van Gogh paintings as well as those of other artists. He writes, "Table, chair and desk came together in a composition that was like something by Braque or Juan Gris, a still life recognizably related to the objective world, but rendered without depth, without any attempt at photographic realism," or "And the texture of the grey flannel—how rich, how deeply mysteriously sumptuous! And here they were again in Botticelli's picture."[15] This experience is unique for each individual who undergoes it. When the artist sees the voluptuous landscape, the musician then hears music, and the intellectual finds startling philosophical discoveries. I recall on one occasion, while under the influence of LSD, sitting by a brook, noting the beautiful jewel-like stones reflecting from the bottom of the stream. Stones appeared to be rubies, emeralds, or sparkling diamonds. Soon I became aware of the rhythmic, tinkling quality of the music as the water ran over the rocks. I was particularly struck by the

* # preceded by F refer to Reference #14.

rhythm, but not being an artist or a musician, I soon lost interest in these visual and auditory effects only to try an experiment. Could I slow the rhythm or speed it up? When I tried, what happened? Instead of slowing the rhythm, the world darkened and the music dropped an octave; trying to accelerate the rhythm induced the reverse, the world became intensely bright, the music now of extremely high pitch but the tempo remained the same. Then I wondered, is that what the French philosopher Henri Bergson meant when he referred to the essence of life as duration. The duration could not be changed.

One unique quality of Monticelli's paintings are small dabs of brilliant reds and luminescent greens and blues which suggest a canvas sprinkled with jewels, an effect which as been perceived by individuals under the influence of psychedelic drugs. Huxley expressed it thusly as he viewed the books on his library shelf under the influence of mescaline (from the peyote cactus), "red books like rubies; emerald books; books in white jade; books of agate, of aquamarine, of yellow topaz, lapis lazuli books whose color was so intense, so intrinsically meaningful, that they seemed to be on the point of leaving the shelves to thrust themselves insistently on our attention." Huxley continued, "Everything . . . is brilliantly illuminated and seems to shine from within." ". . . I become aware of a slow dance of golden lights. A little later there were sumptuous red surfaces swelling and expanding from bright nodes of energy that vibrated with a continuously changing pattern of life."[15] Another example is his description of perspectives so dramatically utilized by Vincent and Munch, "The perspective is rather odd and walls of the room no longer meet in right angles."[15] We have mentioned that Vincent's portraits, which at first glance seem to be caricatures, reveal a striking likeness to the individuals when photographed twenty years later. The caricature aspect of an individual, both beautiful and alarming, is a common experienncce under the psychedelic drugs. At one time when Huxley was scrutinizing a painting by Cezanne he commented, "For the head promptly took on a third dimension and came to life as a small goblin-like man looking out through a window in the page before me,"[15] perhaps like Munch's figures—whose faces had a ghost-like appearance—no unnecessary detail, just enough to convey the appropriate feeling, whether this be terror, anxiety, rage, melancholy, jealousy, or loneliness.

It would have been most fortunate if Vincent had been able to verbalize his perceptual distortions, but unfortunately most of his writings on the subject are vague and, perhaps, somewhat unconvincing. He says, People changed before his eyes; or Millets' Madonna is so dazzling it was difficult to look at; or Nature is so full . . . of feeling; or, Ideas came in swarms. Cezanne reported that Monticelli painted furiously. (See Chapter 4.) Munch must have felt the same way as people remarked that sensory stimulation seemed too much for him, so he would appear to close or shade his eyes.*

All experiences under the psychedelic drugs are not beautiful and pleasant, for there is always an ominous undertone of threatening catastrophe. Huxley comments on this, ". . . the universe is transfigured—but for the worst. Everything in it from the stars in the sky to the dust under their feet is unspeakably sinister or disgusting; every event is charged with hateful significance; every object manifests a presence of an indwelling hold, infinite, all powerful, eternal."[15] Our core subjects expressed this terror, as well as the ecstasy. Charles Lamb wrote, "Dream not Coleridge of having tasted all the grandeur and wildness of fancy—till you have gone mad." And Virginia Woolf said, "As an experience

---

*My own experiences in the use of psychedelic drugs occurred on several occasions between the years 1954 and 1963, or before the drugs "hit the streets." Like Huxley, I believe that such experiences were extremely potent and valuable not only for the behavioral scientists, but also for the creative artists. I was quick to recognize the potential for good and also harm. All my experiments were conducted under the strictest supervision after screening of the participating individuals. Expert psychotherapists were available to calm an individual experiencing a "bad trip" as well as medical backup to administer phenothiazines to abort the psychedelic experience if reassurance failed. Hospital facilities were also available, but fortunately the necessity never arose. It is a well-documented fact that unsupervised use of drugs whose composition is unknown is extremely risky even for the psychologically healthy individual, leading not only to acute and sometimes prolonged psychotic states, but severe damage, even death due to poor judgment. As Huxley states, "This experience left no room so to speak, for the ordinary and necessary concerns of human existence . . ." Needless to say, such an attitude in an unsupervised situation can be disastrous. Eventually it is to be hoped that the unsupervised will properly respect these drugs and the supervised and deserving will be allowed the experience.

madness is terrific,'' and another time ''. . . dark world has its fascinations as well as its terrors.'' (Chapter 5, reference 2.)

It is surprising how often our subjects report these episodes as associated with a cognitive revelation, or deep personal insight. In describing her attacks, Virginia Woolf says, ''. . . and in its lava I still find most of the things I wrote about. It shoots out of one everything shaped, final, not in mere driblets as sanity does,'' or she said ''. . . it taught me a good deal about what is called one's self,'' or again, ''I feel my mind take shape like a cloud with the sun on it,'' or still another comment, ''I'll be quite torpid . . . then suddenly something springs.'' (Chapter 2, reference 3.)

It is also surprising how often the inspirations which occur during these episodes are described in electrical terms. For example, Mary Lamb, drinking a toast with a friend, said (it) ''. . . restored me from the moment as if by an electrical stroke.'' (Chapter 5, reference 2.) Strindberg in describing his experience before the palace when he placed his hands around the iron lamp post, ''Thus forming a psychomagnet which acts on my immediately restored nervous system . . .'' (Chapter 4, reference 6.) And Virginia Woolf said that during her attacks fantasies were like shocks.

Our core subjects all refer to sudden revelations or inspiration that occur during their attacks, and all of us have had the experience of sudden new insight occurring to us seemingly out of nowhere. I described my revelation, ''. . . My God, a van Gogh painting'' while gazing over the garden under the influence of psilocybin (mushroom). This was an inspirational and new perspective for me, but others had discovered it (Huxley). Again, I had the flash of insight into the relationship between ''brainstorms'' and storms of electrical activity deep in the brain—but again, others had thought of and written about this before (Barker). Thus, for me these were inspirational new ideas, but for society as a whole, a repetition of what others had, unbeknownst to me, discovered before. Another example is my sudden realization, when reading Strindberg and Virginia Woolf, that their episodic psychoses might lead to an existential-phenomenologic world view and then I discovered Poole's report on Virginia Woolf as the phenomenologist novelist.

It was a common characteristic of our core subjects that, although their episodic aberrations could at times be an ecstatic experience, more often it was painful, or at least the pain outlasted the ecstasy and this led to intense and sustained introspection. This looking inward was a considerable source for the creative inspiration for all our core subjects, but also included individuals who had chronic aberrations. Perhaps a closer look would reveal undiscovered episodic characteristics of their illnesses too. Certainly Emily Dickinson had a transient psychotic episode superimposed on her chronic neuroses. A similar condition of episodic symptoms superimposed on chronic disorders is likely for Ezra Pound and Adolph Monticelli. Lowell's illness was blatantly episodic and on some occasions was characterized by dyscontrol acts.

It is likely that a more intense investigation of all our subjects would reveal episodic experiences correlated with at least some of their creative inspirations so that their brainstorms might have been associated with storms of neuronal activity in the brain. Thus, Barker is probably right when he proposes there is not so much difference between the epileptic (severe storms in the brain), genius (moderate storms in the brain), and the normal individual (occasional storms in the brain).

Chapter 12

Psychiatric Labels—Are They Necessary?

The medical profession is frequently chastised for retrospectively assigning diagnostic labels to individuals of eminence. A historical diagnosis does little harm to the individual except to devalue his creative product. We have already mentioned the zeal with which physicians have undertaken a retrospective diagnosis of Vincent van Gogh. A Dutch graduate student, Elmira Van Dooren, wrote her doctoral thesis on this subject reviewing all the published accounts from 1922 until 1981. One hundred and fifty-two physicians have offered a medical evaluation of van Gogh; thirteen favoring the diagnosis of schizophrenia, eight the diagnosis of manic-depressive disorder, forty-one psychogenic neuroses, ten character disorders, forty-five a diagnosis of epilepsy and the plethora of other psychiatric and medical illnesses including brain tumors, syphilis, gonorrhea, alcoholic delirium, eye disorders, and digitalis intoxication. It is obvious that it has been great fun for physicians to explore diagnostic alternatives and in many instances the only damage done is the time wasted in such an exercise. However, the implication of these diagnoses has often been to disparage van Gogh's uniqueness. For example, to attribute van Gogh's use of yellow to digitalis intoxication or the halo effect in his paintings as a result of glaucoma is to minimize his creative uniqueness.

I must confess that I am one of the one hundred fifty-two authors who have written on van Gogh's illness and I must insist that precise labels in modern medicine are the essence of helping our patients.[9] If the label applied can be verified through objective laboratory tests and if the diagnosis, once reliably established, indicates a precise and effective medical regimen, and if it can be predicted on the basis of this regimen how the illness will influence the future life of that individual, then labels become important not only for the individual, but for society at large. Unfortunately, such precise diagnostic labeling in most instances still eludes the psychiatrists and did not characterize medicine in general during the epoch in which most of our subjects lived. We will see how an imprecise medical diagnosis in the case of Alfred Tennyson probably had a devastating effect on his life until another diagnosis, equally improbable, but thought to be more benign, was applied which had a salutary effect on his emotional well being.

How does my diagnosis of an episodic behavioral disorder as applied to our core subjects, particularly van Gogh, meet the criteria for useful label? First, I have tried to develop observable behavioral patterns which would differentiate this disorder from other closely related psychiatric illnesses, such as those most often applied, namely schizophrenia, manic-depressive illness, or psychosis with epilepsy. Second, I have identified a specific biologic marker—that is, focal epilepsy within the limbic system—as the most common correlate of this behavioral deviation. Unfortunately, the techniques for objectifying such a biologic marker are too complex to be of practical usefulness, although there are some procedures on the frontiers of neurophysiology which offer hope that in the not too distant future less intrusive measurements of this subcortical excessive neuronal discharge will be possible (see Epilogue). Third, I have proposed that a precise medical regimen, which includes medications that elevate seizural threshold, would be effective in aborting the episodic madness. Fourth, I have tried to clarify the prognosis for such

patients, indicating that if the disastrous destructive consequences, either to self or to others, which are inherent in the
episodic disorders, can be avoided and the individual's productive
years extended then treatment would be of value both to the
individual and society. Finally, I have tried to clarify how successful treatment of these episodic disorders might influence the
creative product of the afflicted individuals. There is some evidence that their creativity would have been different if they had
not been episodically psychotic but in the last analysis only society can say whether this difference would be a loss or a gain.
Nevertheless, it is only the individual afflicted who should decide
whether the "cure" is worse than the disease.

To the extent that most of our psychiatric diagnoses do not
completely meet the criteria of useful labels (as there are not
readily accessible biologic markers to confirm such labels), some
have proposed that mental illness is a myth and that while it
might meet the needs of a particular culture in a particular epoch
the label mentally ill has no scientific consistency.[16] The justification for such a stance is suggested by two of our subjects,
Ezra Pound and Adolph Monticelli. For Pound the question of
whether he was "ill" or "bad" was socially controversial, but
by being identified as ill he was excused from a legal action to
determine guilt or innocence. Some would see this as a socially
justified equivocation while others, and perhaps even Pound,
might feel that the twelve years substitute incarceration in a mental hospital was a miscarriage of justice (either too little or too
much) and inappropriately determined by physicians rather than
by a judge or jury. Pound and his fellow poet Emily Dickinson
also illustrate the difficulty in establishing firm boundaries between creativity and madness in that even the experts argue as
to whether their poetic output at times was psychotically disorganized or just metaphorically obscure. In such individuals the
myth of mental illness may be apropos.

It is important to realize, however, that most of our subjects
did not believe that mental illness was a myth. Even though they
occasionally found psychosis an exhilarating experience, most
often it was a painful interruption in their life which they would

have preferred to have avoided. Most of us have an intuitive sense as to when we are insane so that madness, while still objectively inexplicable, is real to one who has suffered madness. It is not surprising then that the concept of the ''myth of mental illness'' is not widely accepted. Labeling has often been gratuitous, even more frequently meaningless, but history strongly supports the thesis that as medical science advances labels will become more useful to both the individual and society.

TENNYSON

The story of Alfred Tennyson (1809–1892) illustrates the potency of labels, both for better and worse.[11] He was the fourth of twelve children born to an old Lincolnshire family. His father being a minister, Tennyson was raised in the Somersby Rectory which provided the pastorial setting so prominent in his early poems. Few poets have become so widely known and admired. By the age of twenty-four his genius and popularity were established and he continued to write for the following sixty years. He was described as particularly handsome, large in stature and, until age twenty-three, had a zest for physical exercise. Following this he became retiring and was often ill, although details of his affliction are sparse. He married at age forty-one and shortly thereafter was appointed Poet Laureate to succeed Wordsworth. At age seventy-six Gladstone persuaded him to accept a peerage.

It is reported that Tennyson had at least three convulsions during infancy and following these his family thought he was dead. What is not clear is whether Tennyson had true convulsions later in life. His father supposedly had epilepsy as did his paternal Uncle Charles and his grandfather. Tennyson's mother at one time wrote to Uncle Charles stating that her husband was having fits about once a week. Charles suffered from a similar complaint, the fits being described as, ''He sat with his head on his hand as though he was musing—when his wife observed he was not well we spoke—he did not answer—we repeated, he made no effort to speak and was insensible—when he opened his eyes they would roll without meaning and then he spoke incoherently for a moment, this wandering of the intellect is alarming.''[11] Another striking symptom of the Tennysons so afflicted, particularly Alfred's father, George, was intermittent explosive rages which terrorized the family as they felt it would sometime lead to murder. This violence was well known in the community. The taint of mental illness was also remarkable in the Tennyson family. One of Alfred's siblings was insane most of his life and another insane "only a little less so."[11] A third was an opium addict and it is reported the death certificates of many of the extended family indicated they died of a brain affliction of one kind or another. It is not surprising then that the correspondence between Alfred's parents was primarily an exchange of news regarding symptoms, fever, tonics, purges, and medicines. For Alfred there was a constant brooding concern regarding epilepsy. Throughout his life Alfred experienced a number of mental phenomena which he considered quite bizarre. At age sixty-five he described these retrospectively as, ''a kind of waking trance (this for a lack of a better word) . . . I have frequently had quite up from boyhood when I've been all alone, this often comes upon me through repeating my own name to myself silently till all at once as it were, out of the intensity of the consciousness of individuality, the individuality itself seemed to dissolve and fade away into boundless being and this not a confused state but the clearest of the clearest, the surest of the surest, utterly beyond words—where death was almost laughably impossible—the loss of personality (if so it were) seemed no extinction but the only true life.'' The striking similarity of this statement with so many of the creative geniuses we have described is the reason that I say the episodic disorders have given a phenomenologic or existential orientation to their art and/or their writing. This was particularly true of Virginia Woolf, Edvard Munch, and August Strindberg. In retrospect, Tennyson saw this as a beneficent mystical experience, but as a boy it must have been frightening—and perhaps an escape from the painful reality of an unhappy family life. Earlier he alluded to "weird seizures" or to "cataleptic or epileptic spells inherited from the family." He said that a mist would descend upon him, but later as already mentioned he reported some trances that were not confusional states but the "clearest of clear." Tennyson denied that he was ever insane, but admitted feeling close to insanity and did worry about losing control like his father. The description of his symptoms sounds less like epilepsy and more similar to a hysterical dissociation that was self induced. Repeating his name over and over until he lost his identity must have been self hypnosis, so that his episodic disorder was near to the hysteroid pole of the epileptoid-hysteroid continuum mentioned earlier (pp. 208).

During the years 1844–1849, Tennyson admitted himself on several occasions to "hydropathic" establishments for treatment of some disorder. In those times, one could not voluntarily admit oneself to an asylum without seeking a commitment as insane so if one wanted treatment without admitting insanity the hydropathic establishment was the only alternative. This was the same expedient that Munch resorted to fifty years later. Unfortunately, details regarding the reason for Tennyson's admission to these establishments have not turned up so it is impossible to make a retrospective diagnosis. An obvious dramatic difference between Tennyson and those with the more epileptoid episodic disorder is the lack of any evidence that these experiences either contributed to or interfered with his creativity. One can conjecture that, perhaps, his poetic efforts were therapeutic and that by providing an imaginary world may have protected him against madness.

Tennyson lived in constant fear that he had inherited epilepsy and, in fact, delayed his marriage for many years until he was reassured by his doctor that he did not have epilepsy but gout, so he need not be concerned about transmitting his illness to his children. It is important to realize that one of the outstanding authorities on gout, Sir Victor Prichard, described as a prodromal symptom of recurring gout, the state of startling illumination and euphoria as happens according to Dostoevsky before an attack of epilepsy. This change of diagnosis had a potent curative effect and soon thereafter Tennyson was not only able to marry, but also to give up his hydropathic treatments. This illustrates the power of labels, particularly when both doctor and patient are ignorant of the true mechanisms behind the inheritability of illness and for that matter even ignorant regarding an accurate diagnosis. This is an interesting variation of the placebo effect—what has been called the double placebo, i.e., the patient gets better even though the physician's intervention is actually medically impotent (the placebo effect), particularly if the doctor believes erroneously in the potency of his treatment (therefore referred to as the double placebo effect).

There still remains a big debate whether Tennyson's symptoms were purely physical in nature or psychological, but it is highly likely that Tennyson had neither gout nor epilepsy but that his symptoms were hysterical, or what I prefer to call, hysteroid dyscontrol. This could have been related to the fear of his father's violence during childhood and the fear of epilepsy or madness in later life. There is one remote alternative explanation: as part of the therapeutic regimen for gout Tennyson renounced his considerable intake of port. We reported that Munch and Strindberg gave up absinthe or alcohol, which probably precipitated their episodic disorders. At least they got well once having done this, so this could be a possibility in the case of Tennyson.

EPILEPSY AND MADNESS

The family taint of both epilepsy and madness, which in the mid-19th Century were considered incurable and transmittable to offsprings, was a heavy burden for Tennyson. In that time it was thought that epilepsy could be excited in the predisposed by too much smoking and drinking, and also by a tight prepuce in males and if the patient masturbated then his illness was almost incurable. The concept of epilepsy was so broad that it included not only the "falling sickness," but also all possible mental disorders which were noted not only to precede fits or follow fits, but were thought to occur even without fits. Thus, mental illness in general was blamed on epilepsy. Aggression and violence was also considered epileptic (the furor epilepticus of Esquirol). In the middle of the 19th Century Lombroso proposed the epileptoid nature of genius as well as criminaltiy. Nietzsche described "people with intellectual convulsions" and there was also the concept of "convulsions of passion."[17] People of eminence labeled epileptic include Hercules, Socrates, St. Paul, Caesar, Caligula, Mohammed, Pascal, Byron, Dostoevsky, Flaubert, Swinburne, Peter the Great, Napoleon, Alfred Nobel, to mention only a few. However, in 1870 Hughlings Jackson's study on convulsions established the neurologic boundaries of the disorder. During the same epoch Briquet and Charcot distinguished between epilepsy and hysteria designating the latter hystero-epilepsy. Thus, for the first time a dichotomy between neurologic and psychologic seizures was proposed. It was Jackson's study of focal epilepsies with follow-up pathologic studies at autopsy (many patients having focal nervous system lesions due to syphilis) that established the careful empirical data which led to understanding the neurologic basis of epilepsy. Jackson steadfastly maintained Spinoza's two window view of the world that "there is no physiology of the mind any more than there is a psychology of the nervous system."[18] In this he fostered a dualism in his view of illness, relegating physiology to the physician and psychology to the non-physician, although he insisted that the physician must have the appropriate psychological knowledge as it was his responsibility to distinguish between physical and psychological symptoms. Underlying his attitude was an extreme Cartesian dualism because Jackson recognized that although fear could precipitate a seizure, it was fear acting on an organically diseased part of the brain. The concept that fear or any other psychological condition could directly cause anatomic or physiologic changes in normal nerve tissues was counter to Jackson's principles. As specialization in medicine increased, epilepsy became the realm of the neurologist and, following in the tradition of Jackson, it became his responsibility to unequivocally differentiate between a neurologic lesion and conversion hysteria.

Other neurologists, however, continued to espouse the point of view that epilepsy could be the basis for behavioral disturbances without symptoms of motor spasms or loss of consciousness.[17] Kaufmann, in 1862, described ''psychic equivalents'' as epilepsy where seizures were lacking altogether but said that the insanity was really an equivalent of a seizure. In 1875 Samt divided epileptic insanity into two forms, post-convulsive insanity and the psychic equivalents unassociated with convulsions. As an example, Samt's classic case history was a medical student who made homicidal attempts upon his friend and whose amnesia for the event was only partial. Many of Samt's cases of epileptic equivalents included acts of violence and religious ecstasy as we have seen in our patients with episodic disorders. It is not surprising, inasmuch as most of these ideas developed after Tennyson's ''recovery,'' that we have little perspective as to whether Tennyson's problems were organic or psychological. What we do know today is that the dichotomy between the organic and psychologic may be a spurious argument, because as already discussed (pp 217), psychological phenomenon can induce physiologic changes within the brain which in time may become anatomically pathological; i.e., to put it crudely, misfiring neurons may become dying neurons may become dead neurons, whether the process is initiated by an external or internal psychologic or physiologic mechanism. The important point here is that whatever Tennyson's diagnosis was, when the label was changed from epilepsy to gout, an illness with much more benign connotation, Tennyson got well.

Chapter 13

Geniuses and Their Doctors

All of our core subjects were considered sick at some time in their lives so all came under the care of the medical profession. There is considerable data about van Gogh and his doctors while very little on Strindberg. Van Gogh's medical contacts were exceptional even by present day standards, while Virginia Woolf's treatment was grossly inadequate, even taking into consideration the limitations of medical knowledge during the first four decades of this century. She deserved better and such was available in London during her life. Robert Lowell, who died in 1976, is the only one whose psychiatric care can be measured by current standards. Van Gogh's medical treatment included what was undoubtedly a correct diagnosis and prognosis (epilepsy without convulsions) and a specific pharmacological regimen, the best then available for treating epilepsy (e.g., bromides). It also included, as does modern treatment, involvement of the family, rapid hospitalization during acute episodes to protect the patient and others, at the same time offering considerable personal freedom during the essential but prolonged rehabilitative procedures. This was accompanied by talking out problems with the physician, a form of psychotherapy rarely used in his time, as well as an intuitive element of the "human dimension" between the doctor and his patient which only recently has been introduced into the medical curriculum. His doctors recognized his talent, if not his genius, as a painter with a realization that painting aided his recovery. The only aspect of his treatment that might have been neglected was encouragement from his physicians to abstain from alcohol and absinthe. At least such abstinence is one of the more plausible explanations for the Munch and Strindberg ''cures'' and this required a self-discipline that was noticeably lacking in their early lives. This avenue was open to van Gogh who realized himself that his problems were at least aggravated, if not caused by, alcohol and absinthe. Perhaps with more help from his doctors he too could have found such self-discipline.

All subjects including even Virginia Woolf shared some positive factors in their relationship with the medical profession. For us to evaluate retrospectively their treatment we must maintain an appropriate historical perspective. An extreme example would be that one could imagine the psychic trauma today's patient would incur if they awoke from a confused psychotic state and found their head covered with leeches, but this may not have been such a surprise to Mary Lamb during the early part of the 19th Century. Most of our subjects, probably as part of their genius, had a startling psychologic perspicacity; they accepted the concept of the unconscious, recognized that many symptoms and character traits had meaning in terms of their own personal history, particularly their childhood interaction with parents, and that dreams were often an avenue for understanding the meaning of their symptoms. Strindberg and Munch in particular recognized the value of exploring the depths of the ''soul'' in an attempt to attenuate their inner turmoil and this took place a number of years before Freud embarked on a similar enterprise; that is, self-analysis. Munch and Strindberg recognized that such exploration could be utilized in their creative efforts and the creative efforts themselves had therapeutic value in reducing the intense inner dysphoria that they were experiencing.

Fortunately, most of our subjects were not committed to a lunatic asylum. Although reforms had already been proposed at the time they became ill, such institutions were still no more than cruel prisons. Some, like Mary Lamb and Virginia Woolf, had to be hauled off by family and friends, kicking and screaming in straight-jackets, but usually ended up in alternative situations; that is, private sanitoriums, spas or nursing homes, having agreed in time, to family pressure to seek such help. Others, including Munch, Strindberg, and Tennyson, admitted themselves to spas or hydropathic institutions and then, of course, had the option to discharge themselves when they no longer felt the need for such treatment.

VINCENT'S DOCTORS

Inasmuch as we have more details regarding van Gogh's care and have noted how good (although ultimately a failure) this was, we will investigate his care in some depth, using it as a measuring rod for evaluating the care of our other subjects.

Paul-Ferdinand Gachet has been made the scapegoat for van Gogh's suicide and the medical profession raked over the coals for their attitudes toward creative geniuses. In 1947 a French art critic, Antonin Artaud, published a small volume on van Gogh entitled "Le Suicide de la Societe," in which he blames the medical profession for Vincent's suicide. He postulates that the artist in his creative originality challenges society while doctors, being supporters of the establishment, became the agents which destroy this creativity. The polemic of this point of view is elaborated by Ted Morgan[19] who similarly suggests that Vincent's physician, Dr. Gachet, was the direct cause of his suicide. Gachet's philosophy hardly supports Artaud's and Morgan's point of view that all doctors are agents of the establishment because Gachet was not only a medical but a social rebel. He was a homeopathic physician, that is, a member of a deviant group even for those days and was otherwise described as a "free thinker and non-conformist." He subscribed to the new and the original, and as an amateur painter in his own right, was a great enthusiast for the avante garde impressionist movement, hardly a description of a reactionary physician bound by conservative opinions.

Perhaps we can excuse the attitude of Artaud and Morgan if they were uninformed about Gachet but did know of some of the other opinions expressed about art by physicians of that time. In 1896 one physician quoted by Hirsh said that "whoever paints violet pictures has weak nerves, or who paints in the manner of Manet has lesions of the retina." Somewhat later another physician, Hyslop (one of Virginia Woolf's physicians), says, "Only half the post-impressionistic pictures recently exhibited were worthy of bedlam and the remaining being . . . evidence of shamming, degeneration and malingering."[20] Even in the last few years some of the characteristics of Vincent's paintings have been attributed to eye disorders, particularly glaucoma or digitalis intoxication.

What did happen to Vincent following his ear mutilation in December of 1888? He was immediately hospitalized, as he needed both medical as well as psychiatric care. We have evidence that both he and Theo were impressed by his physician, Dr. Rey, who was an intern at the hospital, Vincent remarking how marvelous the "modern" physicians were and how they dedicated their total life to the care of their patients. Such feelings apparently were reciprocated as Rey wrote to Theo, "I have made him come down to my office for a little chat. It will entertain me, and will be good for him."[567]* So it would appear that this was Vincent's introduction to psychotherapy. Vincent developed paranoid delusions and some of these were justified. Upon his release after his second hospitalization, with bandages still on his head, he was jeered and tormented by the adolescent boys in town, and no longer tolerated as merely eccentric by the adults of Arles. The act of mutilation had changed their perception of Vincent as a harmless object of condescending ridicule to that of a person who should be feared, because only a crazy man could mutilate himself. The townspeople petitioned for his commitment, causing Vincent to write to Theo, "So you understand what a staggering blow between the eyes it was to find so many people here cowardly enough to join together against one man and that man ill."[579] It must be remembered, however, that

*3 digit # refers to letter # in chapter 1, reference 1.

Vincent invited martyrdom and then exploited it to elicit sympathy from his family and small circle of devoted friends. As he himself said, he had a propensity for pouring oil on the fire. This rejection and the community's insistence upon his commitment inspired the popular ballad "Vincent." The sentimental lyrics reflect the view that Vincent was persecuted by the world who did not understand his genius, hence, mistook him for mad, thus the refrain:

> Now I understand,
> What you tried to say to me.
> How you suffered for your sanity.
> How you tried to set them free.
> They would not listen—
> They did not know how.
> Perhaps they'll listen now.

It was not the medical profession, however, that was Vincent's enemy; in fact, quite the contrary. His doctors and the hospitals were to be his solace. Freed from legal commitment, he nevertheless stayed at the hospital, saying, "When I have to follow a rule as here in the hospital, I feel at peace."[573] The disturbing experience with the townspeopel and the recent departure of his close friends, including Roulin the postmaster, were compelling reasons for Vincent to request hospitalization at the asylum in nearby St. Remy.

There has been considerable criticism of the medical profession for gratuitously labeling Vincent's illness; however, as we discussed in the previous chapter, labels which can be misused can also have value to both the individual and to society. Whatever connotations labels have, it is helpful to be labeled "sick" and not merely irresponsible. In the sick role one deserves financial aid and other help from relatives and friends. Hospitalized as ill was certainly a preferred disposition to the alternative Vincent proposed of joining the Foreign Legion. Vincent's doctors thought he was suffering from psychoses due to epilepsy even though he never suffered from typical epileptic attacks such as generalized convulsions, short lapses of consciousness, or simple stereotyped automatic behavior. Our current knowledge suggests that Vincent's doctors were correct—he probably had seizural activity in the brain, that is excessive firing of nerves, but this was focal and limited to the limbic system. If such firing had occurred in the area of the brain controlling motor functions, then Vincent would have experienced grand mal seizures. The fact that such abnormality was confined to the limbic system meant that Vincent did not have typical epilepsy but, by intuition, his physicians were right in considering that he had epilepsy even without typical seizural symptoms. Today such a label would suggest a specific pharmacological regimen and Vincent, having been labeled thus, would have been treated with anticonvulsant medication. An indication that this treatment might have been successful is suggested by Vincent's response to bromides, which have weak anticonvulsant action. He wrote to Theo, "However, the unbearable hallucinations have ceased, and are now getting reduced to simple nightmares in consequence of my taking bromide of potassium, I think."[574] It is probable that if he had an adequate regimen on an anticonvulsant his episodic dysphoria and intellectual confusion would have been ameliorated. Vincent still would have had many problems but perhaps he could have coped with these better if he had not suffered from the perplexing episodic psychotic attacks which were so frightening to him. On the other hand, we might ask whether control of these psychotic episodes would have seriously stifled his creativity. Even though he still would have been considered an artistic genius on the basis of paintings completed before his first psychotic attack, he would not have been the Vincent as we know him if he had not experienced these attacks. How did a young intern, Dr. Rey, make this perceptive diagnosis of epilepsy without convulsions? Aaron Sheon (see acknowledgments) called my attention to the detective work of Dr. Gastaut, an internationally known epileptologist from Marseilles, who discovered that Dr. Rey was a close friend of another intern at the medical school in Montpellier, a doctor Aussoleil, who in 1888 was working on his dissertation entitled *Epelepsie Larve Mentale,* a type of disorder similar to van

Gogh's. To Dr. Rey, being acquainted with Aussoleil's work, such a diagnostic possibility must have been foremost in his mind.

Vincent voluntarily committed himself to the asylum and remained there from May 1889 until May 1890. In a letter to Theo he explained this decision, ''I'm paralyzed when it comes to acting and shifting for myself . . . I feel quite unable to take a new studio and stay there alone, here in Arles or elsewhere, I should be afraid of losing the power to work which is coming back to me now by forcing myself and having all the other responsibilities of a studio on my shoulder besides. Temporarily, I wish to remain shut up, as much for my own peace of mind as for other peoples.'' This, and the following statement, would indicate that Vincent had a realistic evaluation of appropriate psychiatric treatment. He continued, ''In my case, nature by itself will do much more for me than any remedies.''[585] He seemed to recognize the chronicity of his illness and to accept medical judgment regarding this matter as he wrote in his next letter, ''This morning I talked a little with the doctor here (St. Remy), he told me exactly what I already thought, that I must wait a year before thinking myself cured, since the least little thing might bring on another attack.''[586]

By September of 1889, less than four months later, Vincent was becoming restless and considered leaving the hospital. He said, ''We shall see if the attacks return about Christmas, and that over, I can see nothing to stop my telling the management here to go to blazes, and return to the North for a longer or shorter time.'' It is an indication that Vincent, like many patients, while respecting his physician, disparages the institution which employs the physician. He says of his doctor, ''M. Peyron has been kind to me and has much experience. I do not doubt that he speaks and judges correctly,'' but in the same letter he remarks, ''But with regard to the management here, we must probably be polite, but we must limit ourselves to that and not bind ourselves to anything.''[602]. His complaints about the hospital are similar to those that are unfortunately still pertinent today, one hundred years later: those of idleness, infrequent medical attention, limited recreational facilities, and bad food.

Peyron, Vincent's doctor at St. Remy, was willing to take risks, allowing him privileges which were denied other patients, such as being given an extra room for a studio where he could keep his paints and brushes even though Vincent abused this privilege by feeble suicidal attempts in eating paints or drinking turpentine. Peyron must have recognized the curative effect of continued creative effort during periods when Vincent was recovering from his psychoses and this was also the attitude of Munch's physician, Dr. Jacobson, who allowed Munch to continue with his painting and writing, one project being the illustrated prose poem "Alpha and Omega." Munch said after he started to work on this, "A strange calm came over me while I was working on this series; it was as if all malice let go of me." (Chapter 3, reference 8.) Vincent was allowed to leave the hospital on excursions to paint landscapes of the nearby countryside and on several occasions visited old friends in Arles. Usually he returned from Arles in an acute psychotic state or, at least, became psychotic shortly after these excursions. Apropos to my current hypothesis that some of Vincent's attacks may have been precipitated by the thujone, the convulsive element in absinthe, Vincent was drinking with old friends in Arles and that this might have precipitated these attacks.

By the winter of 1890, Vincent was frantically pressing for release and suggested that a trip out of the hospital to visit Arles would be a test as to whether he was ready. Similar to previous visits, Vincent had another psychotic episode following this visit, one of his most prolonged attacks, lasting from mid-February to mid-April of 1890. It was no wonder then that Peyron had reservations about releasing Vincent in the spring of 1890, only a month after his recovery from this attack. However, he did accede to pressures from Vincent and furthermore let him travel to Paris alone. I have described elsewhere[1] that such permissiveness is necessary for individuals suffering from episodic reactions, because the onsets of these reactions are unpredictable, and during the lucid intervals between attacks the patients are perfectly competent to care for themselves. In view of this, it is inappropriate to insist upon prolonged hospitalization if other measures to protect the individual from his acute disorder can be devised. For instance, if one can identify prodromals to an attack, the best medical regimen is to arrange for a rapid admission to a hospital as the attack approaches. This provides for close supervision and the protective custody necessary to avoid dangerous psychotic behavior. Once the episode has remitted, early discharge from the hospital should be encouraged, particularly if the patient can be closely supervised. Such a plan is appreciated by the patients themselves, so in the future they are more candid with their doctors, asking for hospitalization as they become aware of an impending attack. The patients must be educated in this recognition of impending danger and the need for close supervision. Such education must be provided during the "normal" intervals between attacks. This regimen means that some hospitalizations last only a matter of days but others are more prolonged, that is several weeks or a month. The decision as to when the risk of dishcarge is reasonable depends on the quality of supervision the patient receives outside the hospital. If van Gogh had had a nearby family that could have provided this supervision he might have spent only two or three weeks in an asylum during most of his attacks, although repeated hospitalizations would have been necessary. Overall, the length of his stay in the asylum would have been considerably less than the one year that he endured. As we saw in the case of Emily Dickinson, an extended family all living together and able to provide supervision may mean hospitalization can be avoided altogether. Some of our subjects—Munch, Strindberg, and Tennyson—accomplished this end by admitting themselves to spas or hydropathic institutions and then left as soon as they no longer felt the need. In this way they retained control over their own destiny. Apparently, such a regimen was never applied to either Virginia Woolf or Mary Lamb and this may be why they were often forcibly sent off to institutions. They both felt that their families were too quick in hospitalizing them and then left them institutionalized for too long. An element of mistrust approaching paranoia developed in each regarding their doctors and family. In view of Mary Lamb's and Virginia Woolf's propensity for violence and lacking proper instruction from the experts, one can hardly blame their families for playing it safe and rushing the patients into the hospital at the earliest possible moment. In fact, until recently, psychiatric institutions functioned predominantly for protecting the families against their lunatic members, the patients being held until it was "proven safe" to return them to family and friends.

Three of our subjects committed suicide (van Gogh, Woolf, and Hemingway) and all were under psychiatric care at the time. This, of course, represents a failure in treatment, but sooner or later in the professional career of almost every psychiatrist, they lose one of their patients in this manner. When this occurrs in the modern psychiatric hospital, the staff engage in a recapitulation of the events that immediately preceded the suicide, hoping to learn from failure and sharpen professional skills to minimize repetition of this unfortunate event. This procedure is referred to as a "psychological autopsy." I will apply such a strategy to each of those who committed suicide to see whether in retrospect one might have predicted the impending suicide. Again, van Gogh provides the most data, particularly, Vincent's relationship with Dr. Gachet, who assumed responsibility for Vincent's care after he was discharged from the asylum at St. Remy.

Vincent's first written opinion of Dr. Gachet was, "I've seen Dr. Gachet who gives me the impression of being another eccentric, but his experience as a doctor must keep him balanced enough to combat the nervous troubles from which he certainly seems to be suffering, at least, as seriously as I."[635] Theo had communicated with Dr. Gachet before Vincent's arrival and the doctor told Theo that he did not believe Vincent's crisis had anything to do with madness. Apparently, after speaking with Vincent, Gachet became more cautious in his prognosis because he was less sanguine about Vincent's chances for recovery. Gachet encouraged Vincent to be frank with him, as all good psychotherapists do, and although he did not promise a cure he assured Vincent that something medically could be done to lessen the depressions should they become intense. He also recommended that Vincent live in a regular and circumspect manner, including adequate sleep, nourishing food, and a sensible work schedule. This is an essential adjunct to any regimen for the treatment of the episodic disorders, as physiologic imbalances induced by irregularities in any of these areas will precipitate limbic seizures responsible for dyscontrol acts, as well as the episodic psychotic reactions that characterize our core subjects.[1] Theo had considerable respect for Gachet as a physician and a friend. Theo realized that Gachet was a man of understanding, and, like Vincent's earlier physicians, Peyron at St. Remy and Rey in Arles, respected Vincent's artistic capabilities, hence would encourage him to pursue those activities while under his care.

In Vincent's opinion of Gachet, one can recognize his ambivalence, that is the vacillating trust which characterized all of Vincent's friendships from early adulthood onward. This attitude had some basis in reality because Gachet was himself depressed as the result of the death of his wife some years before. Furthermore, Gachet revealed his weariness of the responsibilities of a physician. Both of these represent an element of self-revelation that only recently has been accepted by the psychiatric profession as an important part of the therapeutic contract; the point being, if we ask our patients to be frank with us and they discern our own weaknesses we must also be frank with them without excessively burdening them with our own problems. However, several weeks after the first meeting with Dr. Gachet, Vincent wrote, "He is very much the doctor and his profession and faith still sustain him. We are great friends already."[638] This suggests a healthy therapeutic relationship had already developed.

Vincent wrote to Theo, "M. Gachet says he thinks it is most improbable that it (his illness) will return."[638] Gachet may have been too lavish in his optimism. On the other hand, it is more likely that Vincent, in grasping at every straw, may have exaggerated this optimism, for patients usually hear what they want to hear. Gachet may have made a mistake in underestimating the seriousness of Vincent's illness, but in treating a depressed patient it is essential for the physician to remain optimistic with regard to the outcome. The optimism so necessary in treating the depressed patient must be a cautious optimism, for promising too much, too soon, only leads to disappointment when any exacerbation of symptoms occurs. This, in turn, heightens the depressed patient's inherent pessimism, which can be disastrous.

Within the doctor-patient relationship between Gachet and Vincent the inevitable soon happened. There developed what is technically known as a "transference neurosis;" that is, the patient becomes childishly dependent on his therapist, believing that all problems will be solved by the intervention of a loving omnipotent parent figure who will not only take care of the patient but will right all wrongs without any effort on the patient's part. Vincent writes to Theo, "Altogether Father Gachet is very like you and me . . . I feel that he understands us perfectly and that he would work for you and me to the best of his power without reserve for the love of art for art's sake."[638] This transference dependency and love was a heavy burden to place on any doctor, particularly in those days, five years before Freud first described this penomenon.[21] The one realistic note in Vincent's statement was the qualification "to the best of his power." Does it indicate that Vincent fuly realized Gachet's divided obligation, not only to him, but to his other patients and additionaly to his own family? Realistically, Vincent should have been prepared to perceive this because he was becoming frighteningly aware of Theo's divided burden in supporting him as well as a wife and child. The unbearable thought of losing Theo's support, however, may have blocked Vincent's sensitivity to Gachet's divided responsibility. In transference love, the patient can only believe the healer will devote himself fully to him and to him alone.

It was at this time that Vincent's nephew and namesake became ill; hence, Vincent's childish demands were intensely reawakened and he felt desperately threatened by any withdrawal of Theo's support. Furthermore, the mother of his nephew was also ill and finding it difficult to nurse her infant child. These events may offer an explanation for an incident between Vincent and Gachet when Vincent became enraged because the doctor was not taking proper care of a painting by Guillaumin which Vincent considered a masterpiece. This painting now hangs in the Paul Gachet collection in the Jeu De Palme Museum in Paris.

It shows a young, rather small woman lying on a couch naked to the waist who has full round rather large breasts. The skin over the breasts has a slight bluish tinge suggesting engorged veins. Thus, it would seem to be a painting of a lactating female. By association then, this painting must have reawakened Vincent's most infantile need for the tender, feeding care of a mother, a deprivation that was currently being re-enacted between infant and mother in Theo's family.

Several letters written shortly before his suicide become understandable and highly significant if we realize this. In the first letter, written when he had been urging Johanna (Theo's wife), with or without Theo, to visit him in the country accompanied by little Vincent, he says, "I honestly believe that Jo would have twice as much milk here."[645] In a subsequent letter, he addresses Jo directly, "It seems to me that while the child is still only six months old, your milk is already drying up; already like Theo you are too tired. I do not at all mean exhausted, but anyway worries are looming to large and too numerous and you are sowing among the thorns."[647] This described the feelings Vincent was undergoing; that is, his primitive fear of losing the mother's breast was further reinforced by reality for in a letter from Theo in which he describes the illness of little Vincent, Theo discusses a plan to give up his current employment in order to undertake the risky venture of becoming an independent art dealer. The plan could only have been most frightening to Vincent whose very subsistence was dependent on Theo's income. Vincent hastened to Paris to visit his brother and sister-in-law, probably to dissuade his brother from such an enterprise. The excitement of this visit was too much for Vincent, so he returned to the country earlier than expected. In a letter to Johanna, who had written to console him, Vincent replies, "It is no slight thing, when all of us feel our daily bread in danger; it is not a trifle when for other reasons also, we feel that our existence is fragile. Back here, I still felt very sad and continued to feel the weight of the storm which threatened you. What can be done? You see, I generally try to be fairly cheerful, but my life too is menaced at its very root, and my steps also are wavering. I feared—not so much, but a little just the same—that being a burden to you, you felt me to be rather a thing to be dreaded."[649]

At the most primitive level depressed patients act as though they are threatened with starvation by losing the mother's breast. Severely depressed patients often refuse to eat, although they will avidly eat and drink if hand fed by a caring person. In fact, in some instances depressed adults will eat only though a baby's bottle. I believe that Vincent's violent reaction to Dr. Gachet's lack of concern for his Guillaumin painting of the woman naked to the waist resulted from this primitive association between the exposed breasts in the painting and Vincent's preoccupation with symbolically losing the mother's breast, because of the threatened cessation of Theo's support.

If this seems farfetched, one should carefully consider Vincent's letter to Theo, wherein he referred to Jo's lack of mother's milk, saying, ". . . and the prospects grow darker, I see no happy future at all."[648] This too is typical of the severe depressive patient. When such an individual loses hope and sees no future, suicide is the only solution. In the next letter, Vincent says, "I do not need to go out of my way to try to express sadness and extreme loneliness."[649] Without a future there can only be devastating loneliness. Writing to his mother at the same time, Vincent says, "I'm in a mood of almost too much calmness."[650] Vincent once described his mother in the same words, expressing his concern that (as a reaction to his father's death) she would die in the near future. Psychiatrists know that a painfully depressed patient who suddenly shows "too much calmness" has usually made a decision and developed a plan for committing suicide. I suspect that when Vincent wrote this he already had a plan. Salutations that express finalty are also an ominous sign, and on the 23rd of July, Vincent wrote to Theo, "Goodbye now and good luck in business, etc."[651] This was his last letter, except for the one found on his person when he shot himself July 27, dying July 29, 1890.

We know that Vincent's rages were frightening even to his friends and relatives, so it would not be surprising that he frightened Gachet too, particularly because Gachet was well aware of the thwarted attempt on Gauguin's life when Vincent approached Gauguin with a razor. We may say then that Gachet now bore a double burden in caring for Vincent, coping with both his irrational childish dependency as well as the underlying murderous rage when these insatiable needs were unrequited. This is probably the explanation for an event which must have been exaggerated by Morgan as he states that when Gachet was called to Vincent's bedside because of Vincent's gunshot wound he acted almost as a stranger. Morgan, not fully appreciating the dynamics of the transference neuroses, suggests that such rejection by Gachet was tantamount to malpractice or even malevolent neglect. We must keep in mind, however, that Gachet was concerned with Vincent's health but undoubtedly wanted to share this burden for he immediately tried to summon Theo, although this was difficult because Vincent, at first, refused to cooperate by telling him Theo's address. I suggest that Gachet's reaction to Vincent's transference neurosis sufficiently explains this supposed aloofness (if it did exist) at the time he rushed to Vincent's bedside. I cannot accept Morgan's premise that Gachet's supposed "abandonment" was criminal in either the legal or the moral sense. A certain formality between doctor and patient would be appropriate in such a situation and Gachet may have intuitively realized this. To support his thesis that Gachet was a despicable character, Morgan cites his "greed" in hurriedly gathering up Vincent's paintings when Theo offered them immediately after Vincent's death. We must remember that although the paintings were of questionable monetary value at the time, to a friend who shared the last days of Vincent's life as well as familiarity with the scenes and figures painted, they had considerable sentimental value.

In view of our current knowledge of psychotherapy, the biggest mistake Gachet made was to become personally involved with Vincent; that is, the private lives of the doctor and his patient became entwined, a matter which in those days was the rule rather than the exception. We now know, particularly from our psychotherapeutic experiences with dyscontrol patients, that this leads to disaster. One explanation for any possible estrangement between Gachet and Vincent proposed by Marc Tralbaut[22] is that there was a romantic involvement between Gachet's daughter Marguerite and Vincent and that, as in the past, this love was thwarted by parental objection. There is little evidence to support the hypothesis that Vincent was in love with Marguerite, as he mentioned her only casually in letters to Theo when he was painting her portrait and this is quite contrary to prolific correspondence between the two brothers regarding Vincent's previous loves. Morgan's inference that marriage was on Vincent's mind because of comments he made in letters written to Theo is obviously in error. Morgan cites a quote from Vincent's letter to Theo, "I still love art and life very much, but as for having a wife of my own I have no great faith in that,"[646] Morgan believing that this comment was made because Vincent was infatuated with Marguerite. Morgan must not have been aware of the preceding letter from Theo dated June 30, 1890 in which Theo, trying to bolster Vincent's spirits by describing the future the two of them had together said, "I have, and I hope from the bottom of my heart that you will someday have a wife to whom you will be able to say these things."[T39] Vincent's comment then was a rebuttal to this comment in Theo's letter.

There is some evidence that Marguerite might have been in love with Vincent, at least she is supposed to have confided this to a friend and her subsequent life would suggest that she was inconsolably bereaved by Vincent's death, for she suffered a severe depression and remained a spinster recluse the rest of her life. If any love existed between Vincent and Marguerite or even Marguerite alone, one could hardly criticize Gachet for objecting to this liaison. However much Gachet may have admired Vincent as an artist, it would not be surprising if he rejected Vincent as a prospective son-in-law. If Gachet, then, made any serious mistake in light of our present knowledge of psychotherapeutic techniques, it was trying to be a friend and companion to Vincent, as well as a psychotherapist. As already mentioned, such a relationship is particularly difficult, if not impossible, with those patients who manifest the dyscontrol syndrome, but we must remember this was acceptable medical practice in 1890.

Morgan, in placing the blame for Vincent's death on Gachet, ignores our post-Freudian psychodynamic insights regarding the doctor-patient relationship and Artaud's mistake is a projection of his own attitudes onto Vincent because he too had several psychotic episodes, but there was a marked difference in Artaud's treatment as he was forcibly institutionalized for over nine years in contrast to Vincent, who voluntarily entered the hospital and was released upon his own request, one year later.

Gachet arrived at Vincent's funeral with a bouquet of sunflowers because these were Vincent's favorite flowers. In writing to Theo immediately afterwards he says, "The more I think of it, the more I think Vincent was a giant. Not a day passes that I do not look at his pictures. I always find there a new idea, something different each day . . . I think again of the painter, and I find him a colossus because he was a philosopher . . ."

Gachet described Vincent's love for art, "Love of art is not exact; one must call it faith, a faith that maketh martyrs!" Vincent's sister-in-law described Gachet's attitude toward Vincent as, "A form of worship, touching in its simplicity and sincerity," adding that, "None of his contemporaries had understood him better." So neither Gachet's behavior nor the opinion of those closest at hand support Morgan's suggestion that Gachet demonstrated "despicable greed" following Vincent's death.

I have a feeling that there was no intervention which could have prevented Vincent's suicide. Theo was terminally ill at the time, in fact, died six months after Vincent. When a symbiotic relationship such as that which existed between the two brothers is severed by the death of one, the other often dies soon thereafter. Only if both had been in good physical and mental health would their lives have been prolonged, but Theo's health was in the terminal stages; thus, Vincent's death was almost inevitable, so I do not believe Vincent was killed by his doctor.

VIRGINIA'S DOCTORS

As mentioned earlier, van Gogh received surprisingly good medical care, even by modern standards, and this is all the more surprising when one considers the rural setting in which this care was provided. On the other hand, it seems that Virginia Woolf's treatment was not appropriate even by the standards of the early 20th Century and it was equally surprising when one considers that London was a leading medical center during this epoch. Her doctors were selected on the basis that they were treating friends and acquaintances "of her class;" thus, she was cared for by physicians, I presume, who were "social" doctors rather than those who had the most appropriate medical expertise. I wonder what would have happened if early in her illness she could have been under the care of neurologists such as Jackson or Gowers, or later in her life received, if not psychoanalysis, at least psychotherapy under the guidance of the Stracheys who were both early followers of Freud and in her same social orbit.

Virginia did not think much of her doctors, writing, "The doctors call everything nerve exhaustion. So I say, what is nerve exhaustion? And they reply, Ah, that we cannot say." (Chapter 2, reference 4.) Nor did she have much faith in psychotherapy, which she considered rape of the mind. This attitude was not based on ignorance, for the Woolf's Hogarth Press published Freud's collected works and she and Leonard even visited Freud shortly after he escaped to London during the Nazi occupation of Austria. Insight psychotherapy would not have been much help during the height of Virginia's acute agitation, in fact, would have been impossible but, during her convalescence and lucid intervals between attacks such treatment would have been of an inestimable value. Although I have expressed doubts that anything could have saved van Gogh from suicide and also feel the same about Hemingway, I believe that Virginia could have been saved.

How can we explain Virginia's attitude toward her physician, which is in such marked contrast to that of van Gogh and, in fact, to the attitudes of Munch and Strindberg? During the height of her psychosis Virginia was quite paranoid but so were the others. Virginia felt that both her husband Leonard and the doctors were spying on her, talking about her behind her back, and scheming against her, and, in fact, she was right although this was not as malevolent as she thought while psychotic. Virginia is recognized as an early advocate of women's struggle for independence and, as we have noted, so was Mary Lamb almost one hundred years earlier, although this is less generally recognized. This struggle still continues today and has been a slow and torturous process. The "Blue Stockings" of the Victorian Era were far behind their confreres today, but it is important to realize the odds against which intelligent, independent women struggled in order that they might express their creativity. This was true not only for Virginia and Mary but, as we have seen, for Emily Dickinson and Florence Nightingale. Even Virginia's female physician, Dr. Wilberforce, who was caring for her at the time of her suicide, as well as her husband and the male physicians, adopted an extremely paternalistic and condescending attitude towards the "ill" Virginia far in excess of the needs for such even considering the seriousness of Virginia's illness. Virginia's rage against such behavior was obvious only during her illness as reflected by her negative attitude toward Leonard when she would become mute, immobile, refusing to communicate with him, and at times not even recognizing him. To the extent that her novels are autobiographical, Poole points out that this ambivalence was expressed in the conflicts between male and female characters.[23] This would also belie the romanticized version of her marriage proposed by many of her biographers.

Leonard sought consultation with Virginia's doctors regarding her illness even before he became engaged to her. As this was done without her presence and even without her knowledge, this would be, by present standards, psychologically unsound and bound to provide fertile ground for a paranoid attitude. What is even more astounding is that the doctor cooperated, providing a diagnosis and prognosis for Leonard. This must have been unethical even in 1912 and today would be grounds for a malpractice suit. It is no wonder that she believed that Leonard and her physicians were scheming against her.

Virginia's medical regimen was bad, but not all bad. Virginia was supersensitive to outside stimuli and emotionally intense in her creative efforts. This, plus a hectic social life, provided a common sense logic in her doctor's recommendation that she retire to her room and bed, banishing all visitors as well as ceasing active social engagements whenever there were signs of an impending breakdown. Such a regimen must have had considerable value in preventing even more frequent recurrences of her episodic disorder. However, what is good prophylaxis is not necessarily good treatment, so that the proscription of any creative effort during her periods of recovery must have delayed this recovery, at least this is suggested by what we have seen in the treatment of van Gogh and Munch. This must have prolonged her invalidism and probably interfered with her creative output. Fortunately, Virginia did not always adhere to such instructions. We now know that a balanced diet is important in the treatment of the episodic disorders, but that the insistence that Virginia fatten herself by heavy meals and drinking milk between meals ignored Virginia' ectomorphic constitution. Furthermore, as Poole points out, nobody bothered to ask Virginia about her self-image, that being slim was being beautiful while being fat exposed oneself to ridicule. What is surprising, however, is that Virginia did not vociferously express her views to her doctors and friends. She passively resisted, but this was counteracted by forced feedings by her attendants until she became fat and healthy, pleasing both Leonard and her doctors. Her own opinion, that in this state she was disgusting, was not considered. Virginia, who could be so forcefully independent is some ways, was obsequious and dependent in others.

During the bombing of London in World War II, the Woolfs retreated to rural England, making only rare trips back to the city; thus, Virginia was isolated from old friends. The threat of Nazi invasion and Leonard's Jewish origin clouded their future to the extent the they made elaborate plans for a double suicide in such an event. This rural setting must have been particularly difficult for Virginia because, as Poole points out, Leonard and Virginia's view of the world was so disparate, his representing the best of logical positivism while Virginia took a phenomenologic and existential stance. Because of this, communication between the two of them must have been difficult and indeed this was the theme in many of Virginia's novels. What is perplexing is that each read the other's manuscripts and in a sense that these manuscripts expressed their different points of view, one would have thought that this would have encouraged a dialectic discussion which might then have increased the empathy between the two, but at least Virginia seemed to rely on friends, particularly females, to provide such empathy. Virginia needed such companionship because of her insatiable desire for both the mothering and love she received from these female friends. Cut off from these in rural isolation must have left Virginia sad and lonely, which could be tolerated as long as she was writing, but when she finished her novel, *Between The Acts,* she was overwhelmed with the bleakness of her future. She realized quite rightly that even if the Nazi invasion did not come about, the world, and particularly her world, would never be the same after World War II.

Leonard, who recognized the early signs of an impending depression, was not reassured when he and Virginia discussed plans for her new novel. He consulted Dr. Wilberforce, a neighboring friend and female physician, but quite insensitively did not discuss this with Virginia and used the ploy that he had invited Dr. Wilberforce for a social visit, a subterfuge that was soon exposed when the doctor insisted on a physical examination. Virginia panicked in that she feared this was the prelude to another enforced incarceration.

Despite this, Virginia did talk with Dr. Wilberforce and apparently felt better afterwards, perhaps because Dr. Wilberforce was a woman who offered hope for the companionship Virginia had left behind in London. This was a positive sign and perhaps perceived by Dr.Wilberforce as such, so that she reassured a doubting Leonard that Virginia did not need around-the-clock supervision. This, as it proved, was a catastrophic mistake and certainly a risky one in view of Virginia's previous attempts at suicide. If Dr. Wilberforce had been properly informed about Virginia's previous psychiatric history, she might have perceived that Virginia's current behavior was quite different from that during previous suicidal attempts, as Virginia now seemed calm and serene rather than agitated. Such signs are extremely ominous and usually reflect a resolute decision regarding suicide. Planned suicides are much more serious than the impetuous ill-conceived attempts made at the height of overtly psychotic behavior; these ill-timed and ill-conceived efforts are often not successful. We now know from Virginia's letters, just prior to her suicide, that she was hallucinating and, as Nicolsen and Trautmann suggest, had probably been planning suicide for some days.[24]

THE "LISTENING" DOCTORS

If Virginia had been more candid with Dr. Wilberforce the danger would have been recognized, but many years of mishandling her disposition during acute episodes had destroyed her trust even in those she loved. Perhaps Dr. Wilberforce could have more effectively encouraged Virginia's candidness. One vignette suggests how this might have been possible, but it is presented here not so much to criticize Dr. Wilberforce, as hindsight is easy, but to illustrate a point. It is recorded that Virginia said, "I never remember any enjoyment of the body," and Dr. Wilberforce replied, "What exactly do you mean by that?"[23] Regardless of the doctor's tone of voice, this statement is usually perceived by patients as an accusatory comment so shuts off further elaboration. It is like the mother who confronts her "fresh" child with a comment "what exactly do you *mean* by that?" A comment such as "Could you tell me more about that so that I am sure I understand you?" would be more likely to facilitate a continuing self-revelation. The point is that the psychotherapist should not be a "talking" doctor but a "listening" doctor, and apparently Virginia never had a "listening" doctor.* In fact, the modern psychotherapist with an existential bent might say to the patient, "First, let me understand your point of view and your language; that is, put myself in your shoes and see the world through your eyes and then let me show you other possible views of the world."

The listening doctor is important and apparently was a crucial element in Emily Dickinson's recovery. Emily made one of her rare excursions outside the family compound to travel to Boston (and live with relatives) in order to see an opthalmologist regarding her eye trouble. It was the psychotherapy provided by this intuitive doctor that alleviated her symptoms. She lived there three months and saw him several times a week. Catharsis with a sympthetic listening doctor was the essential ingredient in her recovery.[25] Robert Lowell also had a listening doctor, the psychoanalyst Viola Bernard, but it sounds like he did not take this seriously when he said, "Dr. Bernard has decided my dreams are more rewarding than my actuality. This adds great plot, color and imagery to our sessions and seems to remove them for me to the safe and detached world of fiction—my disease in life is something like this."[26] He apparently had little desire to explore the inner workings of his mind, a characteristic typical of manic-depressive patient. It is the euphoric grandiosity of the manic-depressive that leads to this attitude, whereas individuals with the episodic disorders are overwhelmed with anguish—an internal turmoil that demands resolution; hence, they are more cooperative with their physician.

The suicide of Ernest Hemingway is another example of a

---

*This reported interchange sounds "fishy" because one wonders who recorded this interchange. Actually the phrase, "What precisely do you *mean* by that?" was a cliche utilized in the conversations of the Bloomsbury Group who had been members of a secret society at Cambridge, "The Apostles." They were very much influenced by the philosopher G. E. Moore about whom Leonard Woolf said his book *Principia Ethica* "instilled deep into our minds and characters this peculiar passion for truth, clarity, and common sense." In their conversations then, if a statement was made that did not fulfill these criteria, the comment was made, "What exactly do you *mean* by that?" As an aside it was from this same society a generation later that the brilliant young Cambridge Don Anthony Blunt recruited the notorious traitors Guy Burgess, Donald MacLean and Kim Philby. (McDonald, *The Strange Tale of the Traitor-Intellectuals*. Baltimore Evening Sun, Thursday, March 31, 1983.)

suicide that probably could not have been prevented by any
means.[27] Hemingway must have been an introspective and con-
templative man to have become a Nobel laureate in literature.
However, his life style was that of a man of action and so were
most of his characters. Throughout his life he frequently talked
of death and certainly had no hesitation in exposing himself to
the risk of being killed. He once said it was more difficult to live
than to die and frequently talked of suicide. He even taught one
of his wives how she could commit suicide with a shotgun by
resting the butt on the floor, pointing the barrels at one's head
and tripping the trigger with a toe. For one who prized his macho
image, it was easy to predict that he would not grow old gracefully
and because of his prodigious alcoholic intake, his brain might
go before his body. Shortly before his suicide Hemingway sustained severe internal bodily injuries involving liver, spleen, and
kidneys as the result of two plane crashes in Africa. Upon his
return home he felt physically ill and complained that his mind
would not think nor the "creative juices flow." He became de-
spondent, guilty, and paranoid, fearing that he was being followed
by the police. He was obviously arming himself for suicide with
one of his many guns when his wife locked up the ammunition
and guns and flew him in a private plane from his home in
Ketchum, Idaho, to the Mayo Clinic in Rochester, Minnesota,
where he received a thorough medical and psychiatric work-up.
The diagnosis of a major depression was confirmed and he was
treated by electric convulsive therapy (ECT). Within several
months he was discharged home as recovered. I find no mention
of an appropriate plan for outpatient care following his discharge,
but for one as bullheaded as Hemingway this would probably
have not been a successful enterprise. He rapidly relapsed and
had to be hastily returned again by private plane to Rochester.
During a refueling stop he tried to locate a gun in a hangar and
would have walked in front of a landing plane if not restrained.
He received a second course of ECT and was soon judged recovered, although his wife had serious misgivings about whether
he was ready to return home. She proved to be correct as during
the drive back to Ketchum he was agitated because he again felt

he was being followed by the police and threatened with arrest. Within several days he found the keys to the gun closet and early one morning blew his brains out. Like most pessimistic depressed patients he was convinced of his failing physical and mental health, but Hemingway may have been right, and he was certainly not going to allow himself to become a decrepit unproductive invalid. For this reason, I am convinced that no matter how effective his psychiatric regimen, Hemingway would have managed in some way to commit suicide and, in fact, many might agree with his decision regarding this matter. His machismo remained until the end, witness the style of his self-inflicted death.

SELF ANALYSES

We have mentioned that two of our subjects, Munch and Strindberg, seem to have been "cured" of their episodic disorder. These two had friends who were doctors and doctors who became their friends, but it is doubtful whether this is an adequate answer to why they were cured. We also mentioned that both recognized the destructive effect of alcohol and absinthe and both renounced to a greater or lesser extent this indulgence. This probably was responsible for their recovery. This may not be a complete explanation for their cure because there is yet another plausible explanation. Both Munch and Strindberg, as a reflection of their genius, had an uncanny intuitive understanding of the psychological mechanisms behind their behavior years before Freud had published his systematic studies on this process.[21] Munch and Strindberg relentlessly explored the "depths of their soul" as well as early childhood memories and dreams seeking answers for their turmoil. This self-analysis must have played a part in their cure. In both instances they evolved a satisfying solution to their religious and existential perplexities; in finding meaning for themselves, they found meaning in the world. What could be more satisfying and more permanent than this self-healing?

EPILOGUE—MADNESS
AND GENIUS

As originally conceived, this book was to be a clarification of the difference between genius and madness, particularly demonstrating that the insane, while conveying a deviant sense of reality, were quite different from the genius who presented a new or previously unrecognized view of reality. The deviant reality of the mad was thought to be a rigid, stereotypical, confused "unreality," poorly conceptualized and idiosyncratically verbalized. As psychiatrists listen to their psychotic patients they acquire, in time, a capacity to make meaningful connections in the psychotic's ramblings, but these are not startling new revelations and the listener does not experience the excited sense of recognition that Huxley did after reading Darwin's *Origin of the Species,* and exclaimed, "How extremely stupid not to have thought of that."[1] Unlike the genius who fits together what had been disconnected, the psychotic seems to jumble that which to most people is already coherent. The psychotic has difficulty in selecting important detail from the unimportant and confuses the foreground with the background—that is, the "gestalt" or the coherent "whole" such as I suggested characterizes van Gogh's painting "Reminiscence of the North" (pp. 44). In their communications the psychotics abruptly and inappropriately intermingle idiosyncratic personal material with thoughts that have a commonality with all human experience. Creative individuals utilize their personal insights (often regarding their own mental aberrations) in their communications but in doing so attempt to make this meaningful for the "universal mind," while the psychotic does not seem to even be aware that his verbalizations are confusing, rather than clarifying. Often, however, the original discoveries of the genius are not so simply understood. Grappling with the phenomenology of Husserl is an arduous task and only with considerable effort does one discover his meaning and even then his revelations unfold slowly; thus, it is easier for the lazy to dismiss his thoughts as "crazy." Sometimes we may never totally grasp the deeper meaning of the new perspective of the genius, such as Einstein's theory of relativity, but we certainly grasp the implication of Einstein's theory for society, namely, the atomic bomb.

The wife of the Bishop of Worcester (the latter an antagonist of Darwin) when hearing of Darwin's proposal that humans were descendants of the apes said, "My dear let us hope that it is not true, but if it is, let us pray that it will not become generally known."[1] The world might be better today if Einstein's theory had not become generally known—an impossibility of course, but a tactic that society repeatedly attempts—witness the Church's suppression of Galileo and the more recent attempt to legislate against genetic engineering. When the genius first presents his new reality even an intelligent layman may confuse the genius and the insane and it is likely, if we do not approve of what the genius says, that we will dismiss him as mad and thus continue to find comfort in the world as it was previously known.

Psychiatrists identify strongly with their patients, often becoming intense advocates, particularly to counteract society's denigration of the mentally ill. For example, the British psychiatrist Laing[2] has become renowned for his opinion that the schizophrenic break with reality is a constructive creative experience and, in fact, I have reported statements from some of our core subjects which support such a view, but I also report that such breaks with reality at other times have irrevocably terminated creative careers and that our subjects with episodic psychosis were almost never creative during the height of their psychoses, or if they were, the product was inferior to what they created during "normal" interludes. Thus, as Lubin says of Vincent van Gogh, "His case does not aid those who wish to prove that a psychotic man can create great pictures."[3] Madness then in its severe and chronic form permanently terminates creativity while madness in its severe but episodic form temporarily interrupts creativity while insidious madness or madness in remission may enhance creativity.

As my studies progressed I became convinced that at least episodic psychoses not only were compatible with creativity but at times even synergistic with this creativity. Thus, my interest shifted from madness *or* genius to madness *and* genius. There is no reason to believe one must be mad to be a genius but certainly no reason why one could not be mad and still creative. As Barker says, "Having great ideas seems to question whether one is creative or crazy, blessed or damned."[4] I would add that a person may be special just because he is creative and crazy—blessed and damned.

GENIUS—A DESCRIPTION

Looking at the other half of the equation, what are the unique characteristics of the genius? We have mentioned many; some are obvious, such as intelligence and innate skills. Others are not so obvious—for instance, sensitivity leading to a high level of inner turmoil. Another is perseverance often in the face of adversity. This was expressed so well by van Gogh in a letter to Gauguin, "The elan of this bony carcus is such that it goes straight for its goal."[544] Perhaps one of the most important is "passion;" a passion that seems to be the product of an inner conviction that one has something new to give the world or in the more self-serving sense that the world has something new to give to the genius. This may appear to the enthusiastic young psychiatrist as a grandiose delusion of the paranoiac or the manic and, in fact, Munch was labeled a paranoiac by his psychiatric contemporaries. This passsion, however, is also apparent in the neurotically driven, or the intensely ambitious person of eminence. Thus, many of the characteristics attributable to the genius can be observed in the psychotic, neurotic, and "above average" individual.

Pickering[5] says psychoneurosis is passion thwarted while creative work is passion fulfilled. In our core subjects this places the cart before the horse. We see the heightened, even painful perceptiveness, of the outer and inner world which leaves many geniuses with a psychic turmoil that demands attention in the form of some disciplined study of the "soul" or what we would now call the "ego." It is necessary to relieve or at least explain this painful inner turmoil through understanding its origins in one's own personal history. Thus, some of our subjects undertook a self-analysis, considering themselves, as Munch said, a "soul" preparation much as earlier artists used the cadaver as a "body" preparation. The rise of science during the past several centuries, replacing religious explanations such as the "Will of God" made these concerns imperative while the failure of logical positivism to offer satisfying explanations resulted in psychoanalytic, phenomenologic, and existential points of view characteristic of many artists and writers during the last one hundred and fifty years. Explanations, however comforting intellectually, still leave much of the "angst" unrequited; hence, the rise of expressionism at the turn of the century.

Strindberg, in writing about Gauguin, pointed to another seemingly universal aspect of creativity when he said, "Jealous of the Creator (he) makes his own little creation in his free moments," and then Strindberg intuitively saw this as a universal childish trait of the creative person, adding, "The child who takes his toys to pieces in order to make other toys from them."[6] Both the child and the genius have the audacity (or some might say the ignorance) to challenge the Creator through their own creative effort and then persistently say to others, "This is what I see (or do), can't you see (or do) it too?'' Our geniuses not only had this childish audacity but also other childish traits persisting into adulthood—usually at considerable cost to their capacity to cope with the ordinary vicissitudes of life. In fact, many protected their creativity because they established a symbiotic relation with another significant adult who not only looked after their worldly needs but also vicariously lived the life of their genius companion by preserving their creative works for posterity; thus, the companion was assured a place in history which would have been denied without this symbiosis. Again, such dependency is not unique to the genius but also seen in severe neurotic or psychotic individuals. In the case of the mentally disturbed, however, it lacks the mutual rewards of the artistic symbiosis, rather reflecting a parasitic existence which sooner or later destroys one or both of the individuals involved.

GENIUS—A NECESSARY ATTRIBUTE

None of these attributes is sufficient in itself to explain genius and, in fact, I emphasize that such attributes are common to the mentally disturbed, the normal adult, or the child as well. In fact, it is doubtful that all of these together would be sufficient to explain genius. Furthermore, none of these attributes by itself may even be necessary in order to create. The missing ingredient that most closely approximates a necessary attribute of genius is something called the spontaneous thought or action, or as our subjects say the ''inspiration,'' or the ''vision,'' or the ''lucid interval''—a period when previously jumbled concepts and percepts suddenly fit together into a new whole that was not experienced before. In some sense this too is a universal experience. We have all had inspirational ideas and then rushing to report our discovery, to our chagrin, learn that others have thought of our inspirational idea before. Nevertheless, if we have a particular talent in communication and if society is suddenly ''ripe'' for fully appreciating our new discovery we may receive recognition even though our discovery is not entirely original. Freud did not discover the unconscious but gave it a new meaning and could convey this meaning to a world that was, by and large, ready to accept his concept of the unconscious.

The inspirational thought has become apocryphal in describing the genius, particularly the scientific genius. Every school child has a picture of Archimedes running through the streets of Syracuse shouting "Eureka," having jumped from his bath with the startling discovery that his body displaces its own volume of water. There is the story of Newton's inspiration for gravity when hit on the head by the falling apple, or what is probably more realistic, Kenneth Kekulé, in ruminating about the molecular structure of the stable six carbon benzene molecule, dreamt of a snake swallowing its tail and so discovered the benzene ring. What characterizes these inspirational thoughts is that a knowledgeable individual has been ruminating about a problem and then in a state of relaxed free association a jumble of ideas, as if in a dream, all fit together. Again, this is an experience that many of us have had. Furthermore, in the same state of relaxed free floating semiconsciousness, just before we go to sleep or as we wake up, we have been aware of other sensations such as a sudden thump in the head, a pop in the ears, a flash of brilliant light, or a violent jerk of the body. These sensations are directly and obviously associated with bursts of excessive neuronal discharges in the brain and suggest that these excessive neuronal discharges could also be associated with the inspirational thought as well. Thus, the most startling thesis of this book is that these inspirational thoughts are associated with bursts of nerve activity. Thus, I propose that at least often if not always, the inspired insights are associated with mini-fits and such mini-fits have adaptive value; hence, the correlation between storms of electrical activity in the brain and "brainstorms."

I have already mentioned the kindling phenomenon which lowers seizural thresholds in the brain and thus leads to epilepsy, but this process may have adaptive value as well. The kindling phenomenon, as studied in animals, shows that if the animal is electrically stimulated by even subthreshold levels of current, that is, current so low that the neurons do not discharge, in time there develops an increase in the sensitivity so that the original subthreshold current comes to induce electrical discharges in these nerves. Is this a stage when the human animal has a high potential for inspired creative thought but also may be developing an increased risk for spread of these nerve discharges so that the individual tips from creative spontaneity into intense dysphoric emotions and impulsive acts and if the nerve discharge spreads even further the individual is precipitated into an acute psychotic episode or even overt generalized seizures? Animal experiments to support such a concept are difficult to design, but in brief this is the underlying theme of this work. Its value, of course, rests on whether it is a hypothesis that can be tested.

TESTING THE HYPOTHESES

In studying the brain mechanisms and behavior it is hard to imagine the simple crucial experiment of the type Otto Loewi literally dreamt up over sixty years ago regarding the proof of chemical mediation of nerve transmission. Circumstantial evidence suggested this to physiologists of his day because nerve stimulation induced the same organ reactions in the body as did the chemicals noradrenaline and acetylcholine, both known to be present in the body, so it was hypothesized that these chemicals could be essential elements in nerve transmission. The crucial experiment, allegedly revealed to Loewi in a dream, was to connect a dissected nerve-heart preparation of the frog in series with another nerve-heart preparation. He then electrically stimulated the nerve in the first preparation and this slowed the heart as was commonly known. The second preparation was connected to the first in such a way that only the fluid that surrounded the first heart flowed into the fluid surrounding the second or unstimulated preparation, but this heart too slowed in a manner similar to the first, proving that a chemical released into the fluid at the stimulated nerve mediated this slowing. The technical and theoretical simplicity of this experiment reflects the beauty of the inspirational idea, but can such a crucial experiment be designed to prove our present hypothesis, or for that matter many other hypotheses on mind-brain relations? For example, the neurophysiologist Ralph Gerard proposed several decades ago the hypothesis that for every twisted thought there was a twisted molecule. The crucial experiment to prove such a hypothesis still escapes us not because we have any lack of available geniuses, but because we lack the appropriate new knowledge and sophisticated investigative technology necessary before creative scientists can prove such a hypothesis.

The complexity of such an enterprise is reflected in the fact that the number of chemical neurotransmitters or neuron modulators has increased from the two in Loewi's day to over twenty today. Factors which involve these chemical transmitters include synthesis of the chemical transmitter within the nerve cell itself, extrusion from the nerve, hydrolysis—that is, deactivation in the synaptic cleft (the border between the two neurons), and the number of available receptors on the second nerve that the first was to influence. Furthermore, there are feedback mechanisms to the first nerve controlling the synthesis of the neurotransmitter within the cell and feedback to the second nerve causing a proliferation of transmitter receptor sites. There is also a balancing between the nerves of one chemical type and the nerves of another chemical type. There are complex transportation systems within the cell body itself, a study that has opened the new speciality, cell biology.

Classical investigative techniques of staining brain sections of post mortem brain tissue, counting cells, or making lesions with a knife, are not up to the task of discriminating clinically significant dysfunction of nerve transmitters. Meaningful identification of brain lesions before death by x-ray or by brain biopsy is dangerously intrusive, or lacking in the specificity necessary to be of clinical value. New techniques, however, applicable to animals and/or humans, have already proven they can identify crucial biochemical disorders for certain brain diseases and sometimes this has been responsible for the discovery of specific therapeutic interventions. These new techniques have been useful for instance in the organic disorders of the central nervous system that show histologic (cell) abnormalities, such as Parkinson's disease and Huntington's chorea, both movement disorders, and Alzheimer's disease (presenile and senile dementia). For example, in the study of Alzheimer's disease, advances in our knowledge have been obtained by inducing discrete chemical lesions, the chemicals introduced by micropipets through stereotaxic equipment (see p. 211). This destroys the nerve cells in the immediate vicinity without effecting the neurons that are just "passing through." Biochemical markers within the nerve cells specific for a neurotransmitter can now be located through the very sensitive immunocytochemical techniques* so that with a combination of the two techniques one can make specific lesions of cells of one type of neurotransmitter—while leaving the cells with a different transmitter mechanism intact. This is a much more sensitive way to map the brain that the older technique of grossly cutting nerves and then looking for cellular degeneration. Using the analogy of a road map (which we will use again later), the old techniques gave a road map with all the roads identified by black lines. Now we can map the brain and the roads will be multi-colored (red, blue, yellow, etc.), each color reflecting nerves that perform via an identifiable and distinct chemical transmitter. Using such techniques in studying Alzheimer's disease, it could be determined that there were specific dysfunctions of nerves whose transmission was mediated by acetylcholine and furthermore that these nerve cells were particularly located sub-

---

*This refers to a number of variations of a technique which gives us the ability to identify the neurotransmitter's characteristic of a cell. An animal is injected with a chemical (antigen) that is important in the metabolism (often the synthesis) of given neurotransmitter—the cells containing that transmitter develop antibodies to the injected antigen. These cells are studied through the microscope after they have been washed first with antigen (original chemical) and again with the anitbody that has been made detectable—e.g., florescent. As the antigen and antibody fit like a lock and key they indicate cells which contain the specific transmitter substance. The binding, then, is antibody (formed in the live animal)—antigen—antibody (the latter two added to the brain slice) hence, this is often referred to as the "sandwich" technique.

cortically in two cell concentrations.[7,8] Thus, the studies on Alzheimer's disease provide the first example of a major disorder of higher cortical function in which transmitter defined neuronal pathways are identified as dysfunctional and then it was shown that the same dysfunction occurred in at least two other types of dementia. Thus, we may be able to identify "the crooked molecule." However, we also have to identify the crooked thought and despite the intricacies of the biochemistry of the nervous system it may be harder to classify and describe these crooked thoughts. The demented thought (or lack of thought) may be easy to identify, but the innovative thought is more elusive even than some of our chemical interactions and, in fact, many believe the project of correlating crooked thoughts and crooked molecules is a futile enterprise.

THE CRUCIAL EXPERIMENT

In attempting a study of mind-brain relations, scientists must take a stance such as Karl Popper proposes,[9] recognizing that a hypothesis is a provisional conjecture that will always remain so. The strength of the hypothesis, what Popper called its "mettle," depends upon the severity of the test to which it has been subjected or in our words, how crucial is the experiment? In mind-brain correlations hypotheses are most often step-by-step approximations but should lead to refinements of each hypothesis as well as identification of rival hypotheses against which the other can be empirically tested; that is, the hypothesis must be falsifiable. In a preliminary evaluation of the "mettle" of a hypothesis one must:

1. Look at the internal consistency of the system.
2. Rule out the merely tautological.
3. Consider the usefulness of the hypothesis in comparison to other theories.
4. Evaluate the heuristic value of the hypothesis in terms of scientific experiments or technologic application.

The contribution of this volume then should be measured against these criteria. First, I have tentatively accepted what is expressed both in folklore as well as early scientific writings, that many men of genius (at least if genius is defined as men of eminence) have had epilepsy or "falling sickness" which suggests a relationship between the two. I expanded this concept to the assumption that many creative individuals have "epilepsy without convulsions" and, in fact, this may be common among creative individuals and in some sense common to all of us. I then identified the geniuses most likely to have had epilepsy without seizures as those whose disorders had a precipitous onset, brief duration, and abrupt remission. These were recurring illnesses with normal interludes—a "paroxysmal" illness and in this sense similar to seizures. Next, I looked for similarities in early warning signals (auras) and the aftermaths between these individuals and epileptic patients. Then I empirically studied a few individuals with electrical probes deep in the brain directly observing the correlations between storms of neuronal activity and observed behavior, as well as self reports of associated feelings. Finally, I compared the creative individuals with episodic disorders to other creative individuals who suffered from mental aberrations that were not episodic.

The crucial experiment, however, would be direct electrical recordings of subcortical structures demonstrating a correlation of excessive neuronal discharges and the creative inspiration. Current technology, that is, the chronic implantation of subcortical electrodes, is too intrusive to be generally applied and a nonintrusive technique such as the clinical electroencephalogram is too crude because it measures only pools of discharging nerves on the surface of the brain and even this recording is "smeared" by the intervening skull and scalp. Sometimes it is not only smeared but completely blocked so the crucial experiment must await new techniques. I do not believe that we will have to wait long.

What are the new techniques for studying mind-brain relations? The most familiar and the one that already has wide clinical usefulness is computerized tomography (CT), which in essence provides us with x-rays of the head, the individual lying on the x-ray table with the necessary machinery rotating around the head (or for that matter around the whole body). This takes multiple x-ray "pictures" each from a slightly different perspective, and then with the aid of a computer makes a composite picture which vastly improves the "contrast" of the body's tissues when compared to conventional x-ray procedures.[10] This is an example of substituting a non-intrusive for an intrusive procedure that was used previously, namely, injecting air into the fluid spaces surrounding the brain tissue and then taking routine x-rays, a procedure that caused considerable discomfort to the patient and was not without danger. This new technique has already proved valuable for identifying subgroups of disorders, such as schizophrenia, which up to now has been considered a "functional" disorder, that is, a disease that is not associated with structural changes in brain tissues. Utilizing the CT, a subgroup of schizophrenics have been identified that shows enlargement of the spaces surrounding the brain due to atrophy of the brain tissue.[11] This type of data is of little usefulness in testing our hypothesis, however. Referring to our road map analogy this is still a road map when we need a picture of the traffic flow, flow patterns of not only what happens on the surface of the brain but in the subsurface areas as well.

Another road map technique is called magnetic resonance imaging (MRI), which is based on the reception of radio frequency signals emitted by certain atoms and molecules of the cellular elements of the brain following the application of a magnetic field to the area under investigation. This will reveal areas of dead cells that heretofore could only be identified at autopsy, but like the CT this probably has only peripheral relevance in testing the hypothesis under discussion because what we need is not a road map but some image of traffic flow patterns.* Another use of magnetic fields is the magneto-encephalogram MEG.[12] Instead of recording directly the electrical activity of the brain

---

*The technology in brain research is developing so rapidly that since this chapter was first written procedures have become available so that the MRI can now monitor the metabolism of nerve cells, thus provide us with traffic flow patterns as well as the road map.

this measures the influence of this electrical activity on a magnetic field which surrounds the head. This increases the sensitivity of recording nerve activity such as transient waves (short spikes) which characterize the brain waves of epileptic patients between seizures but are difficult to detect on the usual EEG.

Another technique is to study evoked potentials (EP) in the brain. Under standard conditions an individual is exposed to auditory, visual, or other stimuli. A computer analysis of the EEG identifies the associated electrical responses in nerve tracks by separating this response from the background noise ("smeared" recording) of the usual EEG. This data combined with a computer analysis of the frequency and power of the EEG wave forms (Neurometrics) has been used in identifying deviations from age-sex matched normal control subjects. This clarifies important left-right asymmetries in the brain as well as subcortical dysfunctions.[13] Such applications have been useful in studying maturational lag in children; learning disabilities; brain damage following strokes or tumors; irreversible brain changes in the brain stem following trauma (leading to ultimate brain death), and perhaps could be useful in identifying the storms of electrical activity deep in the brain that we postulate are associated with not only epilepsy but the inspirational thoughts.

The most promising of all new procedures is the positron emission tomography (PET). This procedure turns the CT scan inside out;[14] that is, instead of shooting x-rays through the head from the outside, the locations and distribution of molecules labeled with radioactive isotopes within the brain are recorded by multiple radiation sensitive detectors outside the head. A computer converts this into two-dimensional "slices" of brain tissue. For example, brain energy, like muscle energy, comes from glucose, so that if the glucose is tagged with radio-isotopes the metabolic activity in the brain can be traced and is visually imaged by color code from white and red for the highest activity through orange, yellow, green, blue, to indigo for the lowest. Other molecules can be labeled to examine other metabolic functions in the brain. Areas of storms of neuronal activity are certainly high energy-using areas so we can localize electrical storms in the brain. Continuing our analogy, this would be a measure of the traffic flow.

In summary then the CT and the MRI image atomic structures. The PET and the biochemical and immunocytochemical procedures mentioned earlier (p. 271) measure chemical nerve transmitter activity while the modifications of the EEG including MEG, and Neurometrics measure rapid electrophysiologic transients reflecting neuronal activity. One of these techniques, or perhaps several in sequence, could provide a rigorous test of our hypothesis that the creative individual may be an individual who has a propensity for excessive neuronal discharges in certain localized areas deep in the brain; thus, in one sense these individuals could be thought of as suffering from focal epilepsy even though in the sense that they do not have characteristic seizures are not considered as epileptic. Furthermore, the hypothesis could be tested as to whether even the average individual may not show such patterns while experiencing the "lucid" cognitive and perceptual experiences which is subjectively similar to the "eureka" experience of the genius.

As I repeatedly emphasized in this book, no neurophysiologic explanation will be sufficient to explain creativity and, in fact, we seem to have come full circle, that is, why do the universally experienced storms in the brain lead to creativity in some individuals but not in others, but then just as Popper proposes, experiments on one hypothesis will lead to new hypotheses to test while striving for a closer approximation to the ever elusive "truth" regarding the relationship between madness, genius, brainstorms, and storms of electrical activity deep in the brain.

CHRONOLOGY
VINCENT VAN GOGH

1853-1868 **Childhood and Early Adolescence**

Born March 3, 1853—Zundert, Holland. Father a minister.
Age 4, Younger brother Theo born.
Age 11-15, Attends boarding school.

1869-1876 **Late Adolescence and Early Adulthood**

Age 16-23, Art dealer at the Hague, Brussels, London and Paris.
Age 20, Falls in love. When rejected, idiosyncracies first appear.
Age 23, Dismissed from job.

1877-1879 **Identity Crisis**

Age 23, "Curate," London. Following in his father's footsteps.
Age 24, Amsterdam to prepare for University. Gives up within year.
Age 25, Brussels. Attends missionary school, but fails.
Age 26, Missionary work with miners at Borinage in Belgium. Again fails.

1880-1885 **Finds Calling as an Artist**

Age 27, Studies drawing and perspective in Brussels.
Age 28, Returns home. Falls in love, again thwarted.
Age 29, Angrily leaves home. Establishes symbiosis with his brother Theo.
Age 30, Lives with prostitute, Sien, for the next one and one-half years.
Age 31, Returns to family home now in Nuenen. Seriously paints.
Age 32, Vincent's father dies. Begins work on his first masterpiece.

1886-1887 Emergence into the Art World

Age 33, Moves to Paris. Exposed to impressionism. Addicted to absinthe.

1888 Feverish Creativity

Age 35, Leaves Paris for Arles. Gauguin joins him in October. December 24th mutilates ear. During 10 months completes over 300 works.

1889-1890 The World of Madness

Age 35-37, Suffers seven transitory psychotic episodes.
Age 36, Voluntarily commits self to asylum at St. Remy.
Age 37, May, leaves asylum for Auvers, cared for by Dr. Gachet.
Shoots self July 27, 1890 and dies in his brother's arms two days later. Six months later, brother Theo dies.

CHRONOLOGY
VIRGINIA WOOLF

1882-1895 An Unusual Child

January 25, 1882, Birth—Second marriage for both parents. Three maternal half sibs (Duckworths), one paternal half sib, three full sibs. Age 13, Mother dies, three months later first episode. Desire to write.

1896-1904 Caring for Father

Age 13-22, Virginia and sister nurture a demanding father.
Age 22, Father dies. Three months later second episode.

1905-1915 Birth of the Author

Age 23, Founding of the Bloomsbury Group.
Age 25, Sister marries—Virginia begins first novel *The Voyage out*.
Age 30, Marries Leonard Woolf
Age 31, Another episode.
Age 33, First novel published—another episode.

1916-1923 Critical Acclaim

Age 38, Novel *Night and Day* published.

Age 40, Novel *Jacobs Room* published, another episode.
Age 41, Still another episode.

1924-1929   Healthy and Productive

Age 43, *Mrs. Dalloway* published.
Age 45, *To the Light House* published.
Age 46, *Orlando* published.

1930-1938   Recurrent Illnesses, But Productive

Age 47, Another episode, *Room of One's Own* published.
Age 48, Fainted, ill for ten days.
Age 49, Ill again.
Age 50, Finishes *The Waves,* but ill again.
Age 51-56, *Flush, The Years, Three Guineas* published.

1939-1941   End of World as Virginia Knew It

Age 57, Moves from London to country.
Age 59, Finishes *Between the Acts.*
March 28, 1941, Drowns herself.

CHRONOLOGY
EDVARD MUNCH

1863-1879 Youth

Birth, December 12, 1863. Father Army doctor.
Second of five children.
Age 1, Family moves from Löten to Christiania
(Oslo) Norway.
Age 4, Mother dies of TB.
Age 13, Sister dies of TB.
Age 15, Enters technical college.
Age 16, Gives this up to paint seriously.

1880-1889 Meteoric Entrance to World of the Artist

Age 17, Enters School of Design.
Age 19, Works first exhibited.
Age 20, Receives grant for further studies.
Age 21, Paints three major works—*The Sick Child,
The Morning After* and *Puberty.*
Age 25, First one-man exhibit (Oslo). Father dies
in November.

1890-1897 Secession from Conventional Art

Age 28, Invited to exhibit in Berlin. Caused violent
protests.
Age 29, Painted *The Scream.* Lives mostly in Germany.

Age 31, Starts etchings, lithographs and woodcuts.

1898-1907   Illness, Travel and Poverty

Age 35, Sanitarium in Norway.
Age 36, Travels Berlin, Florence, Rome, then sanitarium in Switzerland.
Age 38-43, Irritable, explosive, fights with friends.

1908-1944   Illness with Cure

Age 44, Enters Dr. Jacobson's clinic (Copenhagen) in October, 1908 and leaves May 1909 for Oslo.
Age 45, Actively productive for remainder of his life.
Age 48, First exhibit in U.S. One year later exhibits in Armory Show.
Age 53, Unveiling of Murals in University banquet hall (Oslo).
Age 74, Works in German museums confiscated by Nazis.
Age 80, Dies January 23, 1944.

CHRONOLOGY AUGUST STRINDBERG

1849-1876 **Developmental Years**

Birth January 22, 1849, Stockholm. Father a steamship agent, mother a servant. Strindberg had six living siblings, two with mental problems.
Age 12-15, Religious guilt.
Age 18, Entered University, but left without a degree.
Age 22-28, Thought he was going mad, feeble suicide attempt. Writing plays, acting.
Age 23, Thought he was a failure as an author, so tried painting, had hallucinations.
Age 25, Worked at Royal Library.

1877-1893 **Paranoia**

Age 28, Marriage to Siri—episode of paranoid mania and pathological jealousy.
Age 30, Published *Red Room*.
Age 41, Sought a "Certificate of Sanity."
Age 43, Path of Munch and Strindberg cross in Berlin—blackouts.
Age 44, Second marriage to Frieda Uhl.
Age 45, "Scientific" experiments.

1894-1897 **Psychoses "The Inferno"**

Age 45-48, Five psychotic episodes in 33 months.

1898-1912 Cure

Age 49, Published *To Damascus*
Age 52, Married third time, Harriet Bosse.
Age 55, Divorced.
Age 60, In love with Fanney Falkner, 19 year old
actress.
Age 63, Died May 15, 1912.

CHRONOLOGY
MARY LAMB

1764-1795 Early Symptoms

Born December 3, 1764, one of three surviving children, a brother one year older and Charles 10 years her junior. Father was the valet and clerk for a London lawyer.
Age ? Nervous breakdown during childhood.
Age 30, Mary's first identified breakdown.
Age 31, Charles' only hospitalization six weeks duration.

1796-1804 The Tragedy and Four Relapses

Age 32, Mary stabs mother in the heart, sent to asylum.
Age 33, Made a ward of brother Charles.
Age 33-39, Four confinements.

1805-1817 Creative Period

Age 40-45, Mary and Charles publish jointly *Tales of Shakespeare* and *Mrs. Leicesters' School.*
Age 45, Mary publishes *Poetry for Children.*
Age 53, Publishes *"Embroidery"*—ten episodes during these years.

1818-1833   Both Lambs Ill

Age 55-68, Mary suffered eleven episodes.
Age 60, Charles retires from East India
Company—three months later ill.
Age 63, Charles ill again.

1834-1847   Chronic Illness

Age 69, Charles dies.
Age 69-77, Seven illnesses. Several lasting for many
months.
Age 77-82, Three episodes, but senile between ep-
isodes.
Age 78, Last known letters written by Mary.
Age 83, Dies May 20, 1847.

REFERENCES
AND
BIBLIOGRAPHY

Prologue
1. Monroe, R. R. The Episodic Psychoses of Vincent van Gogh. *J. Nerv. Ment. Dis.*, 166:7, 480-488, 1978.
2. Monroe, R. R. *Episodic Behavioral Disorders*. Cambridge, Mass.: Harvard University Press, 1970.
3. Barker, W. *Brainstorms: A Study of Human Spontaneity*. New York: Grove Press, 1968.
4. Heath, R. G. *Studies in Schizophrenia*. Cambridge, Mass.: Harvard University Press, 1954.
5. Goddard, G. U. and Morrell, F. Chronic progressive epileptogeneses induced by focal electrical stimulation of the brain. *Neurol.*, 21:393, 1971.
6. Monroe, R. R. Limbic Ictus and Atypical Psychoses. *J. Nerv. Ment. Dis.*, 170:711-712, 1981.
7. Poole, Roger *The Unknown Virginia Woolf*. Cambridge, Mass:, Cambridge University Press, 1972.
8. Monroe, R. R. DSM III Style Diagnoses of the Episodic Disorders. *J. Nerv. Ment. Dis.*, 170:664-669, 1982.

Section I - Chapter 1
1. van Gogh, V. *The Completed Letters of Vincent van Gogh, Vols. I, II and III*. New York Graphic Society, New York, 1959. (Letter numbers in the text apply to this reference.)
2. Tralbaut, M. E. *Vincent van Gogh*. New York: Viking Press, 1969.
3. Monroe, R. R. The Episodic Psychoses of Vincent van Gogh. *J. Nerv. & Ment. Dis.*, 166:480-488, 1978.
4. Nagera, H. *Vincent van Gogh: A Psychological Study*. London: George Allen and Unwin, 1967.

5. Lubin, A. J. *Stranger on the Earth*. New York: Holt, Rinehart and Winston, 1972.
6. Westermann Holstijn, A. J. The psychological development of Vincent van Gogh. *J. Ment. Sci.*, 103: 1-17, 1957.
7. Perry, I. H. Vincent van Gogh's Illness. *Bull. Hist. Med.*, 21:146-172, 1947.
8. Welsh-Ovcharov, Bogomila (Editor) *van Gogh in Perspective*. Englewood Cliffs, New Jersey: Prentice Hall, 1974.
9. Evensen, Hans *Die Geisteskrankeit Vincent van Goghs "Zeithschreft fur Psychiatrie USW."* Drack und Verlag von Walter de Gruger & Co., Bd 89 Berlin W. 10.
10. Wilkie, Denneth *The van Gogh Assignment*. New York: Paddington Press Ltd., 1978.
11. de la Faille, J. B. *The Works of Vincent van Gogh*. New York: William Morrow and Company, 1970.
12. Hemphill, R. E. The Illness of Vincent van Gogh. *Proceeding of the Royal Society of Medicine*, 54:27-32, 1961.
13. Monroe, R. R. *Episodic Behavioral Disorders*. Cambridge, Mass.: Harvard University Press, 1970.
14. Temkin, O. *The Falling Sickness. 2nd Ed, Baltimore, Maryland: Johns Hopkins Press, 1971.*
15. Bett, W. R. *Vincent van Gogh (1853-90) Artist and Addict. The British Journal of Addiction,* 51:7-12, 1954.
16. Saintsbury, G. *Notes for a Cellar-Book*. London: Macmillan, 1920.
17. Zolotow, Maurice "Absinthe" *Playboy,* 171-178, June, 1971.
18. Ferguson, M. *The Brain Revolution*. Traplinger, New York: 1973.
19. Barker, W. *Brainstorms: A Study of Human Spontaneity*. New York: Grove Press, 1968.
20. Canaday, John. *Mainstream of Modern Art,* New York: Simon and Schuster, 1959.

Section I - Chapter 2

1. Bell, Quentin: *Virginia Woolf A Biography*. New York: Harcourt Brace Jovanovich, 1972.
2. Poole, Roger: *The Unknown Virginia Woolf*. Cambridge: Cambridge University Press, 1972.
3. Nicolson, Nigel and Trautmann, Joanne (Ed.): *The Letters of Virginia Woolf*. New York: Harcourt Brace Jovanovich, 1980.
4. Bell, Ann Olivier (Ed.): *The Diary of Virginia Woolf*. New York: Harcourt Brace Jovanovich, 1982.
5. Woolf, Leonard: *The Journey Not the Arrival Matters: An Autobiography of the Years 1939-1969*. New York: Harcourt Brace Jovanovich, 1969.
6. Woolf, Virginia: *Moments of Being: Unpublished Autobiographical Writings*. Edited by Jeanne Schulkind. New York: Harcourt Brace Jovanovich, 1976.
7. Woolf, Virginia: *Mrs. Dalloway*. London: Hogarth Press, 1925.
8. Woolf, Virginia: *Between the Acts*. New York: Harcourt Brace Jovanovich, 1941.

9. Love, Jean O.: *Virginia Woolf: Sources of Madness and Art.* Berkley: University of California Press, 1977.
10. Nobel, Joan Russell: *Recollections of Virginia Woolf.* London: Peter Owen, 1972.
11. Rosenthal, M. *Virginia Woolf.* New York: Columbia Univ. Press, 1979.

Section I - Chapter 3

1. Heller, Rinehold: Love as a Series of Paintings and a Matter of Life and Death: Edvard Munch in Berlin 1892-1895, Epilogue 1902, pp. 87-108. In *Edvard Munch: Symbols & Images,* Washington, D. C. National Gallery of Art, 1978.
2. Woll, Gerd: *The Tree of Knowledge of Good and Evil,* pp. 229-247. In *Edvard Munch: Symbols & Images,* Washington, D. C. National Gallery of Art, 1978.
3. Hodin, J.P.: *Edvard Munch.* New York: Praeger Publishers, 1972.
4. Lathe, Carla: *Edvard Munch and His Literary Associates: An Essay on the Interpretation of Art and Literature Around the Turn of the Century,* Norwich England, Library University of East Anglia, 1979.
5. Heller, Rinehold: Edvard Munch's "Night" The Esthetic of Decadence in the Context of Biography, *Art Magazine,* pp. 80-105, October, 1978.
6. Heller, Rinehold: *Edvard Munch: The Scream.* New York: Viking Press, 1972.
7. Steinberg, Stanley and Weiss, Joseph: The Art of Edvard Munch and Its Function in His Mental Life. *Psychoanalytic Quarterly,* 23:409-423, 1954.
8. Stange, Ragna The Aging Munch: New Creative Power. In *Edvard Munch: Symbols & Images,* pp. 77-85, Washington D.C. National Gallery of Art 1978.
9. Monroe, R. R.: *Episodic Behavioral Disorders.* Cambridge, Mass.: Harvard University Press, 1970.
10. Eggum, Arne: The Landscape Motif in Munch's Art, pp. 246-251. In *Munch's Exhibition,* Tokyo, The National Museum of Modern Art, 1981.
11. Eggum, Arne and Börnslad, Sissel: Edvard Munch Alpha and Omega, Oslo The Munch Museum, 1981.

Section I - Chapter 4

1. Strindberg, August: *The Confession of a Fool* (Translated by E. Schleussner), London: Latimer, 1912.
2. Lidz, Theodore: August Strindberg: A Study in the Relationship Between His Creativity and Schizophrenia. *International Journal of Psychoanalysis,* 45:399-406, 1964.
3. Anderson, E. W.: Strindberg's Illness. *Psychological Medicine,* 1:104-117, 1971.
4. Harding, Gosta: Comments on Dr. Lidz's Paper. *International Journal of Psychiatry, 406-410, 1964.*

5. *Campbell, G.A.: Strindberg.* New York: Haskel House Publishers, 1933.
6. Brandell, Gunnar: *Strindberg in Inferno.* Cambridge, Mass.: Harvard University Press, 1974.
7. Sprinchorn, Evert (Ed.): *Inferno, Alone and Other Writings by August Strindberg.* New York: Anchor Books, 1968.
8. Strindberg, August: *Six Plays of Strindberg.* Translated by Elizabeth Sprigge. Garden City, N.J.: Doubleday Anchor Books, 1955.
9. Temkin, O. *The Falling Sickness.* 2nd Ed. Baltimore, Maryland: Johns Hopkins Press, 1971.

Section I - Chapter 5

1. Anthony, Catherine: *The Lambs: A Story of Pre-Victorian England.* New York: Alfred A. Knopf, 1945.
2. Marks, Edwin W. (Ed.) - *Letters by Charles and Mary Lamb.* Ithica, N.Y.: Cornell Unversity Press, 1975.
3. Ashton, Helen & Davies, Catherine: *I Had A Sister: A Study of Mary Lamb, Dorothy Wordsworth, Caroline Herschel, Cassandra Austin.* London: Lovat Dickson, 1937.
4. Monroe, R.R.: DSM III Style Diagnoses of the Episodic Disorders. *J. Neuro. Ment. Dis.,* 170-664-669, Nov. 1982.
5. Richter, Curt Paul - *Biological Clocks in Medicine and Psychiatry.* Springfield, Illinois: Charles C. Thomas, 1965.
6. Ross, Ernest C.: *The Ordeal of Brigit Elia.* Norman, Oklahoma: Univ. of Oklahoma Press, 1940.

Section II - Chapters 6 - 10

1. Hamilton, Ivan. *Robert Lowell: a Biography.* New York: Random House 1982.
2. Baker, Carlos. *Ernest Hemingway: a life story.* New York: Charles Scribner's Sons, 1969.
3. Cornell, Julien. *The Trial of Ezra Pound: A Documented Account of the Treason Case by the Defendant's Lawyer.* New York: John Day Co., 1966.
4. Kapp, Frederick T. Ezra Pound's Creativity and Treason: Clues from his Life and Work. *Comprehensive Psychiatry,* 9:414-427, 1968.
5. Norman, Charles. *The Case of Ezra Pound.* New York: Funk and Wagnalls, 1968.
6. Wing, J.K. *Reasoning About Madness.* New York: Oxford University Press, 1978.
7. Stock, Noel. *The Life of Ezra Pound.* New York: Pantheon Books, 1970.
8. Sheon, Aaron, *Monticelli: His Contemporaries and His Influence.* Pittsburgh: Museum of Art, 1978.
9. Cody, John. *After Great Pain: The Inner Life of Emily Dickinson.* Cambridge Mass.: Harvard Univ. Press, 1971.
10. Kubie, L. S. *Neurotic Distortions of the Creative Process.* Lawrence, Kansas: Univ. of Kansas Press, 1958.

11. Catalog - Collection L'Art Brut. Introduction by Jean Dubuffet and Michel Thevory. Chateau De Beaulieu 11, Av. Des Bergieres 1004 Lausanne, Suisse, 1976

12. Unger, Richard *Hölderlin's Major Poetry: The Dialectics of Unity.* Bloomington, Ind.: Indiana University Press, 1975.

13. Buckle, Richard. *Nijinsky,* New York: Simon and Shuster, 1971.

14. Pickering, G. *Creative Malady.* New York: Dell Publishing, 1974.

15. Jones, E. *The Life and Work of Sigmund Freud.* 3 Volumes. New York: H. Wolff, 1953.

16. Clark, R. W. *Einstein: The Life and Times.* New York: World Publishing Company, 1971.

17. Frank, P. *Einstein: His Life and Times.* Translated by George Rosen. New York: Knopf, 1947.

Section III - Chapters 11-13

1. Monroe, R. R. *Episodic Behavioral Disorders.* Cambridge, Mass.: Harvard University Press, 1970.

2. Boss, M. *Psychoanalysis and Daseinanalysis.* New York: Basic Books, 1963.

3. Heath, H. G. *Studies in Schizophrenia.* Cambridge, Mass.: Harvard University Press, 1954.

4. Goddard, G. U. and Morrell, F. Chronic Progressive Epileptogeneses induced by focal electrical stimulation of the brain. *Neurol.* 21:393, 1971.

5. Heath, H. G., Monroe, R. R. and Mickle, W. A. Stimulation of the amygdala nucleus in a schizophrenic patient. *Amer. J. Psychiat.,* 111:862-863, 1955.

6. Heath, R. G. Electric self-stimulation of the brain in man. *Amer. J. Psychiat.,* 120:571-577, 1963.

7. Heath, R. G. Pleasure and brain activity in man. *J. Nerv. and Ment. Dis.,* 154:3-18, 1972.

8. Monroe, R. R. Heath, R. G. Mickle, W. A. and Llewellyn, R.C. Correlations of rhinencephalic electrograms with behavior. A study on humans under the influence of LSD and Mescaline. *EEG Clin. Neurophysiol.,* 9:623-642, 1957.

9. Monroe, R. R. The episodic psychoses of Vincent van Gogh. *Nerv. and Ment. Dis.,* 166:480-488, 1978.

10. Lesse, H., Heath, R. G., Mickle, W. A., Monroe, R. R. and Miller, W. H. Rhinencephalic activity during thought. *J. Nerv. and Ment. Dis.,* 122:433-440, 1955.

11. Martin, R. B. *Tennyson: The Unquiet Heart.* New York: Oxford University Press, 1980.

12. Barker, Wayne *Brainstorms: A Study of Human Spontaneity.* New York: Grove Press, 1968.

13. van Gogh, V. *The Complete Letters of Vincent van Gogh.* 3 Volumes. New York: New York Graphic Society, 1959.

14. de la Faille, J. G. *The Works of Vincent van Gogh.* New York: William Morrow and Company, 1970.

15. Huxley, Aldous *The Doors of Perception.* New York: Harper and Row, 1954.
16. Szasz, T. *The Myth of Mental Illness.* New York: Harper and Row, 1961.
17. Temkin, O. *The Falling Sickness.* 2nd Ed. Baltimore: Johns Hopkins Press, 1971.
18. Taylor, James (Ed.) *Selected Writings of John Hughlings Jackson.* 2 Volumes. New York: Basic Books, 1958.
19. Morgan, Ted *The Strange End of Vincent van Gogh. Horizons,* Autumn, 1974.
20. Hirsh, William *Genius and Degeneration: A Psychological Study.* New York: D. Appleton and Company, 1896.
21. Breuer, Joseph and Freud, Sigmund *Studies in Hysteria.* New York: Nervous and Mental Disease, Monograph, 1947.
22. Tralbaut, Marc (Ed.) *Vincent van Gogh.* New York: Viking Press, 1969.
23. Poole, Roger *The Unknown Virginia Woolf.* Cambridge, Mass.: Cambridge University Press, 1978.
24. Nicolson, Nigel and Trautmann, Joanne (Eds.) *The Letters of Virginia Woolf.* New York: Harcourt, Brace and Jovanovich, 1980.
25. Cody, John *After Great Pain: The Inner Life of Emily Dickinson.* Cambridge, Mass: Harvard University Press, 1971.
26. Hamilton, Ian *Robert Lowell: A Biography.* New York: Random House, 1982.
27. Baker Carlos *Ernest Hemingway: A Life Story.* New York: Charles Scribner and Sons, 1969.

EPILOGUE

1. Darwin, Charles. *Origin of the Species* - Forward by Patricia G. Horan, New York: Avenel Books, 1979.
2. Laing, Ronald D. *The Divided Self: A Study of Sanity and Madness,* Chicago: Quadrangle, 1960.
3. Lubin, A. J. *Strangers on the Earth,* New York: Holt Rinehart and Winston, 1972.
4. Barker, W. *Brainstorms: A Study of Human Spontaneity,* New York: Grove Press, 1968.
5. Pickering, G. *Creative Malady,* New York: Delta, 1974.
6. Sprinchorn, E. (Ed.) *Inferno, Alone and Other Writings by August Strindberg,* New York: Anchor Books, 1968.
7. Coyle, J. T., Price, D. L., and Delong, M. R. Alzheimer's Disease: A Disorder of Cortical Cholenergic Innervation, *Science,* 219:1184-89, March 1983.
8. Kolata, Gina. Clues to Alzheimer's Disease Emerge, *Science* 210:941-42, February, 1983.
9. Popper, Karl. *The Logic of Scientific Discovery,* New York: Harper & Row, 1968.
10. Pearlson, G.D. Veroff, A.E. and McHugh, P.R. The Use of Computer Tomography in Psychiatry, *Johns Hopkins Med. Journ.* 149:194-202, 1981.

11. Buchsbaum, M.S. The Mind Readers. *Psychology Today,* July 1983, pp. 58-62.
12. Hughes, J. R. et al. Relationship of the Magneto-encephalogram to the electroencephalogram. *EEG and Clin. Neurophys.* 40:261-278, 1976.
13. John, E. Roy et al. Neurometrics, *Science,* 196:1393-1409, June, 1977.
14. Bunney, William E. Jr., Garland, Blynn and Buchsbaum, M. Advances in the Use of Visual Imaging: Technique in Mental Illness. *Psychiatric Annals,* 13:420-426, May 1983.

Author Index

SUBJECT INDEX

Absinthe 4, 27, 28, 36, 37, 76; Creativity 40; Hemingway 140; Monticelli 154; Strindberg 109, 110; van Gogh 39; see also Thujone
Abstinence 233, 261
Alcoholism 52, 76, 82, 91, 93, 94, 140
"Almond Tree Branch in Blossom" 44
"Alpha and Omega" 96; "Alpha's Progeny" (Munch), fig. 8, p. 95
Asch., Dr. 104
"Ashes" (Munch) 88
Archimedes 268
Artaud, A., 239
Art: mad and sane 187, 189
Astrup, Dr. C. Ack 1
Auden, W. H. 149
Aura 107
Aussoleil, Dr. 242, 243
Authorship, denial of 111, 112, 185, 186, 187, 220
Autopathography 5
Awareness, levels of 1, 13, 63, 119, 209
Awareness, self 1, 75, 99; see Self-analysis

Baltimore Museum of Art Ack 4
Bankhead, W. 157
Barker, Dr. W. 224, 225
Bell, Clive 56
Bell, Quentin 66, 68
Bergson, H. "Duration" 222
Bernard, E. 25

Bernard, Dr. V. 135, 259
Biologic markers, 228
Biopsychosocial perspective 8, 90, 153
Birnbaum, Dr. K. 108
Bishop of Worcester 264
Black Pig 81, 103, 104; see Zum Schwarzen Ferkel
Bleuler, Dr. E. 192
Bloomsbury Group 56, footnote 259
Böe, A., Ack 2
Borderline syndrome 178, 179
Botticelli, S. 221
Brainstorms 2, 131, 219-225, 268, 276; see Barker, Storms in the brain
Brain wave, see Electroencephalogram
Braque, G. 221
Brentano, F. 209
Briquet, P. 234
Bromide 33
Browning, E.B. 195, 196
Byrd, H. 151
Byron, G. 234

Caesar 234
Cailleux, Jean, Ack 2
Caligula 129, 234
Camphor 35
Carboni, R. 187
Chagall, M. 186
Charbonniers' Collection 159
Charcot, Dr. J. M. 234

THE COLLECTED PAPERS
OF MILTON H. ERICKSON
ON HYPNOSIS

Edited by Ernest L. Rossi

Erickson, a pioneer in the uses of trance for psychotherapeutic purposes, has written in a style that is as original and personal as his technique. These four volumes (edited by a collaborator) are fascinating to read or just browse through.

Psychology Today

Erickson succeeded in becoming the foremost exponent of hypnosis in the Western world. He influenced more professionals to pursue hypnosis as a study than any other person in modern times. He was an indefatigable worker, a stimulating teacher, and a gifted writer whose style was at the same time lucid, instructive, exciting, and entertaining. These qualities become apparent in the present collection, and the editor has done a splendid job collating and organizing Erickson's papers, as well as resurrecting and introducing some previously unpublished material.

American Journal of Psychiatry

VOLUME I: **THE NATURE OF HYPNOSIS AND SUGGESTION**
A first-hand demonstration of Erickson's development of a nonauthoritarian approach to hypnotic suggestion.
570 pages. 0-8290-1206-0 $24.95

VOLUME II: **HYPNOTIC ALTERATION OF SENSORY, PERCEPTUAL**
AND PSYCHOPHYSIOLOGICAL PROCESSES
Describes actual mind/body mechanisms involved in the induction of an hypnotic state. 367 pages. 0-8290-1207-9 $19.95

VOLUME III: **HYPNOTIC INVESTIGATION OF PSYCHODYNAMIC**
PROCESSES
Explores the psychodynamic context underlying the development of hypnosis and its approaches to the unconscious.
367 pages. 0-8290-1208-7 $19.95

VOLUME IV: **INNOVATIVE HYPNOTHERAPY**
Presents Erickson's unique approaches in achieving a wide variety of symptom resolution through hypnosis.
561 pages. 0-8290-1209-5 $24.95

MILTON H. ERICKSON received his MD from the University of Wisconsin. He was president of the American Society of Clinical Hypnosis and A Life Fellow of the American Psychiatric Association and the American Psychopathological Association. Dr. Erickson was the founder and editor of the *American Journal of Clinical Hypnosis* and co-author of *Hypnotic Realities, Hypnotherapy, Experiencing Hypnosis,* and *Time Distortion in Hypnosis,* all published by Irvington. He received the Benjamin Franklin Gold Medal of the International Society of Clinical and Experimental Hypnosis.

ERNEST L. ROSSI received his PhD from Temple University. He is a Diplomate in Clinical Psychology, a Jungian analyst, and a pioneer in psychobiological theory. He is co-author of *Hypnotic Realities, Hypnotherapy,* and *Experiencing Hypnosis.*

The Collected Papers of Milton H. Erickson on Hypnosis is also available in a clothbound edition.

IRVINGTON PUBLISHERS, INC.   MC/Visa orders may be
740 Broadway, New York, NY 10003   telephoned to (603) 669-5933.

The Wisdom of Milton H. Erickson
Volume 1, Hypnosis & Hypnotherapy

Ronald A. Havens, Editor

The psychiatrist Milton Erickson was a master hypnotist, capable of inducing trances by the most unexpected means—even a mere hand-shake. Erickson also published numerous books, articles, transcripts, and audiotapes. Erickson's books have sold more than 250,000 copies. *The Wisdom of Milton H. Erickson I: Hypnosis and Hypnotherapy* is the first work to provide a unified survey of the philosophy behind Erickson's techniques.

The material in this volume has been selected from the psychiatrist's lectures, seminars, articles, and books and is carefully organized to offer a clear account of how Erickson conceived of hypnosis, particularly its access to the unconscious and its role in the process of psychotherapy. The reader discovers what hypnosis actually does, explores general considerations on inducing the state, learns specific techniques, and most importantly, comes to understand the contribution that hypnosis can make in the healing or therapeutic process. *The Wisdom of Milton H. Erickson I: Hypnosis and Hypnotherapy* is a valuable guide to the work of one of psychiatry's most original and innovative minds.

...a heroic effort to bring clarity to a hard-to-grasp theory...(This book) is a major reference for students and scholars who want to know what Erickson said and when and where he said it.

Contemporary Psychology

ISBN 0-8290-2413-1 (Paper)
298 pages
$14.95

IRVINGTON PUBLISHERS, INC.
740 Broadway, New York, NY 10003

MC/Visa orders may be telephoned to (603) 669-5933.

The Wisdom of Milton H. Erickson
Volume 2, Human Behavior & Psychotherapy

Ronald A. Havens, Editor

Milton H. Erickson was one of the most creative, dynamic, and effective hypnotherapists and psychotherapists of the twentieth century. Erickson's books have sold more than 250,000 copies. He used unconventional techniques with remarkable success. An indication of the respect Erickson gained from his peers are the words inscribed on his 1976 Benjamin Franklin Gold Medal, the highest award that the International Society of Clinical and Experimental Hypnosis can bestow: "To Milton H. Erickson, M.D.—innovator, outstanding clinician, and distinguished investigator whose ideas have not only helped create the modern view of hypnosis but have profoundly influenced the practice of all psychotherapy throughout the world."

Although he wrote hundreds of papers, articles, and books in his lifetime, Erickson himself never put his techniques and methods into a clear and centralized body of work. *The Wisdom of Milton H. Erickson, II: Human Behavior and Psychotherapy* is an effort to do just that. Along with its companion volume, *The Wisdom of Milton H. Erickson I: Hypnosis and Hypnotherapy*, this book is a collection of Erickson's methods and lessons, including his feelings on the uses of objective observation, the uniqueness of the conscious mind, the realities and abilities of the unconscious mind, the creation and use of a therapeutic environment, and many other aspects of the life and work of this remarkable thinker and teacher.

...a heroic effort to bring clarity to a hard-to-grasp theory...(This book) is a major reference for students and scholars who want to know what Erickson said and when and where he said it.

Contemporary Psychology

ISBN 0-8290-2414-X (Paper)
258 pages
$14.95

IRVINGTON PUBLISHERS, INC.
740 Broadway, New York, NY 10003

MC/Visa orders may be telephoned to (603) 669-5933.